POLITICS, ADMINISTRATION AND PUBLIC POLICY IN DEVELOPING COUNTRIES

POLITICS, ADMINISTRATION AND PUBLIC POLICY

IN

DEVELOPING COUNTRIES

Examples from America, Asia and Latin America

EDITED BY

H.K. Asmerom and R.B. Jain

VU University Press   Amsterdam   1993

Copyright © 1993 by VU University Press, Amsterdam
De Boelelaan 1105
1081 HV Amsterdam
the Netherlands
tel. 020-6444355 fax 020-6462719

Cover design by D PS, Amsterdam
Printed by Wilco, Amersfoort

ISBN 90-5383-187-8/CIP/NUGI 661

CONTENTS

PREFACE

This book is the result of an internationally-coordinated research project in the field of politics, administration and the policy process. As such, it is the third consecutive product of the ongoing research activities of IPSA Research Committee No. 4: Public Bureaucracies in Developing Societies (formerly IPSA Study Group No. 27). The central theme and problem area of the book is to re-examine the linkages and relationships between politics and administration vis-a-vis the formulation and implementation of urgent public policies and other nation-building tasks. In this sense, the perennial debate regarding the dichotomy between politics and administration is the focus of many of the essays. Further, as a prelude to the substantive and concrete discussion of this global theme with the help of concrete case studies, an attempt is made in the *introductory chapter* to review the politics/administration dichotomy in the light of theoretical trends and developments.

The case study areas addressed by the essays are diverse in character and geographical location. Brazil, Surinam, Egypt, Ethiopia, India and Bangladesh have many traits that are unique to each country. They also display common characteristics of underdevelopment, especially in the area of socio-economic malaise. Some, indeed, like Egypt, Ethiopia and Thailand, have long and almost unbroken continuity with their historical past. Others like India, Bangladesh, Brazil and Surinam have had relatively long periods of colonial rule. Countries like India, Egypt and Brazil are practising democracies. In others like Ethiopia, democracy is still on the far horizon. On the other hand, almost all of them are heterogenous and multi-ethnic societies and face comparable hurdles in their efforts to create viable, responsible and accountable political and administrative institutions within the framework of democratic values and norms. It should be made clear, however, that these complex issues are not discussed in detail in the essays presented in this volume. What is more, without deviating from the main theme, the approaches and research strategies adopted by each author are dictated by the case at hand. Consequently, there are different emphases on how the linkages and relationships between politics and administration are addressed. Regardless of the diverse approaches, the case studies reveal the complex problems of linkages between political and administrative institutions in particular, and state/society relationships in general. To this extent, the essays clearly demonstrate the relevance of such a reappraisal at a time when Third World countries, despite their tremendous difficulties, are re-orienting themselves towards becoming truly democratic societies.

In preparing this book we have received support and assistance from many quarters. Firstly, we would like to record our gratitude to the IPSA Secretariat in Oslo for its moral and institutional support in our research activities under the umbrella of the International Political Science Association. Second, we have received constant support from the Department of Political Science and Public Administration of the Free University in Amsterdam and the Department of Political Science of the University of Delhi. In particular, we are thankful for the administrative and related assistance we received from the secretariat staff of the Department of Political Science and Public Administration of the Free University. Last, but by no means least, we are grateful to the VU University Press for accepting the manuscript for publication and for presenting it in such a magnificent format.

H.K. Asmerom,   R.B. Jain

THE CONTRIBUTORS

Asmerom, H.K. Senior Lecturer in Comparative and Development Administration at the Department of Political Science and Public Administration, Free University Amsterdam, The Netherlands.

Elsenhans, Hartmut, Professor at the Department of Political and Administrative Sciences, Faculty of Social Sciences, University of Constance, Constance, Germany.

Hoppe, R. Professor of Political Science and Public Administration at the Faculty of Socio-Cultural Studies, University of Amsterdam, Amsterdam, The Netherlands.

Jain, R.B. Professor of Political Science at the Department of Political Science, University of Delhi, Delhi, India.

Otto, J.M. Director, Van Vollenhoven Institute of Law and Administration of Non-Western Societies, State University of Leiden, Leiden, The Netherlands.

Mahtab, N. Professor of Public Administration at the Department of Public Administration, University of Dhaka, Dhaka, Bangladesh.

Reis, Elisa P. Professor of Political Science, University of Rio de Janeiro, Rio de Janeiro, Brazil.

THE EDITORS

R.B. Jain is at present professor of political science at the University of Delhi, India. Earlier he has been the Dean of the Faculty of Social Sciences and Head of the Department of Political Science, University of Delhi; Professor of Public Administration, Indian Institute of Public Administration, New Delhi, and Professor and Head, Department of Public Administration, Punjabi University, Patiala. He has held a number of visiting appointments at several universities in Canada, the USA and Europe, and is currently the Convenor and Chairman of the IPSA Research Committee No.4: Public Bureaucracies in Developing Societies. He is the author/editor of several books including *Contemporary Issues in Indian Administration; Bureaucratic Values in Development; Comparative Legislative Behaviour; Bureaucratic Politics in the Third World* and a number of research articles and papers published in reputed International Journals like, International Social Science Journal, International Political Science Review, Participation and Development, Indian Journal of Public Administration, Indian Journal of Political Science among others.

H.K. Asmerom is senior lecturer in comparative and development administration at the Department of Political Science and Public Administration, Free University Amsterdam. In the 1960s he was staff member at the Institute of Public Administration in Addis Ababa where he worked as a counterpart to various UN experts in Administrative Reforms and Legal Matters. Later he was a staff member of the Public Administration Courses at the Institute of Social Studies in the Hague. He completed his post-graduate studies in the late 1970s at the Free University in Amsterdam with a doctorate thesis entitled: *Emergence, Expansion and Decline of Patrimonial Bureaucracy in Ethiopia (1907-1974)*. Further, he has published articles in a number of National and International Journals and contributed chapters on administration and politics in the context of Eastern Africa. Together with R. Hoppe and R.B. Jain, he edited *Bureaucracy and Developmental Polocies in the Third World*. He is the current secretary of the IPSA Research Committee No.4: Public Bureaucracies in Developing Societies. He is also a board member of the Study Group on Development Administration of the Netherlands' Society for Public Administration.

1 POLITICS AND ADMINISTRATION : SOME CONCEPTUAL ISSUES

R.B. Jain and H.K. Asmerom

A Glimpse at the Politics/Administration Dichotomy

Politics and Administration are two classical concepts that are crucial for establishing linkages and relationships between state and society. They have been part and parcel of organized human activity since immemorial times. They could sometimes be used as instruments for propping up repressive and totalitarian regimes. At other times, and in the majority of cases, they are shaped into responsible and humane means for achieving material and non-material goods, articulated and aggregated by various interest groups in the name of the people at large. To state all this in a slightly different manner, the rise and fall of nation-states cannot be isolated from the good and the bad attributes of political and administrative systems at a particular epoch in their history. Thus, as aptly recorded by Toynbee in his seminal work, *A Study of History*, " the Hellenic Civilization had broken down because, in the internal economy of this society in its growth stage, at some point something had gone wrong with the interaction between individuals through which the growth of every growing civilization is achieved " (as quoted in Gladden 1974: 340). Or, as Heady stated it with reference to ancient Egypt, "one of the reasons for Egyptian institutional longevity was the high level of administrative services achieved, ranking the Egyptians with the Chinese as creators of the most impressive bureaucracies in the ancient world" (Heady 1984: 150-51). These quotations clearly recognize that administration and politics have been important elements of an integrated social behaviour at all time. Indeed, as Merghani has correctly formulated it, "the political system comprising all the institutions and instruments by which public decisions are made represents the framework within which the administrative system operates. The two systems in a sense complement each other and together represent the means by which the new state maintains its unity and deals with its responsibilities, domestic and international" (as quoted in Diamant 1964: 16).

Ever since Aristotle first attempted to define the political realities of the Greece of his day, relentless efforts have made throughout the ages to formulate appropriate definitions (van Dyke 1960: 131-157). For instance, Robert Dahl defined "politics" or "a political system" as any persistent pattern of human relationships that involves, to a significant extent, power, rule, or authority" (Dahl 1963: 6). To be sure, this definition is not fully accepted by all political scientists. In fact, Dahl himself was the first to admit that this definition is very broad and devoid of any value connotation at that. Its only utility lies in the fact that it is applicable to any type of political system, ranging from pluralist liberal democracy to dictatorships of the right and of the left which nurture and defend a particular brand of ideology and economic system (Dahl 1963: 7-9).

The question as to how far administration should be separated from politics, or in how far both politics and administration should be conceived as intertwined dimensions of the same process, has been a lively issue for sustained debates ever since the emergence of public administration as a distinct field of study following the publication of Woodrow Wilson's celebrated essay on *"the study of administration"*(1887; reprinted 1941: 481-506). However, as rightly stated by Riggs several years ago, to treat politics and administration as two separate disciplines "is unrealistic and has injured the study of politics as well as administration, for neither can be understood apart from the other" (Riggs 1965: 70). Indeed, in the day-to-day business of government there is always a genuine mix or a random overlap between the political and administrative processes. In other words, wherever there is a government, legitimate or otherwise, there will be policy initiatives by both politicians and civil servants. These policy initiatives are eventually formalized by the former and implemented by the latter.

Public administration as a distinct field of study has grown by stages in which earlier schools of thought and timely input from other disciplines have formed the foundation for the next stage. Vigorous or mild criticisms of older school(s) of thought were essential to legitimize the relevance of a new one. No school of thought was completely abandoned, however, as the result of this new approach to the study of public administration. Depending on the situation, it has always been a matter of hitting the right mix and not of outright rejection of previously formulated theories and approaches. The recognition of the cumulative nature of administrative theories and thus the contribution of earlier schools of thought to the next has been systematically described by McCurdy in the form of four distinct phases: (a) *the orthodox era* (1880-1945) with its emphasis on good administration, more efficiency, better productivity and practical application. This period was known for its strong prescriptions accentuated by reform, the science of administration and human relations; (b) *the period of description* (1945-1965), characterized by two broad schools of thought: the political approach, a central pillar of public administration that considers the latter to be an extension of the governing process, and the behaviourial revolution with its emphasis on the study of organizational behaviour with the help of input from disciplines like sociology, anthropology, psychology, and business administration, among others; (c) *the era of applications*

(1965-1980)in which public administration has been firmly established as a multi-disciplinary field of study. The movements and schools of thought which came to prominence during this period include, among others: 1. the rational school (operations research, cost-benefit analysis, etc) ; 2. the policy and public choices approaches; 3. management science, including the application of computer sciences to public administration; 4. organizational development with its emphasis on the building up of knowledge about small group behaviour and human motivation; 5. comparative public administration with its emphasis on cross-cultural study of administrative systems, especially those of developing countries; and lastly, (d) *a period of reconsideration* (present) which tries to reestablish the principle that good administration remains as much a question of political philosophy as managerial efficiency. This cumulative body of knowledge in the study of public administration is derived from various disciplines including sociology, psychology, political science, law, economics and business administration (McCurdy 1986: 14-72). This brief discourse on the cumulative nature of public administration as a discipline is presented here merely to provide a clue as to how fresh studies like the ones included in this volume, can utilize multiple theories and approaches advanced by various schools of thought from different vantage points.

Regardless of the cumulative and evolutionary character of theory building in administrative science, the thin border line where politics stops and where straightforward execution of public policy begins, varies from one situation to the other. In some countries, where there is a tradition of a relatively neutral civil service with its own identity as a group and having discretionary powers, policy formulation and policy implementation can be conceived as distinct and yet complementary elements of the same process. In cases, where the neutrality of the civil service is unknown or has been abandoned in favour of politicized outlook and loyalty to the only party in power, and where higher-level civil servants are recruited on ideological or on patron-client considerations, the borderline between what is truly political and what is essentially administration can be completely blurred. In this type of situation, political control and supervision in the day-to-day administration by party cadres or loyal protégés of the ruler permeates the bureaucracy. These distinctions are not always watertight. The empirical situations are much more complex and intractable than the ideal images would seem to suggest. What is more, with the advent of the democratization process which has been sweeping across the political landscapes of Eastern Europe and many third world countries, the link between politics and administration has become extremely fluid and unsettled in character. Even in countries with long traditions of democracy, where governments are regularly replaced by competitive elections, and where the neutrality of the civil service is an established fact, the precise borderline between politics and administration in day-to-day government business is not always easy to demarcate.

The contradictions and dilemmas implicit in this time tested paradigm of the relationship between politics and administration vis-a-vis various changes in ideology and regime types are analysed and appraised in many of the essays contained in this volume. How to establish the precise linkage between politics and administration has been the concern of students of both political science and public administration for a very long period of time. Accordingly, numerous models and theoretical frameworks have been regularly advanced in the form of normative and/or explanatory guidelines to the study of political and administrative systems in the context of both the developed and developing countries. It is beyond the scope of this short introduction to deal exhaustively with this vast literature on models and frameworks of administration and politics. While some models and frameworks are more enduring and relevant than others, it would be profitable, especially now in the face of the declining socialist ideology, to make an inventory to establish which ones are still relevant, which ones are obsolete, what new ones are emerging in the *context of the transition to democracy in third world countries*, and so on. These are all relevant issues which need to be addressed in a much more comprehensive research undertaking. As a rough guideline to the collection of essays in this volume, however, it would be sufficient to pay passing attention to some of the standard models that are reviewed in Ferrel Heady's standard work, *Public Administration: A Comparative Perspective* (1984). Following Heady's systematic inventory, the currently most relevant models of political and administrative systems are classified as: (a) traditional elite systems, (b) personalist bureaucratic elite systems, (c) collegial bureaucratic elite systems, (d) polyarchal competitive systems, (e) dominant-party semicompetetive systems, (f) dominant-party mobilization systems, and (g) communist totalitarian systems. Notwithstanding the variety of models and regime types, there are a number of common administrative characteristics that are applicable to all the developing societies. These include: 1. deliberate imitation of some version of western-type administration; 2. lack of skilled manpower needed for development programmes, resulting in emphasis on one's own interests at the expense of the larger public; 3. a widespread discrepancy between form and reality; and 4. a near monopoly on technical expertise (Heady 1984: 281-285). In addition to these common characteristics, which in themselves may not be necessarily applicable to all the developing countries in exactly the same manner, the position and role of the public bureaucracy vis-a-vis each one of these ideal types of political systems vary from bureaucracies characterized by *total subservience* to those in power (dictators and authoritarian rulers of one type or the other) to those bureaucracies that have constitutionally recognized positions of *neutrality* ready to serve the general public under an elected government and to participate in the formulation of realistic and responsible policies and in the implementation of the same with confidence and trust in themselves. Bureaucracies of this latter type are expected to carry out their duties not only in accordance with established routine procedures, but also following ethically sound codes of behaviour and discretionary judgements.

A related topic that has received considerable attention in a number of the essays in this volume is the link between politics, administration and development. In this sense, the concept of *development* refers to the changes and improvements that have to be made in the socio-economic and political aspirations of society as integral components of the nation-building process. In particular, development is closely associated with nationally and locally initiated concrete socio-economic programmes and projects and with the creation of national and grassroots organizations in which the people can meaningfully participate in the formulation and implementation of policies. From the 1950s until relatively recently, it has been generally assumed, or even taken for granted, that the complex and often difficult nation-building process would be achieved with the help of a development-oriented administrative system - a thoroughly reformed variety of the law-and-order administration which was left behind by the departing colonial powers. This process of reorientation of the administrative system is valid for countries with long histories of colonial rule such as Bangladesh, Brazil, Egypt, India and Surinam, or for those which had very little or no colonial background such as Ethiopia. This new approach of conceptualizing the administrative systems of developing countries both as part of the development process itself and as primary agent for implementing various developmental projects has come to be known as *development administration*. The following paragraphs present a birds'- eye view of this trend in historical perspective.

Some Pertinent Models and Frameworks for the Study of Development Administration.

Despite the fact that the meaning of development administration has been subjected to various interpretations depending on one's own commitment and scientific interest (Schaffer 1969; U.N. 1975; Gable 1975; Springer 1977; Gant 1979; Hope 1984), it is generally accepted that development administration refers to an aspect of public administration in which the focus of attention is on organizing and managing public agencies and government departments at both the national and sub-national levels in such a way as to stimulate and facilitate well-defined programmes of social, economic and political progress (Gant 1979: 3-28).

The theoretical foundations for the study of development administration can be traced to earlier theories and models of administration as advanced by Max Weber, Riggs, Weidner, Ilchman and others. With regard to Max Weber, we are mainly referring to his ideal types of *the legal rational, charismatic, and traditional authority patterns* and their corresponding

administrative systems. More by accident than by design, Weber's legal rational model
was found to be a critical prescriptive guideline for the study of political and administrative
systems in both developed and developing societies, although the norms and value considerations implicit in this model of bureaucracy have been found to be inadequate as a framework
for development administration in the context of developing countries. For one thing, the
characteristics of the legal rational model of bureaucracy which evolved in the western
context and are generally recognized as such as preconditions for efficiency and effectiveness,
were not necessarily the departure points for institutionalizing development-oriented administrations capable of coping with the new and urgent tasks of nation-building (La Palombara
1963). Nor were the other two ideal types of Weber constructed on the basis of the prevailing
socio-economic, cultural, political and administrative characteristics of present-day developing
societies. To be sure, they have some utility as explanatory models of the administrative
and political systems of many developing countries where traits of tradition and charisma
still have influence on the structure and functioning of state institutions. These influences
can be detected in some of the contributions such as the Chapters on Egypt, Ethiopia and
Brazil, but their usefulness for promoting development administration is negligible. This
gap had to be filled by something new. Accordingly, the search for new models and theoretical
frameworks began in earnest and Fred W. Riggs became the first to advance a model
exclusively designed in the context of contemporary Third World Societies.

Riggs' original model was known as *agraria and industria-toward a typology of
comparative and development administration*. It was an inductive method meant to provide
"a system of hypothetical categories for the classification and analysis of realities, including
patterns of political and administrative transition" (Riggs 1957:23-100). It relied heavily
on the structural functional approach and was designed to show the interdependence of
the administrative systems and the societies in which they functioned at two extreme stages
of development (Raphaeli 1967: 12). Observers were quick to criticise it as being too general,
too abstract, too static, too deterministic, and too incomplete to be applicable to societies
that are found in between the two extreme situations let alone to situations in the developed
countries like the United States (Hahn-Been Lee 1967; Kasfir 1968; Monroe 1970). Riggs
then came with a thoroughly updated and revised framework consisting of: a) the *fused
(undifferentiated) model* intended to be applicable to traditional societies; b) the *prismatic
(semi-differentiated) model* intended to be applicable to the developing countries; and c)
the *refracted (differentiated) model* intended to be applicable to the economically advanced
and industrialized societies along the lines of Weber's legal rational model (Rigg 1964,
1973). The main characteristics of each model in terms of the economic sub-system, the
political sub-system and the administrative sub-system are given extensive treatment. For

instance, the economic subsystem of the second model is characterized by the so-called bazaar-canteen, an agrarian economy with an undetermined and irregular price system; the nature of the political sub-system can range from neo-traditional authoritarian to semi-democratic; while the administrative sub-system is characterized by the so-called sala model, which is supposed to display traits such as formalism, overlapping, nepotism, poli-communalism and heterogeneity.

Riggs revised framework was still found to be inadequate. It merely tended to magnify the negative aspects of the cultural, social, economic, political and administrative characteristics of the developing countries. As such its restricted utility for undertaking research in development administration became obvious in the course of time. And yet, despite all the valid criticisms, Riggs' theory of prismatic society is still a useful yardstick for appreciating some of the peculiar traits of the political and administrative systems of African, Asian and Latin American countries.

Weber and Riggs are not the only sources for models and frameworks in comparative and development administration. For instance, Eisenstadt advanced four types of bureaucracies: a) service-oriented bureaucracies intended to serve both the ruler and the major social groups in society; b) sub-servient bureaucracies which are entirely under the control of the ruler and carry out functions that are approved by him; c) autonomous and self-oriented bureaucracies which are not subordinated to any other interest group in society and are largely inclined to maximize their own interests; and d) compromising bureaucracies which promote their own interests as well as those of the ones who are in control of the political system (Eisenstadt 1963: 276-370). These typologies are derived from extensive historical investigations, but, depending on the adopted research strategy, they can still be useful as normative and explanatory conceptual tools in understanding the administrative and political systems of the developing countries of today.

In a slightly different perspective, and with the expressed intention of clarifying the meaning of development administration, Weidner advanced five types of administrative systems reflecting the priority task of the regime in power: (a) production - oriented, an administrative system which has the commitment and capacity to provide goods and services to society; (b) consumption - oriented, an administrative system which gives priority to the provision of goods and services with clear intention of maximizing consumption; (c) defense - oriented, an administrative system which is devoted to continuously strengthening its armed forces to combat real or imagined internal and external threats; (d) law-and-order - oriented, an administration which is preoccupied in the management of social control making sure that people are law-abiding; and (e) non - development - oriented, an administrative system which is essentially concerned with the balancing of interests and forces within society and, in particular with satisfying the needs of groups who could pose a threat to the regime if their interests are neglected (Weidner 1962: 97-98). Again, these are ideal types which stress the most glaring areas of regime activity. In actual fact, most administrative systems carry out a combination of activities ranging from law-and-order to developmental programmes.

On the other hand, Ilchman's approach to development administration is entirely different in its aim and strategy. Thus, as he argues, if it is to achieve the increasing demands generated by society, development administration needs to be periodically subjected to either drastic or piecemeal reforms. With this in view, Ilchman identified two possible alternative approaches on how to bring about reforms in development administration:

(a) the administrative systems approach, which is subdivided into:

1. the balanced administrative growth strategy, which is geared to the overall improvement of the administrative system (including the personnel system, budgeting and fiscal procedures , planning processes and organizational development); and

2. unbalanced administrative growth strategy, which is concerned with the piecemeal approach to administrative reform by concentrating on key and urgent elements in the administration.

(b) the social systems approach, which, like the first one is subdivided into:

1. the balanced social growth strategy, which holds that effective administration is dependent on the simultaneous presence of a healthy and semi-independent economic system, a strong political system and functionally specific interest groups. (The argument here is that without effective political systems, power is bound to be concentrated in the bureaucracy, which means that political institutions no longer perform their "interest articulation" and "interest aggregation" functions); and

2. the unbalanced social growth strategy, whose advocates believe that a mature and well-functioning bureaucracy can serve as a catalyst to the development of autonomous and yet interdependent centres of power (Illchman 1965: 315-318).

Without doubt, Ilchman has provided a neat classification of various and often conflicting approaches to improving the performance of development administration. How and to what extent the various approaches are to be operationalized is not explained. This apparent missing link may be bridged by Caiden's fourteen normative guidelines, which he believes that strategists of administrative innovation should follow step by step when engaging in administrative reform programmes (Caiden 1969: 16-18).

Others, like Bjur and Zomorrdian (1986) and Hoppe (1992), believe that the study of development (and comparative) administration has to be understood primarily from the point of view of the cultural values, norms, customs and ideological orientations of the developing countries themselves. The main argument that is advanced by Bjur and Zomorrdia is that cultural values that are of direct relevance to good administration have to be systematically identified and applied, while administrative norms and values borrowed from another culture have to be modified to the local value and cultural systems. However, Bjur and Zomorrdia have weakened their argument by admitting that they are more intuitive than rational, more heuristic than replicable (Bjur and Zomorrodian 1986: 397-416). The framework put forward by Hoppe, on the other hand, seems to be more assertive as it contains systematically derived hypotheses relevant for bureaucracies in different cultural contexts (Hoppe 1992: 334).

Rondinelli and Montgomery have provided a new conceptual framework for assessing development administration vis-a-vis the dynamics of policy-making and implementation (Rondinelli and Montgomery 1991: 89). They define development administration as the efforts of governments to promote and guide activities aimed at achieving social and economic change. As such, development administration encompasses policy issues identified in terms of public administration, economic growth, social development and international transactions (Rondinelli and Montgomery 1991: 91-100). With the help of this theoretical framework, the authors have made a worthwhile attempt to evaluate the successes and failures of a number of governments in the Third World in their efforts to promote socio-economic development (Ibidem: 100-114). The problems of public policy making, planning and plan implementation, in the context of their environmental settings highlighted in a number of the contributions to this volume, have to a certain extent utilized the theoretical framework charted by these two authors. Implicit in this conceptualization are (a) the policy-making process in its entirety, and (b) the need to create decentralized structures and other local institutions to carry out integrated and well-coordinated development programmes with the full participation of the people at the grassroots level.

Apart from its role in understanding development administration, the study of bureaucracy has also been the study of political power (Smith 1988: 229). When bureaucracy is denigrated, it is done so to show support for political interests and values that the bureaucracy is thought to threaten. This is true, whether one is thinking of the state at large or conditions within large-scale formal organizations. However, bureaucratic and political power may feed off each other, and those in government may welcome their alliance with bureaucracy and the political benefits that bureaucracy brings, including the secrecy in its dealings with the political opposition. Democratic politics should not be viewed as a struggle between politicians and bureaucrats. The collusion between the two actors is implicit in the corporalist interpretations of modern politics. As has been observed by Smith "the distinction between bureaucrats and politicians as well as politics and administration increasingly becomes mystification in the corporalist state. The principles of indirect, informal quasi-public and covert administration under corporatism complete the politicization of bureaucracy in the capitalist state" (Smith 1988: 232).

Smith further contends that Third World countries have provided an equally receptive environment for the development of bureaucratic power even beyond the 'over developed' conditions in which it was bequeathed by the colonial powers to the newly independent state. The growing involvement of state in the direct management of economy in society, the absence of alternative centres of expertise, the colonial heritage of bureaucratic dominance and the frequent fusion of party and state in single party systems, have given rise to familiar concerns about the capacity of non-bureaucratic political institutions to fulfil the requirements of political democracy. All these concerns have led to a most crucial dilemma for modern societies: whether the bureaucratic organization has any advantage despite the costs of maintaining it in terms of its own dysfunctional potential and the political vigilance required (Smith 1988: 237); and the concomitant search for debureaucratization and alternatives to the administrative state (Dwivedi and Jain 1985).

However, scholars like B.Guy Peters (1988) have bemoaned the relatively few theoretical developments concerning relations between political executive and administration, which he thinks is true not only for individual nations, but also for the comparative study of their interactions. He outlines five theoretical models of such interactions, which he believes can enhance our understanding of politics within the executive branch in different countries. The first is the 'formal legal model' in which the bureaucracy is reduced to saying yes to the political executives. This model, which is similar to the approach of Wilson and Weber, is important as a normative standard against which to compare real patterns of interaction and policy making. The second model of the relationship, according to Peters, may be termed the 'village life' model. In this, senior civil servants and political executives are conceptualized as having relatively similar values and goals, the most important being maintenance of the government and the smooth functioning of the executive branch. In this conception of executive branch politics, the political and the bureaucratic coalesce against outside interference in their tightly constrained little world (Guy Peters 1988). The third model, which he calls the 'functional model', posits an integration among elites along functional lines. In this model there would be close ties among civil and political executives within the same functional area (for example, health, education, or defence) and links to other actors in that issue area, such as legislative committees and interest groups. There will be little or no linkage to other civil servants or to other political elites outside that issue area. Such a model fits into the newest descriptions of corporatism in a number of European countries (Ibid). The fourth model is to a great extent the converse of the second in which the political executive and the senior civil servants are assumed to be competitors for power and control over policy (Ibid). The fifth is the 'administrative state' model. This model reflects an increasingly common perception that the decision-making of government is dominated by bureaucracy (Ibid). This type of model is perhaps most applicable to situations prevailing in most of the developing countries, where the political executive often does not know its mind, or is incapable of decision-making in most crucial socio-economic policy areas.

Another interesting theoretical framework for study of the relationship between politics and administration is furnished by Barbara Wake Carroll who, in a recent article, examines the relationship between the two as a *trichotomy* rather than a *dichotomy* (Carrol 1990 :345-66). Analysing the changes at senior management level of the Canadian Federal Public Service from 1967 to 1987, the author considers "the management of a department" as consisting of "a group of senior executives", rather than only the deputy-ministers, and by breaking down the administrative component of the organization into managerial and technical systems. When these are combined with the institutional (or political) sub-system, there is a trichotomy rather than a dichotomy to consider. Focusing upon the administrative components of that trichotomy, the author shows that there has been a major shift in emphasis towards the management sub-system and away from the technical sub-system over the past twenty years. The article suggests that the functioning of public bureaucracies is better understood by considering them as organizations composed of three inter-dependent essential sub-systems. The concept of the policy or politics/administration dichotomy overlooks the fact that there are three functions which must be carried out within any organization, including public organizations. While institutional representation remains through the person of the minister and the ethic of public service, the more serious shortcoming lies with the increasing underrepresentation of the technical sub-system. Thus one of the causes of non-adaptiveness and the inability of public bureaucracies to resolve policy problems may be that the technical aspects have come to be under-represented within its senior management (Carrol 1990: 347). This is often the case in most developing countries.

One of the latest conceptual frameworks to the study of politics and administration vis-a-vis regime types is the *governance approach* advanced by Goran Hyden and others in the context of Africa (Hyden 1992). Hyden argues persuasively that governance is a promising and better strategy to the study of comparative politics. As a framework, governance is defined in global terms to accommodate all shades of political systems that are located in between four dominant models, namely, the libertarian, the statist, the communitarian and the corporalist (Hyden 1992: 17-20). One can detect a fair degree of resemblance between this framework and the one advanced by David Apter three decades ago (Apter 1965), although the latter's theoretical setting and scholarly aims were different from those now presented by Hyden and his associates. At any rate, the governance approach takes into account the significance of cultural variables and the importance of diversity and flux characterizing all political regimes. On the face of it, the framework is meant to be neutral and value-free inasmuch as it is applicable to all political systems. Beyond that, however, it seems to endorse positively the universal and seemingly irreversible move away from totalitarianism of any kind in the direction of democracy and pluralist political systems. Thus, in the words of Hyden, the framework

> "provides a means of conceptually linking up more closely with the broader field of comparative politics, yet it offers a meaningful way of relating to the ongoing efforts in the continent to reverse autocracy and build democracy" (Hyden 1992: 23).

To this extent, the framework is meant to serve as a strategy on how to improve politics and the conditions that have to be met if viable democratic institutions and other state organizations are to be created in Africa and, by extension, in other relevant Third World countries (Bratton and Rothchild 1992: 263-284).

As these reviews amply demonstrate, *the link between politics and administration and its significance for nation-building and developmental processes*, have been the subject for extensive research by both scholars and practitioners since the 1950s. This admittedly brief insight into the literature of politics, administration and development administration, is not meant to serve as an explicit theoretical guideline for the contributions in this volume. However, in one way or another, all the contributions examine these central issues and appraise their significance for nation-building and socio-economic development in the context of each of the eight respective case studies from Africa, Asia and Latin America. The seventh essay concentrates on a new approach to the understanding of politics and development administration in global terms and from the socio-cultural perspective of political economy. And to that extent, it enriches this volume by providing an additional dimension to the understanding of administration, politics and economic development of Third World countries, including the ones examined in the other six essays.

References

Apter, David E. (1965), *The Politics of Modernization*, The University of Chicago Press, Chicago and London.

Bjur, Wesley E. and A. Zomordian (1986), Towards Indigenous Theories of Administration: An International Perspective, in *International Review of Administrative Sciences,* Vol. 52, 397-420.

Bratton, Michael and Donald Rothchild (1992), The Institutional Bases of Governance in Africa, in Hyden and Bratton eds., *Governance and Politics in Africa,* Boulder and London, 263-284.

Caiden, Gerald E. (1969), Development Administration and Administrative Reform, in *International Social Science Journal,* Vol.21, No.1, 9-22.

Carrol, Barbara Wake (1990), "Politics and Administration: A Trichotomy"? in *Governance,* Vol. 3, No.4,1990: 345-366.

Diamant, Alfred (1962), The Bureaucratic Model: Max Weber Rejected, Rediscovered, Reformed, in Heady and Stokes eds. *Papers in Comparative Public Administration,* 59-96.

Diamant, Alfred (1964), *Bureaucracy and Developmental Movement Regimes: A Bureaucratic Model for Developing Societies*, Comparative Administration Group, Occasional Papers (Seminar) University of Michigan, June 15-July 24.

Dwivedi, O.P. and R.B. Jain (1985), *India's Administrative State*, New Delhi, Gitanjali Publishing House.

Eisenstadt, S.N. (1963), *The Political Systems of Empires*, The Free Press of Glencoe.

Esman, M. J. (1968), The Maturing of Development Administration, in *Public Administration and Development,* Vol. 8, 125-134.

Gable, Richard W (1975), *Development Administration: Background, Terms, Concepts, Theories and a New Approach*, AID/TA/DA.

Gant, George F. (1979), *Development Administration: Concepts, Goals, Methods,* The University of Wisconsin Press.

Gladden, E.N. (1976), Toynbee on Public Administration, in *The International Review of Administrative Sciences,* Vol.XLII, 338-348.

Hahn-Been Lee (1967), From Ecology to Time: A Time-oriented Approach to the Study of Public Administration, in *International Review of Administrative Sciences*, Vol.33, No.2, 103-113.

Heady, Ferrel (1984), *Public Administration: A Comparative Perspective, Second Edition, Revised and Expanded*, Marcel Dekker, New York and London.

Heady, Ferrel Sybil L. Stokes eds. (1962), *Papers in Comparative Public Administration*, Ann Arbor, Michigan.

Hope, Kemp Ronald (1984), *The Dynamics of Development and Development Administration,* Green Wood Press.

Hoppe, R. (1992), Bureaucracy and Public Policy in the Third World: A Culturalist Approach, in Asmerom, H.K., R. Hoppe and R. B. Jain eds., *Bureaucracy and Developmental Policies in the Third World,* VU University Press, Amsterdam, 317-340.

Hyden, Goran and Michael Bratton, eds. (1992), *Governance and Politics in Africa,* Lynne Rienner Publishers, Boulder and London.

Illchman, Warren F. (1965), Rising Expectations and the Revolution in Development Administration, in *Public Administration Review,* Vol.25, 314-322.

Kasfir, Nelson (1968), Prismatic Theory and the Emerging Shape of African Administration, Unpublished paper, Makerere University College, 1-26.

LaPalombara, J. ed. (1963), *Bureaucracy and Political Development*, Princeton, N.J., Princeton University Press.

Monroe, Michael L. (1970), Prismatic Behaviour in the United States? in *The Journal of Comparative Administration,* Vol.2, No.2, 229-242.

McCurdy, Howard E. (1986), *Public Administration: A Bibliographical Guide to the Literature*, Marcel Bakker, New York and Basel.

Peters, B. Guy (1988), *Comparing Public Bureaucracies: Problems of Theory and Method*, The University of Alabama Press.

Raphaeli, Nimrod (1967), Comparative Public Administration : An Overview, in Raphaeli, Nimrod ed., *Readings in Comparative Public Administration*, Allyn and Bacon, Inc., Boston, 1-24.

Riggs, Fred W. (1957), Agraria and Industria, in Siffin, William J. ed. *Toward the Comparative Study of Public Administration,* Bloomington, Ind., Indiana University Press, 23-100.

Riggs, Fred W. (1962), An Ecological Approach: The Sala Model, in Heady and Stokes eds. *Papers in Comparative Public Administration*, Ann Arbor, Michigan, 19-36.

Riggs, Fred. W. (1965), Relearning An Old Lesson: The Political Context of Development Administration, in *Public Administration Review, Vol.25,* No.1, 70-79.

Riggs, Fred W. (1973), *Prismatic Society Revisited*, Morristown, New Jersey, General Learning Press.

Rondinelli, Dennis A. and John D. Montgomery (1991), Methods and Problems of Analysing Administration in Developing Countries: Development Administration as a Conceptual Framework, in Elsenhans, Hartmut and Harald Fuhr eds. *Administration and Industrial Development*, National Book Organization, New Delhi, 83-118.

Schaffer, B.B. (1969), The Deadlock in Development Administration, in Colin Leys ed., *Politics and Change in Developing Countries,* Cambridge University Press, 177-211.

Smith, B.E. (1988), *Bureaucracy and Political Power,* Sussex, Wheatsheaf, Books.

United Nations (1975), *Development Administration: Current Approaches and Trends in Public Administration for National Development,* New York.

Weber, Max (1964), *The Theory of Social and Economic Organization,* tr. by Henderson, A.M. and Talcott Parsons, The Free Press, New York, 56-77.

Weidner, Edward W. (1962), Development Administration: A New Focus for Research, in Heady F. and Sybil L. Stokes ed., *Papers in Comparative Public Administration,* The University of Michigan, Ann Arbor, Michigan, 97-115.

2 INTEGRATING POLITICAL ECONOMY IN THE COMPARATIVE STUDY OF ADMINISTRATION

Hartmut Elsenhans

Introduction

The comparative analysis of development administration has long ago left the area of narrow concentration on the internal structures, settings and rules of the bodies to be analysed. In line with North American theory of political modernization, it has more recently concentrated on values and socio-cultural norms which are considered part of an inherited socio-cultural environment (Riggs 1964). In this essay a different approach is followed, one based on political economy. The principal contention is that political and administrative behaviour, as part of a greater variety of social behaviours, cannot be explained without referring to the overall politico-economic texture of society. Following the principles of the mode of production, we consider a society as being determined by the way production is organized: who organizes the work processes; who appropriates the surplus, and on the basis of what type of entitlement; how and according to what principles is the surplus used; and what are the resulting macroeconomic outcomes (Elsenhans 1989: 111). If such a mode of production proves to be stable, microeconomic factors should create incentives for patterns of behaviour that stabilize the macroeconomic setting. This should result in social and political practices that stabilize the meso and macro-social and political settings in a similar way. Values and norms may have their origins in history, but their reproduction is only guaranteed if they are not in conflict with the reward structure at the micro-economic and micro-social levels.

The essential problem in transferring western notions of administration from developed capitalist countries to non-capitalist underdeveloped countries lies in the fact that the non-capitalist sector engaged in the non-market production of public goods in capitalist countries is largely controlled through the power of capitalists and labour, who are able to dictate the economic use of (artificially) scarce surplus and therefore produce rational administration of the Weberian type, at least in some areas and at some levels (Elsenhans 1987b: 378-380). A look at the history of administration in general, as well as that of actual administration in the Western industrial countries reveals that this type of rationality has been achieved through goal limitation. Only some general purposes can be dealt with by means of uniform and general rules that limit the discretionary power of the administration. It is not so much the expansion of the size of the administration, but of the scope of goals to be pursued that changes its mode of operation and results in segmentation, the withholding of information, the establishment of formal networks, and capture by clients. One particular mechanism operates in a capitalist society: The major part of surplus is appropriated as profit for investment and increases of surplus available for consumption do not appear as surplus per se, but rather as rising wages that are directly used for consumption, eliminating the need to channel such surplus to "needy" groups. Administrations make decisions in only a very limited way on the direction of investment and growth and therefore their procedure can be organized in such a way that appropriateness to specific situations is neglected, allowing the imposition of general rules at the expense of discretionary powers.

The dominant form of surplus in a non-capitalist society is rent or tax (Elsenhans 1986a: 6-15). Even the profits appropriated by private entrepreneurs are based not only on their efficiency in the market place and their total net investment, factors that determine one's profitability in a capitalist society, but also on monopoly, state regulations and promotional programmes benefitting particular enterprises. The appropriation and allocation of surplus in the form of rent does not depend on the market, with its automatic allocation procedures, but on politico-administrative decision-making. This process is not regulated by profit rate and the "law of values", but depends on the complicated and often opaque interplay of influences of the most varied types of groups, none of which represents the consumptive interests of the masses. Furthermore, the allocation of additional consumptive power in non-capitalist societies is not realized through general increases in incomes, but through particularistic programmes that favour groups that have been established on the basis of the so-called "objective criteria", reflecting a large measure of discretionary power on the part of the awarding authorities.[1] This process can be summarized as constituting the pervasiveness of rent (Elsenhans 1986b: 31-34).

Central and regional administrations in a capitalist economy are limited to general purposes which can be executed on the basis of rather easily enforceable rules. The discretionary power of directing the process of growth and accumulation is mediated through the rate of profit, which in its inter-branch and inter-enterprise variation, depends on the purchasing power of private households.

Where administration is engaged in the management of specific or local public goods, whether in developing countries or in the West, the Weberian form of bureaucracy never did and does not exist, since the mixture of politics and administration is under the control of local forces which are more or less democratically constituted.[2]

These elements of control limit the process of political bargaining for the allocation of surplus and allow for the enforcement of economically rational decisions, i.e. decisions where the stated purposes are achieved without fringe-benefits for special interest groups. To the extent that cultural environments are characterized by this rationality, it is impossible to introduce other interests into the decisionmaking process than those of the beneficiaries of the decision. The cultural traits of the decision makers cannot be introduced in the decision-making process to a substantial degree and thus become irrelevant to the decision-making process, but they may be especially important in the day-to-day operation of the administrative machinery. If, on the other hand, rent is channelled into specific programmes, such cultural values become important not only for the formal aspects of the decision-making process but also for the material results of this process, since discretionary power is a key element at any level of the decision-making process.

The discretionary power associated with rent is limited in various ways. Firstly, rent is based on the production of goods that are sold at prices above the costs of production. Individuals associated with the production of goods can be in a position to influence the appropriation and allocation of rent. Rent is also channelled through decision-making bodies that are influenced in varying degrees by competing interests. The critical evaluation of Third World development administrations has concentrated at this level and has identified a strong autonomous tendency among the groups that are in control of this process. It is especially claimed that they are not very sensitive to mass interests. This evaluation tends to expound one of two theories, either the theory of the dominance of privileged groups that are linked to the decision-making bodies (Thomas 1984:60; Smith 1979:102; Siebold 1988:3; Sackey 1979:46; Ledda 1967:597f; Cabral 1974:15ff), or the theory that those in control of the administrative machinery form a separate dominant class in themselves (Luke 1984: XVIII; Callaghy 1986: 49; Bergschlosser 1979: 650). In both theories, the analysis of administration concentrates on the values and norms of the elitist groups. This limits proposals for reform to those directed at the improvement of the ethical norms of the administrators, instead of those dealing with the problem on how more efficient outside control can be introduced.

The more the processes of allocation of surplus are locally decentralized, the more they are influenced by social groups which are not highly organized. Since large organizations are characterized by very hierarchical structures, the concentration of discretionary powers over rent at the top levels of the political system may lead to the cooptation of leadership of competing organizations. Only the decentralization of decision-making is able to lead to control by lower strata of society through their participation. In brief, it can be said that an underdeveloped society is characterized by a cloud of revenue, rent, the use of which - as opposed to wage and profit - is not economically determined, but rather politically determined. This results in hierarchies of avenues of access that are weakened and insufficiently replaced by mechanisms of self-control in those in the upper echelons of the system. Therefore any attempt at comparative theorizing should insist on identifying the origins of rent, the link between strategy of development and the relative importance of rent versus profit, the characteristics of the upper echelons of power and their impact on the degree of decentralization should be clarified. These and related themes are discussed in the remaining paragraphs of this essay.

Types of Rent and Its Control through Associations of Producers

Any rent is related to at least two production processes and channels through which redistribution takes place. The first is the one in which the goods are produced, the control of which creates entitlements to rent; the second is the one in which the goods are produced that are appropriated through rent. Goods can be appropriated through rent by means of international transactions, in which case the production process of the products consumed is located outside the territory of the respective society. The rent element is not based on the denial of access to more remunerative outlets for the products and producers of the supplied goods have nothing to complain about except possible customs duties. If the production of goods which are consumed for rent is local, however, it often results in denial of free marketing and leads to producer protests against compulsory marketing.

Entitlement to rent normally results from the production of goods, whose sales price is higher than the cost of the production. In the case of underdeveloped economies, differences in productivity compared with the leading industrial countries, who determine the relative prices of goods on the world market, result in production lines within Third World economies that differ in productivity as measured by prices (Baerresen, Carnoy, Grunwald, 1965:33; Diaz-Alejandro 1965:209; Lydall 1977:26; Tidrick 1986: 23; Aydalot 1968:42). By varying the exchange rate, and hence the international value of national factors of production, a continuum of situations between the following two extremes can be constructed. First, if the exchange rate is fixed at a level where only the most productive production line is able to pay a wage rate that is average for the local economy and a profit rate that conforms to international standards, no one formally earns rent, but those in control of the export products have a high international purchasing power. Second, if the exchange rate is fixed at a level where even the marginal factors of production are fully employed, export products can be taxed and will yield rent to the amount of the difference of their local costs of production and the world market price. In case of perfect specialization, this rent disappears due expansion of the quantity of production and, if exports are price-inelastic, this may lead to net decreases in export earnings. The acquisition of discretionary power on the part of development administrations requires some movement away from the first extreme situation so that there is a possibility of taxing exports.

The larger the groups that participate in the production of exports, the more probable a large participation in the political process of allocation of the rent. In the cases of mineral and oil production, the high performance of capital-intensive technologies imported from the West has led to low employment levels. Appropriate technology is rarely available and hence there are only a few connected activities. In order to avoid general claims for rent redistribution, the structure of rent control takes the form of high wages paid to the labour force in these islands of high productivity. Hence we find the typical labour aristocracies who are sufficiently aware of their own privileged character to seek collaboration with those in control of the rent.

On the other hand, rent may result from labour-intensive production involving large parts of the labour force. If this is wage labour, its strategy will be determined by its chances for success. If unemployment is high, the emergence of political organizations is to be expected rather than trade-unions with limited objectives (Paige 1975: 6ff). As long as the sectors concerned remain limited in size, the result will not be very different from the political practices of plantation workers, with limited gradualism facing strong opposition against reform from the dominant classes. If employment is high, however, such a rent-generating sector would probably be a leading force in the transformation of the society, and have a very high impact on the political process, and, hence the control of rent.

A more interesting alternative is the organization of production into small units such as small-scale cash crop farming or small-industry export or export-related subcontracted production. Here the fight against political allocation of rent takes the form of a struggle against monopolies and could lead to an alliance of all non-rent financed classes, including peasants, workers, small entrepreneurs, and larger non-subsidized enterprises. Creation of a self-sustained market-regulated capitalist economy, however, would require that the marginalized population be absorbed without redistribution of assets (Georgescu-Roegen 1960: 32-40; Breman 1985).

Rent may also be allocated in the form of subsidies to privileged producers to enable them to acquire foreign technology through direct subsidies or through allocation of foreign exchange at overvalued exchange rates. Here the political process will take the form of a fight between "monopoly" capital and non-subsidized capital. The prosperity of the non-subsidized sector as it thrives due to monetary expansion resulting from the inefficiency of the public sector will tend to be an effective check to rent abuse. If rent is generated by export-import operations, its volume can be increased through the expansion of the privileges of the public sector or of state-financed private enterprises in the input markets or even in the outlets. With respect to the internally generated volume of resources, a counteracting process of wealth accumulation, triggered by state-sponsored development, will lead to the emergence of opposing forces that will challenge the unproductive use of resources.

There are forms of rent which are not at all dependent on production. The major one is foreign aid. One can describe many aid-dependent countries as exporters of an entitlement to a good conscience (Sen 1981 :162). The Western donors "buy" these entitlements because they help justify getting funds from public treasuries in the West. The economies of the South, which are specialized in such "production" lines, experience exchange rates far too high in relation to the productivity of the rest of the economy. This discourages development through economic diversification. Rent normally discriminates against diversification of production (Sid Ahmed 1989 :182f; Benachenhou 1971: 925-929), as can be seen in the examples of 16th century Spain (Vilar 1974:109; Keman 1984: 60-1; Bagu 1949: 47,95,105; Wiebe 1895: 287), Poland in the 17th and 18th centuries (Kula 1970: 96; Malowist 1959:188; Pach 1966: 1222) or America's ante-bellum South (Aldrich 1973 :399; Huertas 1979: 95). In the case of aid-dependent countries, this may lead to the absurd situation of transforming the whole economy into a poverty-stricken rentier system. Some aid-giving organisations argue that aid raises the awareness of the poor who receive aid-financed services. It is doubtful this process of awareness creation is more important than the process of displacement of potential producers that can result from even well-intentioned aid. Aid-dependent countries are characterized by the gate-keeping activities of those in power, who in effect, "levy customs duties" on the delivery of services to the poor in the form of "mis" allocation of part of the aid to their own use.

A review of the aid/rent problem shows that the more aid is automatically allocated through the pressure of large groups associated with the production of rent-generating goods, the less probable will be abuses. On the other hand, cases can be identified where the rent is entirely used for non-productive purposes such as the financing of military forces (Iraq) or the subsidizing of predominantly upper-class consumption (Kuwait) without stimulating even limited development of productive forces. In such cases, the discretionary power of those in control of the rent increases, along with the probability of abuse.

The analysis of the forms of the rent leads to the following conclusions: Dependent on another set of factors still to be dealt with, an optimum inflow of rent depends on two factors:

- the consequences of the production of rent-generating goods for the labour market and on the formation of small and medium-scale entrepreneurs. Whether these entrepreneurs and labourers are in agriculture or in industry will influence the political process according to the often- described differences in communication capability of the social groups in either setting. It is clear, however, that agriculture per se does not inhibit mobilization as was once thought.
- the importance of the rent element in the production of rent-generating goods and the total production, both of which are dependent on the overall level of economic development. The more diversified and developed an economy, the less the dangers inherent in rent and the greater the possibilities that it will be controlled by classes to the difference to clienteles that share common interests and can be organized according to their dependence on the division of labour.

Control of Rent and Different Types of Development

The strategy of development chosen has an important impact on the possibilities of the control of rent through the classes which are not financed from it. It is widely held that deregulation will allow for the disappearance of rent. This view, however, is connected to the rent-seeking literature (Krueger 1974 :290-303; Olson 1982), which considers rent only as a result of politically imposed monopoly or oligopoly. I have shown elsewhere that this approach does not take into account the necessary divergence of relative productivity between specific production lines within underdeveloped economies with respect to the developed economies as a whole where productivity (not productivity incomes) tends to be average in all production lines (Elsenhans 1986c :276-289). This approach also argues that there is an automatic disadvantage in machinery production in underdeveloped economies. I will show that, in addition, a more egalitarian distribution of income leads to the greater possibility of utilizing global interventions than does a more non-egalitarian strategy.

Global interventions for steering an economy target fiscal and monetary policy. Any change in mix and volume of the final demand will lead to flexible adaptation to growth, only, if at least in case of declining exchange rates, diversification can occur. Where underdeveloped economies are characterized by structures that lead to new export lines, which become profitable only at high rates of devaluation whereas price-elasticity of demand for traditional export lines is low, the gap between the consumptive and productive capacities of the economy cannot be bridged through additional export earnings. The adjustment process requires, rather, the reorientation of local factors of production to meet new local demands.

This is possible if the economy is flexible, i.e. if required new equipment is produced locally (Bitar 1979: 259; Muller-Plantenberg, Hinkelammert 1973:225; Sideri: 1979: XIII-XXIII). Monetary policy affects the volume of investment through regulating the price of credit. Actual local production will be influenced only if decreases or increases in investment change the volume of local demand. This situation will occur only if equipment is produced locally.

Fluctuations in the business cycle are due to changes either in export or in investment demands. Variations in export demand are difficult to control. Variations in equipment (i.e. investment) demands are smoothed out in a developed economy by the following mechanisms: A technological innovation is only profitable (i.e. economically efficient) if it reduces total labour requirements (direct labour used in its operation plus indirect labour is used for its production). Reduction of new investment during crisis will lead to physical depletion or economic obsolescence of existing plant, creating new demands for investment. At some point of the cycle, this built-up demand will trigger new investment, leading to a concentration of new equipment order, with the result of rapidly increasing employment - (Montgomery 1938:38; Aldcroft 1986: 152; Stevenson/Cook 1977: 55; Keynes 1939:35-6; Richardson 1939:431-441; Habakkuk 1972: 275; Cole 1961: 12). This tendency toward cyclical concentration of investment in developed capitalist countries in combination of sticky monetary wages in the downswing, falling prices and hence rising real wages has regularly led to the redistribution of income in favour of mass consumption resulting in long-term growth (Elsenhans: 1979:101-148; 1983a: 1-15; 1983b: 187-205; and 1991: 36-45).

None of the above-mentioned mechanisms exists in an economy which does not possess locally generated means of production. The strategy for overcoming underdevelopment through mass consumption, mass production, and greater reliance on locally produced equipment (Elsenhans 1975: 293-313, 1982: 152-182) requires a comprehensive view of the future structure of the economy that allows for a greater reliance on market mechanisms. It is obvious that production of a higher percentage of traditional products in comparison with industrial goods, a smaller selection of modern products lower the quality requirements for goods and technologies, and higher economies of scale are the results of a more egalitarian distribution of demand that favours local equipment production (Burch 1987:11; Steel/Takagi 1978:28; Chinn 1974:90; Strassmann 1956:425-440; Sideri 1972:14; King/Byerlee 1978:205).

Strategies based on a non-egalitarian distribution of income are associated with punctualistic interventions in which development administrations select single projects with doubtful criteria of usefulness (Murelius 1981: 12-16; Little/Mirrles 1974: 86; Tower/Pursell 1986: 131). Strategies based on an egalitarian distribution of income may require large-scale economic projections, but can be implemented sector by sector programmes of promotion that do not favour individual beneficiaries or projects. The domain of possible patronage and rent abuse shrinks. Rent control is facilitated as rent finances either general programmes with broadly based benefits or very limited projects which correct specific problems and which engage a relatively small amount of resources (rent). One of the mishaps which have befallen the Third World is that elites committed to egalitarianism distrust the market, although they could use it to good advantage, whereas elites committed to non-egalitarian distribution of income favour market regulation, especially because the existing market mechanism is imperfect and allows for gate-keeping.

The Structure of the Rent-Controlling State-Class

Due to the control of rent which requires politico-administrative decision-making for its appropriation and allocation, development administrations tend to become major elements of a dominant class in which administrators, the political leadership, the officer corps and the managers of public enterprises are merged (Elsenhans 1981: 118-192). I have described these new classes as being State-classes which are segmented (Elsenhans 1976: 257-258, 1977: 34-35). The segments strive to increase their influence, income and prestige. An analysis of types of such classes in developing countries requires consideration of the socio-cultural norms. Such norms are not easily changed and have greater relevance to the political realm in these countries than in a capitalist society. Thus, even if all these classes tend to waste resources, such behaviour is influenced by the accepted norms.

With regard to the control of rent, I suggest distinguishing between three sets of variables: The degree of routinization, the degree of policy-relatedness of the segmentation, and the position of a given State-class in the cyclical movement between waste/privilege and reform.

One way of reducing waste is the routinization of administrative procedures. Limiting areas of competence leads to limited discretionary power which in turn, allows for abuse of resources. In Algeria, for instance, superiors were not permitted to perform administrative acts devolved to their inferiors, effectively limiting the amount of pressure that could be exerted from above. By increasing the number of administrative levels involved in making an administrative decision, the cost of bribery increases and the returns may become so low that unlawful practices are no longer attempted. The more a development strategy is project-oriented, the more its routinization leads to heavy procedures that may result in rent finally being wasted through increasing administrative costs.

Granting more discretionary power may enhance the possibility of well-intentioned segments of State-classes promoting development, but it also opens up avenues for patronage, clientele-building and even corruption. Routinization without heavy procedures results from interventions that are programme-oriented instead of project-oriented. It has also been shown that strategies based on egalitarian distribution of consumption are more capable of being implemented by routinized procedures than those based on non-egalitarian distribution.

Segments of State-classes arise out of shared characteristics that build mutual confidence, such as common educational background, common ethnic or regional origin, or shared religion or caste. The more these characteristics are policy-related (Elsenhans 1991), such as shared convictions about the appropriateness of certain strategies, the more the rivalries between segments will bring out alternatives in development. As development strategies have different impacts on the interests of different social groups outside the State-classes, a crystallisation of segments around policy issues tends to allow coalition-building between segments and such impacted social groups on the basis of shared economic interests. In such cases, this coalition-building does not tend to separate the leadership of the non-State-class organizations from the membership and thus increases the cohesiveness of these organizations.

On the contrary, the predominance of "ascribed" roles in segment formation leaves only the personal interests of directly concerned leaderships of organizations representing non-State-class interests as basis for coalition-forming. Personalization of power is a subtype of this type of segment-building (Callaghy 1984: 163).

The existence of several parties does not necessarily lead to policy-oriented segmentation since these parties may be machine-parties or parties of notables based on patronage. It does, however, open up avenues for policy-segmented orientation when there is real competition among parties. This competition tends to increase the sizes of networks that are fed by patronage favours, which can result in the emergence of non-satisfied strata of the population. These can become political forces which do not accept the minor advantages patronage and clientelistic networks may offer to them. They may assess these short-term advantages as insignificant in comparison to hoped-for advantages from policy changes and press for the latter. Here, again, diversification of the economy and society will favour such a process of policy-oriented segmentation of the State-class through the activities of policy-oriented class-based organizations.

There is an in-built tendency in State-classes to decrease the degree of policy-orientation in segment-building during the course of their tenure in power. This is due to two main factors. First, the inefficiencies in planning and implementing development projects are compensated for through patronage and clientele building , since power would otherwise be lost. Second, and related to the first, is a process of decreasing openness in discussion and dissemination of information. On the political level, there is no check to patronage-building.

With regard to planning, the interests of segments in promoting their incomes, power and prestige leads to attempts to maximize the financial resources under their control. Even if rent were required to be used for investment, the selected investment projects would not primarily be selected on the basis of their benefit to the macro-economic structure, but rather on the basis of the ability of the segments to which they will belong to push them by presenting them in an over-optimistic light. Costs and expected delays are systematically underestimated while contributions to production are systematically overstated. As a result, competing plans lack internal consistency compared with one another.

At the level of implementation, scarcity, as measured by prices, cannot be used as the basis for allocating resources. Consequently, enterprises have to use other means to ensure adequate supplies of raw materials and markets for their products. Since, scarcities are not reflected in planning documents, enterprises cannot base their claims on them. Networks of connections thus become vital in achieving set targets. Achieving defined targets is necessary in order to maintain one's competitive position among rival segments and other friendly segments, who also expect support in return. The more unrealistic the plans and the more difficult their implementation, the more pronounced becomes the switch from policy-oriented to patronage/clientele-building exercise.

Patronage and clientele systems can be interpreted as mechanisms of adapting the perceptions of the real world held by the dominate State- classes to the objective economic and social reality. Quite rightly, economic results in such a society are not measured by statements of gains and losses achieved on the market by particular enterprises. The reason given for this is that the objective of development is structural transformation through investment projects which are not already profitable, but will be in the future if complementary projects can become operative and/or if complementary measures (i.e. income redistribution) are implemented. On the other hand, bad results reflected on statements of gains and losses may not necessarily be attributable to the pursuit of such long-term objectives, but could merely be the result of bad management, if not fraudulent practices. The dividing line between the two is difficult to establish. Results therefore have to be negotiated among the members of the State-class (Elsenhans 1987a: 86-93). In order to improve one's position in actual or potential negotiating processes, one must take care to create an image which conveys to partners and competitors the impression that one has power, influence, resources and relations. Therefore it is not only economic data which have to be manipulated but even information about relations has to be carefully monitored. The result of this pursuit of self-interest is that the State-class itself, loses more and more knowledge about the society it controls and even about its own structure. The distance between the world one perceives and the world one is expected to believe can become as great as in the tale about the Emperor's new clothes.

It is obvious that the "age" of those in power is important. A newly installed ruling segment may be policy-oriented. Repeated failures in the economic field, however, may lead to patronage/clientele building. This, together with successive repression of rival groups, allows for the emergence of less policy orientation, less realism and more patronage. This continues until either the limits of financial resources are reached or a sudden decrease in the volume of rent occurs (debt crisis) or the regime is violently overthrown or the regime falls down due to the biological end of its head.

The only possible checks to such patronage building would be found in opposition groups within the State-class or competing outside social forces that are powerful enough to impose their own will. In both cases, the leaders of such groups would themselves have to recognize that the short-term benefits from accepting patronage are considerably lower than the long-term benefits or avoided misfortunes from other strategies. Competing groups within State-classes who wish to change the policy are likely to emerge only when the wastefulness of the dominant group threatens the survival of the system. Opposition from competing classes will occur earlier if it is not based only on despair but can offer to hope of achievements if there is a change in development strategy. The more diversified and developed the economy, the greater the probability of the emergence of such opposition.

Underdeveloped economies are characterized by lacunae in the web of their economic activity, especially due to low qualification of labour. Rent is a source of income that seems to provide finance for the overcoming of such lacunae. By favouring the emergence of State-classes, however, rent actually allows for the misuse of such financial resources. As a result, State-classes may become more and more distant from society. The weakness of civil society makes collaboration with members of other classes, especially their leaderships, economically promising to the State-classes. Instead of the horizontal organization of class interests, this vertical cooptation of the leadership of potential class organizations is used to further consolidate the power of the State-classes, which appear as a great octopus with tentacles reaching down to all spheres of society. Whether the horizontal organization of interests is possible this process of verticalization of social and political interaction is decreased and the multiplication of policy-oriented groups within the State-class is increased. Nation-building through the State-class appears to be like placing concrete on top of a pyramid which stands on a pile of sand and is suspended from the top by a rope attached to a crane (rent) which has its power base outside.

Typologies of development administration should be constructed in a way that allows for the positioning of a particular state class between the poles of patronage/personal rule with waste of rent and high discretionary power, on the one hand and policy-oriented regimes with consistent macroeconomic plans and large areas of routinized procedures on the other. The latter are favoured because of their achieved level of economic and social diversification and their economic strategies that are based on growing markets, due either to egalitarian distribution of incomes or to exports. Both of these elements lead to free civil society because the inbuilt incentive structures are capable of providing accumulated knowledge and growth of productive forces through decentralized private entrepreneurs.

Rent and Decentralization

The distinctive problem of developing societies that are dominated by the bureaucratic elements of state-classes is the weak link between the interests of the society and those of the bureaucratic elements themselves. There seem to be an impossibility of aggregating the particular interests of actual existing social forces to a collective interest which could serve as a basis for coherent economic and political development of the society concerned. The argument that distributional conflicts without prior reorientation of the economy will result in balance of payments deficits or in inflation, is based on one of the manifestations of this weakness in cohesiveness in the underdeveloped economies of third world countries. There is no real "belly" in Third World societies which keeps the parts together and allows for absorbing shocks. The State-classes are not forced to defend long-term social interests, even though their economic position would allow them to do so, whereas society is unable to get integrated on the basis of such long-term goals.

Due to the fact that disintegrative tendencies increase with size - larger organizations being coopted by State-classes - decentralization seems to be the key element for maintaining democratic control (including the control of rent). My argument here is in line with the conclusion of many commentators on Third World administration, but is based on a principally different analysis. Due to the importance of rent, the low degree of diversification of the economy, the necessary dominance of a State-class and the tendencies to deepen the related distortions in the economy and the society, the organization of countervailing social power will lead to the cooptation of the leaderships of such organization or to extremism.

Cooptation of leadership will destroy the organizations concerned and limit their capacity to engage reforms in the interest of the social groups they may represent. In order to avoid such cooptation, opposing groups may choose patterns of organization which are designed to preclude such cooptation. Syndicalist and anarchist organizations are often to be found in such societies. Both cooptation and anarchism, are forms of unsuccessful integration of societies.

If integration at the "national" level tends to fail, lower levels can provide the possibility of democratic control of organizations and institutions which are able to cooperate with higher levels. The reason for this is that the process of adjustment of interests at the decentralized level can (but need not) be sufficiently open so that outcomes are considered legitimate by all concerned. From this analysis, decentralization to local levels appears to be the major instrument for nation-building, since a nation cannot be built at the central levels which are cut off from the lowest strata as the result of the mechanisms which have been described.

The conditions for this needed decentralization are rather unfavourable. Rent as a major source of surplus becomes visible mostly at central levels. Export taxes, import duties and monopoly pricing by state enterprises on external or internal markets serve as additional income of the centre. On the other hand, property-related taxes largely favour decentralized bodies, because the taxable asset is localized. Income-related taxes will also not necessarily accrue to the centre. Indirect taxes on products will normally accrue to rather central authorities. The revenue structure of Third World economies has rarely been analysed from the point of view of decentralized control of expenditures, but it seems obvious that public revenue is much more concentrated at the centralized level than in the West.

Despite the widely publicized autonomy of pre-capitalist villages, local autonomy in the Third World has rarely led to local government. There is nothing comparable to the sturdy struggles of the villages for their "liberties" in European feudalism (Schulze 1982:26-43; Heitz 1982: 180), nor to the emergence of city governments (Davey 1975:33; Lewis 1937:35; Stern 1970:36; Sauvalet 1934: 455f; Breuer 1987:195; Lapidus 1969:73; Lagarde 1939:104). Nor is there even research on the extent of such autonomies in the precapitalist Third World.

National liberation movements were largely based on the initiative taken at the central level. The leadership of these movements had to deny the colonial authorities any access to potential pro-colonialist bridge-heads in the local population. Local autonomies could also easily appear as structures quite opposed to national unity. In many of the independent countries, state-classes seem to project a fear of being dependent on locally elected democratic bodies for their actions. I have not yet found a Third World country in which the local government can dispose of assured revenues without far-reaching political interference from above.

Local government can be developed on the basis of rather direct participation by the people at grassroots levels. But such participation will not necessarily be equal for all social groups. The view that devolution of power to local bodies can go without increasing control of local elites is probably not true. A bureaucracy which is in charge of local government may have initially better intentions with regard to the local poor than local elites, but it is less responsive to the local population than are the local elites who must obtain electoral support (Jain 1985:206). Rigging elections may certainly be difficult to overcome. On the other hand, the organization of the poor through voluntary agencies can produce countervailing power which may find ways and means of exercising its influence on the elected local government bodies. Restricting participation in voluntary agencies to the poor does not contradict the devolution of powers and resources to local bodies. Rather it serves as a complementary strategy. Here the solution should be the retention of the meagre local tax resources for local government, together with automatic transfers of money from the centre to local government to be based on a per capita basis, instead of project-related transfers of grants based on approved projects.

Concluding Considerations

The analysis presented in this essay does not deal with the irrelevance of specific administrative set-ups for the improvement of administrative efficiency. Rather it has tried to demonstrate that there is another approach to the understanding of development administration and decentr-alization other than the ones normally followed in the developing countries. To be sure the Weberian type of control is an important instrument for limiting the discretionary power of bureaucracies. In the context of the developing countries, however, discretionary power cannot be completely avoided due to the immense scope of tasks intended to be accomplished by development administration. The essential problem of administrative organisation is to define those areas where Weberian principles can be applied and to restrict discretionary power to a smaller range of agencies.

I have argued that this pattern is greatly enhanced by a more egalitarian distribution of income and by the industrial structure that is related to such a distribution. Even then, "administration" has to perform roles of investment in specific projects. The scope of these projects, however, can be narrowed down as more market-regulated activities become possible.

Agencies specialized in investment are inclined to reduce rewards of their members if their importance in the overall economic decision-making and administration decreases. Fewer decisions are made by the public as more bodies are excluded from discretionary decision-making. This situation seems to favour the proliferation of a greater number of bodies whose members jealously observe the more freely operating agencies.

Some of these freely operating agencies may be limited to carrying out projects only with local bodies, which could lead to further interaction with beneficiaries. Although such participation will favour rich local elites, the enlargement of participation is nevertheless bound to create additional avenues for claims by the neglected elements of the population. The internal functioning of such agencies with limited resources and competencies, and the awareness of the public concerning the existence of competing administrative bodies and outside agencies will contribute to the emergence of new orientation to the stated goals instead of orientation to the particular interests of the agencies.

Therefore, types of development administration may be analysed with regard to the proportion of rent in the overall allocation of resources. On the other hand, the share of discretionary power over financial resources vis-a-vis the amount distributed under general rules is also part of this analysis. The smaller the discretionary power, the greater the possibilities of combining macro-economic projections with implementation through generally accessible advantages for all enterprises. The greater the scope of such programmes, where individuals cannot benefit from "personal" relations, the smaller the possibility of creating networks of patronage and clienteles. In that case, the policy orientation of the development administration and the interest of state-classes are enhanced and patronage as a source of power decreases. This stops the "involutionary" degeneration of the State-classes into self-privileging waste through politicking in the process of allocation of rent. The more "entitlements" are broadly distributed, the greater the limits to waste.

The performance of the administrations according to stated goals and objective rules can certainly be promoted by educating the administrators. New norms will, however, be stable only if the incentives are perceived as worthy of being adhered to. The more the market, with its checks on those in control of economic surplus, is revitalized, the more powerful the groups that demand that administrations adhere to such norms, even if some administrative units or agencies continue to dispose of discretionary powers in order to promote particular projects. The rationale for this assertion is the fact that continuing underdevelopment will not be sanctioned by net returns of the market. The stronger these market-oriented producers and consumers, the more probable the emergence of a diversified economy which is capable of responding flexibly to the needs of the population as a whole.

Notes

1. If access to fair-price shops depends on a ration card to be issued by local authorities only if residence is legal, access becomes dependent not on poverty but on more "complex" criteria.

2. Results of the Konstanz research project B5, cf. Universität Konstanz, Sonderforschungsbereich 221 (1987): *Verwaltung im Wandel, Wissenschaftlicher Arbeits- und Ergebnisbericht für die Finanzierungsperiode 1985-1987,* Konstanz: Universität Konstanz, 31-34.

References

Aldcroft, D.H. (1986), *The British Economy (1): The Years of Turmoil, 1920-1951,* Brighton, Wheatsheef Books.

Aldrich, M. (1973), Flexible Exchange Rates, Northern Expansion and the Market for Southern Cotton, 1866-1879, in *Journal of Economic History,* 33, 2, 399-416.

Aydalot (1968), "Essai sur les problémes de la stratégie de l' industrialisation en économie sous-développée. L'exemple tunisien", Tunis/Paris, in *Les Cahiers du CERES,* 1-175.

Baerresen, D.W. Carnoy, M. and Grunwald J. (1965), *Latin American Trade Patterns,* Washington, The Brookings Institution.

Bagú, S. (1949), *Economía de la sociedad colonial: Ensayo de historia comparada de América Latina,* Buenos Aires, El Ateneo.

Bergschlosser, D. (1979), *The Social and Economic Basis of Politics in Kenya: A Structural and Cultural Analysis.* Berkeley, University of California Press.

Benachenhou, A. (1971), "Le renversement de la problématique ricardienne des coûts comparés dans la théorie économique contemporaine" in *Revue algérienne des sciences juridiques, économiques et politiques,* 8, 4, 913-934.

Bitar, S. (1979), *Transición, socialismo y democracia: La experiencia chilena,* Mexico: Siglor, Veintiuno.

Breman, J. (1985), *Of Peasants, Migrants and Paupers: Rural Labour Circulation and Capitalist Production in West-India,* New Delhi, Oxford University Press.

Breuer, S. (1987), *Imperien der Alten Welt,* Stuttgart, Kohlhammer.

Burch, D. (1987), *Overseas Aid and the Transfer of Technology: The Political Economy of Agricultural Mechanization in the Third World,* Aldershot, Avebury.

Cabral, A. (1974), *Die Revolution der Verdammten: Der Befreiungskampf in Guinea-Bissau,* Berlin, Rotbuch.

Callaghy, T.M. (1984), *The State-Society Struggle: Zaire in Comparative Perspective*, New York, Columbia University Press.

Callaghy, T.M. (1986), "Politics and Vision in Africa: The Interplay of Domination, Equality and Liberty" in Chabal ed., *Political Domination in Africa: Reflections on the Limits of Power*, 1986, Cambridge et al., Cambridge University Press, 30-51.

Chinn, D.L. (1974), *Potential Effects of Income Redistribution on Economic Growth Constraints: Evidence from Taiwan and South-Korea,* Berkeley, Ph. D. Thesis.

Cole, M. (1961), *The Story of Fabian Socialism*, London et al., Heinemann.

Davey, B. (1975), *The Economic Development of India*, Nottingham, Spokesman Books.

Diaz-Alejandro, C.F. (1965), "Industrialization and Labour Productivity Differentials" in *Review of Economics and Statistics*, 47, 2, 207-213.

Elsenhans, H. (1975), "Overcoming Underdevelopment: A Research Paradigm", in *Journal of Peace Research*, 12,4, 293-313.

Elsenhans, H. (1976), " Zur Rolle der Staatsklasse bei der Überwindung von Unterentwicklung", in Schmidt ed., *Strategien gegen unterentwicklung: Zwischen Weltmarkt und Eigenständigkeit,* Frankfurt, Campus, 250-265.

Elsenhans, H. (1977), " Die Staatsklasse/Staatsburgeoisie in den unterentwickelten Ländern zwischen Privilegierung und Legitimationszwang", in *Verfassung und Recht in Übersee,* 10, 1, 29-42.

Elsenhans, H. (1979), "Grundlagen der Entwicklung der kapitalistischen Weltwirtschaft", in Senghaas ed., *Kapitalistische WeltÖkonomie: Kontroversen über ihren Ursprung und ihre Entwicklungsdynamik*, Frankfurt, Suhrkamp, 101-148.

Elsenhans, H. (1981), *Abhängiger Kapitalismus oder bürokratische Entwicklungsgesellschaft: Versuch über den Staat in der Dritten Welt,* Frankfurt, Campus.

Elsenhans, H. (1982), " Die Überwindung von Unterentwicklung durch Massenproduktion für Massenbedarft - Weiterentwicklung eines Ansatzes", in Nohlen/Nuscheler eds., *Handbuck der Dritten Welt (1): Unterentwicklung und Entwicklung - Theorien, Strategien, Indikatoren*, Hamburg, Hoffmann & Campe, 152-182.

Elsenhans, H. (1983a), " Rising Mass Incomes as a Condition of Capitalist Growth: Implications for the World Economy", in *International Organization*, 37, 1, 1-38.

Elsenhans, H. (1983b), " Égalité et développment: L' experiénce européenne et le monde sous-développement d'aujourd'hui", in *Cultures et développment,* 15, 2: 187-216.

Elsenhans, H. (1986a), "Rente, sous-développment et Etat dans le Tiers Monde", in *Les Cahiers du CREAD*, 5: 5-52.

Elsenhans, H. (1986b), "Rente, Strukturelle Heterogenität und Staat: Entwicklunsperspektiven der Staatsklasse in der Dritten Welt", in *Journal für Entwicklungspolitik*, 4: 21-36.

Elsenhans, H. (1986c), "Der Mythos der Kapitalintensität und die notwending falsche Technologiewahl der Entwicklungsländer", in Kohler-Koch ed., *Technik und Internationale Entwicklung*, Baden-Baden, Nomos, 267-290.

Elsenhans, H. (1987a), "Dependencia, Underdevelopment and the Third World State", in *Law and State* Vol.36: 65-94.

Elsenhans, H. (1987b), "Der Sonderforschungsbereich 'Verwaltung im Wandel' an der Universität Konstanz", *Jahrbuch zur Staats- und Verwaltungswissenschaft*, Baden-Baden: Nomos, 369-388.

Elsenhans, H. (1989), "Zur Theorie und Praxis bürokratischer Entwicklungsgesellschaften", in Körner ed., *Zur Analyse von Institutionen im Entwicklungsprozess und in der internationalen Zusammenarbeit*, Berlin, Duncker und Humblot, 101-141.

Elsenhans, H. (1991), *Development and Underdevelopment: The History, Economics and Politics of North-South Relations*, New Delhi/Newbury, Park/London, Sage Publications.

Elsenhans, H. (1993), "Analyse Comparative de l'Etat dans le Tiers Monde - notamment en Afrique Noire", in *Revista Internacional de Estudos Africanos,* No. 16, forthcoming.

Georgescu-Roegen, (1960), "Economic Theory and Agrarian Economics", in *Oxford Economic Papers*, 12, 1: 1-40.

Habakkuk, H. (1972), " Fluctuations and Growth in the 19th Century", in Robertson/Kooy eds., *Studies in Economic and Economic History,* London, Macmillan, 259-279.

Heitz, G. (1982), " Der Zusammenhang zwischen den Bauernbewegungen und der Entwicklung des Absolutismus in Mitteleuropa" in Schulze ed. 1982, *Europaische Bauernrevolten der fruhen Neuzeit*, Frankfurt, Suhrkamp, 171-190.

Huertas, T. (1979), "Damnifyng Growth in the Antebellum South", in *Journal of Economic History,* 39, 1, 87-100.

Jain, L.C. (1985), *Grass Without Roots - Rural Development under Government Auspicies,* New Delhi, Sage Publications.

Keman, H. (1984), *European Society 1500-1700*, London, Hutchinson.

Keynes, J.M. (1939), "Relative Movements of Real Wages and Output", in *Economic Journal,* 49, 193, 34-57.

King, R./Byerlee, D. (1978), "Factor Intensities and Locational Linkages of Rural Consumption Patterns in Sierra Leone", in *American Journal of Agricultural Economics*, 60, 2, 197-206.

Krueger, A.O. (1974), " The Political Economy of the Rent-Seeking Society", in *The American Economic Review,* 290-303.

Kula, W. (1970), *Théorie économique du système féodal: Pour un modèle de l' economie polonaise, 16e-18e siècles,* Paris/Den Haag, Mouton.

Lagarde, G. de (1939), " La structure politique et sociale de L'Europe au XIVe de siècle", in Coville ed., *L'organisation corporative du Moyen Age à là de l' Ancien Régime (Etudes présentées á la Commission Internationale pour l'Histoire des Assemblées des Etats)*, Leuven, Bibliothèque de l'Universite de Louvain.

Lapidus, I. (1969), " Muslim Cities and Islamic Societies", in Lapidus ed. 1969. *Middle Eastern Cities: A Symposium on Ancient Islamic and Contemporary Middle Eastern Urbanism*, Berkeley, University of California Press, 47-79.

Ledda, R. (1967), "Classes sociales et lutte politique" in *International Socialist Journal*, 4, 22, 594-615.

Lewis, B. (1937), " The Islamic Guilds", *Economic History*, 8,1, 20-37.

Little, I.M.D./ Mirrles, J.A. (1974), *Project Appraisal and Planning for Developing Countries*, London, Heinemann.

Luke, D.F. (1984), *Labour and Parastatal Politics in Sierra Leone: A Study in Working-class Ambivalence*, New York/ Hamburg, Lanham Institut fur Afrika-kunde, XVIII.

Lydall, H. (1977), *Distribution During the Process of Development*, Geneva, International Labour Office.

Malowist, M. (1959), " The Economic and Social Development of the Baltic Countries From the Fifteenth to the Seventeenth Centuries", in *Economic History Review*, 12, 2, 177-189.

Montgomery, A. (1938), *How Sweden Overcame the Depression*, Stockholm, Alb Bonniers Boktryckeri.

Müller-Plantenberg, U. /Hinkelammert, F. (1973), " Condiciones y consecuencias de una politica de redistribución de ingresos", in *Cuadernos de la realidad nacional*, 16.2, 203-228.

Murelius, O. (1981), *An Institutional Approach to Project Analysis in Developing Countries*, Paris , OECD.

Olson, M. (1982), *The Rise and Decline of Nations: Economic Growth, Stagflation, and Social Rigidities*, New Haven, Conn./ London, Yale University Press.

Pach, Z. (1966), "L'activité commerciale des seigneurs et leur production marchande en Hongrie au XVIe siècle", in *Annales E.S.C.*, 21,6, 1212-1231.

Paige, J.M. (1975), *Agrarian Revolution, Social movements and Export Agriculture in the Underdeveloped World*, London/ New York, Free Press Collier Macmillan.

Richardson, H. (1939), " Real Wage Movements", in *Economic Journal*, 49, 195, 425-441.

Riggs, F.W. (1964), *Administration in Developing Countries: The Theory of Prismatic Society*, Boston, Houghton-Mifflin.

Sackey, J. A. (1979), " Dependence, Underdevelopment and Socialist Oriented Transformation in Guyana", in *Inter-American Economic Affairs*, 33, 1, 29-50.

Sauvalet, J. (1934), "Esquisse d'une histoire de la ville de Deamas", in *Revue des Etudes Islamiques*, 8, 4, 421-480.

Schulze, W. (1982), " Europäische und deutsche Bauernrevolten de frühen Neuzeit (Probleme der vergleichenden Betrachtung)", in Schulze ed. 1982. *Europäische Bauernrevolten der frühen Neuzeit,* Frankfurt, Suhrkamp, 26-43

Sen, A.K. (1981), *Poverty and Famine: An Essay on Entitlement and Deprivation*, Oxford, Clarendon Press.

Sid Ahmed, A. (1989), *Economie de l'industrialization à partir de resources naturelles (I.B.M.) Vol.1, Faits, pratiques et théories,* Paris, Publisud.

Sideri, S. (1972), " The Industrial Development Deadlock in Latin America: From Import Substitution to Export Promotion", in *Development and Change,* 3, 2, 1-17.

Sideri, S. (1979), "Introduction", in Sideri ed. 1979, *Chile 1970-73: Economic Development and Its International Setting. Self-Criticism of the Unidad Popular Government Policy,* Martinus Nijhoff, Den Haag etc. XIII-XXIII.

Siebold, T. (1988), *Ghana 1957-1987: Entwicklung, Rückentwicklung, Verschuldung und IWF-Intervention,* Hamburg, Institut fur Afrikakunde.

Smith, H. (1979), *Labyrinths of Power: Political Recruitment in Twentieth Century Mexico,* Princeton, Princeton University Press.

Steel, W.F./Takagi, Y. (1978), *The Intermediate Sector, Unemployment-Output Conflict: A Multi Sector Model. (World Bank Staff Working Papers No.301),* Washington D.C., World Bank.

Stevenson, J./Cook, C. (1977), *The Slump: Society and Politics During the Depression,* London, Jonathan Cape.

Stern, S.M. (1970), "The Constitution of the Islamic City", in Hourani/ Stern eds., (1970). *The Islamic City,* Oxford, Cassirer, 25-51.

Strassmann, W. (1956), "Economic Growth and Income Distribution", in *Quarterly Journal of Economics,* 70, 3, 425-440.

Thomas, C.Y. (1984), *The Rise of the Authoritarian State in Peripheral Societies,* London, Heinemann.

Tidrick, G. (1986), *Productivity Growth and Technological Change in Chinese Industry. (World Bank Staff Working Paper No.761),* Washington D.C., World Bank.

3 BRAZIL : THE POLITICS OF STATE ADMINISTRATION

Elisa P. Reis

Introduction

The politics of state administration in Brazil from the 1930s on serves to illustrate the range of problems affecting bureaucracies in third world societies. The present overview of the Brazilian historical experience during this period begins with a brief review of discussions of the bureaucratic question among latecomers, as the issue originally appeared in the development literature and as it was later influenced by the critiques of bureaucracy raised in advanced capitalist as well as in existing socialist contexts

Section two then explores the innovations brought to administrative structures and the role attributed to public bureaucracies across different regimes from 1930 to the present. Given the extent to which state structures have played a key role in economic growth, I focus on the administrative options characterizing each regime, examining these as political options made by the state. While I do not deny the usefulness of an analytical distinction between politics and bureaucracy, what I propose here is to concentrate on the interaction between bureaucratic patterns and structures and the nature of the prevailing political order.

Section three presents concluding remarks on Brazil's current attempt to consolidate a democratic political order while responding to the bureaucratic dilemma. I call attention to the fusing of the political and economic crises in this postdictatorial era and argue that bureaucracy has remained a key variable in the economic growth equation, while its participation in the democratizing challenge seems to have expanded. I believe this conclusion justifies the quest for a better understanding of the politics of bureaucracy in Brazil and in other postdictatorial contexts, as a contribution to democratizing theory and practice.

The Bureaucratic Phenomenon in Historical and Comparative Perspective

It is a commonplace to affirm that during this century the role of the state has been paramount in national development. Already in the nineteenth century, Germany set the standard that was to be reinforced by successful and unsuccessful developmental experiences all over

the world, both capitalist and non-capitalist. The 1960s brought the apex of the development
ideology in which public bureaucracies play a key role in the production of political, economic,
and social goods. As LaPalombara stated in the preface to a prestigious collection of articles
that he edited in 1963:

> "Whereas much of the Western world developed with relatively little direct intervention
> by the 'public sector', this history will clearly not repeat itself. For reasons that
> range from economic necessity to ideological rigidity, the developing nations insist
> that government - particularly the bureaucracy - should play a major, even exclusive,
> role in affecting the changes that are thought. Thus, whether it is the building of
> roads, the creation of new industries, or the radical transformation of traditional
> villages, one can usually expect to find the bureaucracy intimately involved. Even
> in those places where some concessions are made to the participation of the 'private
> sector', such activity will be and probably must be carefully integrated with what
> government itself does" (LaPalombara 1963: ix).

Coherent with the above 'creed', reforms aimed at equipping the state with modern
bureaucratic agencies were promoted throughout the third world and involved the channelling
of international aid funds, the creation of numerous training programs, and the fuelling
of endless academic discussions There was little doubt that in due time the newly created
bureaucracies would dominate the scene, supplanting the typical dual pattern of transition
to modernity that combined legal-rational structures with traditional ones, the latter based
on old commitments and thus not adequate to meet developmental challenges.

The most optimistic versions of the modernizing ideology saw bureaucratic innovation
as the remedy to more than just inefficient administration. The creation of new administrative
posts based upon universalistic criteria was also meant to create an opportunity for the
emergence of a new leadership capable of ousting long-entrenched elites from power. Thus,
much of the developmental literature has explicitly or implicitly assigned governmental
bureaucracy a key role: identified as strategic actors, bureaucrats were either deliberately
or by default supposed to constitute the political opposition to traditional interests and
backward sectors.

To a large extent, the endeavour to bureaucratize public power -- something which
has been intrinsic to development projects -- responded not only to economic requirements
but also to a concerted effort to promote the nation-state. Thus, the inauguration of public
agencies in sparsely populated rural areas constituted a powerful instrument of state penetration
and affirmed public authority against private powers, thereby enhancing the state-building

enterprise. At the same time, the provision of services and goods by the newly established bureaucracies helped to foster social identification with public authority, in turn encouraging loyalty, the substratum of nationbuilding.

The optimistic developmental expectations prevailing in the sixties evolved, matured, and in most of the third world were laid to rest. Now, three decades later, bureaucracy has become the villain and is held responsible for economic inefficiencies, for the vicissitudes of public finances, for the arbitrary allocation of public services, and for the inhibition of social creativity. Paraphrasing LaPalombara, one could say that for reasons that range from economic necessity to ideological rigidity, 'bureaucratic shrinkage' has become the key word in the third world. Privatization, budget reductions, fiscal shock, small government, de-bureaucratization, and similar formulas popular in the new state imagery all entail drastic steps to re-dimension the size and scope of public bureaucracies.

While latecomers have grown disillusioned with public bureaucracies mainly due to the failure of development projects, most current critiques echo discourses elaborated in both the first and second worlds. Within mature capitalist societies, opposition to the 'big state' comes from both the left and the right. What mainly comes under attack by the left is the reemergence of patrimonial features of the welfare state that curb social initiatives and consequently prevent the strengthening of social bonds (Keane 1984). The right, on the other hand, aims its criticisms at the usurpation of market functions by the state and at the inefficient bureaucratic use of resources, where this use could be optimized through competitive mechanisms (Revel 1983). Vigorous opposition to bureaucracy is heard within the socialist sphere as well, where deep frustrations spring from the inefficient fulfilment of economic functions as well as from the predominance of authority over social solidarity resources.[3]

No doubt, many of the problems faced by existing socialism as well as by mature capitalism find close correspondence across the third world. In experimenting with more or less orthodox developmental strategies, the latecomers have usually found themselves encumbered with a huge state machine accused of technical rigidity and the despotic use of power and blamed for the fiscal crisis.

While from a generic perspective these recurrent criticisms of bureaucracy remain universally valid, third world countries run the risk of importing misplaced ideologies. For example, much of the privatised discourse popular among nco-conservatives in mature capitalist societies addresses situations where citizenship was long ago extended de jure and de facto to all social sectors. The society-wide granting of full citizenship rights typical of mature capitalism means that the state does not have to compensate for a deficit in social solidarity as it does in less developed societies. Moreover, within the latter, the fulfilment of economic functions by the state has itself served to crystallize privileges among private sectors, which in turn has contaminated the market and made it heavily dependent upon authority mechanisms.

Much of the competitive vigour usually associated with the market consequently has thus never found expression among latecomers. While this brings to mind the problems currently confronting Eastern Europe, any parallel must again be carefully qualified. As far as social structure is concerned, the differences between existing socialism and Third World capitalism are so dramatic as to make the implications of a move toward a restitution of market functions radically different here and there.

In brief, public bureaucracies in third world countries today share many of the vices plaguing the developed capitalist world as well as many of those afflicting existing socialism, while they at the same time preserve their own peculiarities, augmenting the complexity of these situations and posing the need for original theoretical elaborations and original policy solutions.

Comparisons with first and second world societies are of paramount importance, but equally critical is the effort to arrive at generalizations concerning the peculiar blend of market and of authority that characterizes the latecomers. The discussion that follows, while somewhat superficial and restricted to the experience of a single country, seeks to place Brazilian historical processes in an analytical perspective that might prove a fruitful basis for generalizations on public bureaucracies in the third world.

The Role of Bureaucracy in the Brazilian Economic Growth

Brazilian public administration has a long-standing negative reputation for being too centralized, inefficient, parasitic, and oversized. Both official and popular explanations of this state of affairs usually stress the influence of Portuguese patrimonial structures. Our colonial heritage is blamed for the proliferation of state agencies whose main function is to offer an opportunity for the exercise of patronage power and also for the endless bureaucratic routines that Brazilians must cope with in daily life.

Genetic explanations do in fact seem to play an important role. The colonial administration forced Brazil to adopt a rigidly centralized system of control based on prebendal jurisdictions, a formalistic legal tradition, and excessive concern with the regulation of societal development.[4] The fact that national independence was attained without a liberation struggle certainly contributed to preserving administrative continuities.[5]

It has, however, never been satisfactorily explained just how and why objective conditions permitted the persistence of this tradition, despite explicit efforts to reverse it. Even if we take the notorious resilience of bureaucratic structures into account, the fact remains that the dynamics of the Brazilian state-building process and the strategies of economic development that were adopted greatly stimulated further proliferation of bureaucracy and centralization of power (Reis 1979: chapter IV). Historically, the expansion of the state apparatus became particularly noticeable after the Revolution of 1930 (Vieira da Cunha 1963; Baer, Kertzenetzky and Villela 1973; Martins 1976). As the country was transformed under the aegis of the state into an increasingly urban and industrialized society, the bureaucratization of public authority expanded greatly. Vargas, in power from 1930 to 1945, led a successful drive toward modernization from above, with the politics of state administration playing the key role.

Under Vargas came a major effort to modify public administration, especially after 1938. The landmark of these efforts was the creation of the DASP (DePartamento Administrativo do Servico Publico), a federal agency entrusted with the formulation and implementation of norms governing the functioning of the central government administration and the civil service. The new agency introduced a meritocratic system into the federal administration and made job entrance and promotion exams mandatory within bureaucratic agencies. The DASP also placed critical legal-rational limits on bureaucratic initiatives, particularly those related to resource allocation and accounting controls (Vieira da Cunha 1963; G. Siegel 1978).

The general idea behind this administrative reform was to equip the Brazilian state with a modern, efficient, and reliable administrative structure in order to promote national development. To this end, deliberate efforts were made to approximate the Weberian ideal-model of a legal-rational administrative instrument. The administrative reforms undertaken by Vargas' modernizing dictatorship most certainly constituted a significant departure from the old patrimonial tradition.

It is possible to identify multiple goals in the politics concerning bureaucracy that was implemented during the Vargas years. Analytically, I would distinguish four different, although inter-related purposes behind the administrative model pursued during that period: First, as indicated above, innovations in recruitment and training practices, career patterns, and civil service conceptions were intended to respond to a critical need to improve the efficiency of the bureaucratic machine. That is to say, reforms altering administrative practices and bureaucratic behaviour were intended to increase state performance.

Second, administrative innovation under Vargas sought to fashion instruments that would promote rapid economic growth. The industrialization model adopted granted the state the leading role in basic economic activities, with the aim of laying down pre-conditions and creating incentives for private industrial investments.[6]

Third, administrative reforms were used as an instrument to create public power. In other words, the establishment of new public structures provided an opportunity to affirm state authority vis-à-vis the power pretensions of long-standing oligarchies. In this sense, bureaucratic politics played a decisive role in the state-building enterprise, sharpening the distinction between public and private power.

Fourth, bureaucratic growth during this period also reflected a significant nation-building effort. Since political incorporation followed the premises of state-corporatism, it was mainly through the bureaucratic dispensation of social rights that the state invested in the legitimation of power. Popular political support was basically built upon the extension of labour rights to urban workers who were tied to the state through the bureaucracy of the Ministry of Labour and through statepatronized unions (Schmitter 1971; Werneck Vianna 1976). In practice, the sustained growth of the industrial sector made the expanding labour market the critical source of political incorporation. The labour card became the instrument of access to citizenship rights (dos Santos 1979).

It is undeniable that during the period of 1930-45 the politics of state administration scored high as far as the state- and nation-building enterprises are concerned. There is also consensus as to the remarkable success of newly established state agencies assigned productive functions. Yet most analysts today would agree that results were far from satisfactory in terms of efficiency and accountability.

In relation to bureaucratic efficiency, not only did many longstanding problems persist, but the very modifications that were introduced themselves had pernicious effects (Graham 1968; Garcia 1983). The demands of political compromise forced the continuation of patronage recruitment patterns, wherein hirings were officially justified as only temporary but would in fact become permanent appointments. At the same time, new agencies established to meet developmental challenges were placed under the direct responsibility of the executive, furthering the growth and concentration of state power. In short, this first attempt to modernize bureaucracy was a de facto sanctioning of what would become a well-established dualistic tradition in Brazilian administration: parasitism and inefficiency, on the one hand, and lack of accountability, on the other.

The 1945 return to democratic-constitutional politics did not greatly alter these established patterns. Under the pressure of reactivated party politics, public sector patronage expanded. So did the creation of new executive agencies as a solution for overcoming the incapacity of already existing ones. Thus, during the so-called liberal period from 1945 to 1964, a series of piecemeal initiatives were undertaken to counteract bureaucratic impasses; instead of an all-encompassing attempt to reform the administration, the government opted for multiple and ad hoc remedies to administrative problems.

In retrospect, one could say that during this period bureaucratic innovation was no longer perceived as part of a state-building strategy, essentially becoming instead a means of stimulating economic growth.[7] This is most clearly visible under the Juscelino Kubitschek administration (1955-60), when task forces became the typical bureaucratic solution in the implementation of development projects. In addition, through the creation of autarchic agencies and state foundations, the government managed to circumvent bureaucratic inefficiency without challenging established patron-client networks or pork barrel practices.

Thanks to the above-mentioned strategy, the gap between the traditional civil service and the more recently established agencies became institutionalized (Nunes and Geddes 1987: 147-78). Worst of all, this gap lent grounds to the generalized belief that the efficiency of the new administrative sector was based on its organizational autonomy and its technocratic independence from social demands. By implication, endeavour to improve the traditional sector began to be seen as worthless. Ironically, the period we usually think of as the 'democratic intermezzo' in Brazilian history thus sanctioned administrative practices and related beliefs that ran contrary to the notions of accountability and social responsiveness normally associated with the democratic model.

In short, the politics of administration that characterized the 1945-64 democratic regime was directed essentially toward economic growth. No bureaucratic reforms were attempted, and the proliferation of new agencies did not come in response to any concerted institutional plan. Rather than representing an attempt to improve the performance of existing bureaucracies, what took place looked more like a pragmatic strategy to adopt ad hoc solutions to new administrative challenges. Given Brazil's relative economic prosperity and the multiplication of new sources of investments, the door was open to widespread bureaucratic corruption. The development ideology substituted state- and nation-building projects. More precisely, the strengthening of the nation-state was mainly dependent on economic development. National development became more important than state growth. But to the extent that state involvement in economic production was already deeply ingrained, there was ample room for a variety of alliances and compromises between public and private sectors.

All in all, during the democratic intermezzo the state managed to bypass the obstacles posed by the heavy administrative structure inherited from the previous period, thanks to the ability to introduce new administrative structures to cope with developmental challenges. However, solutions remained shaky and provisory and administrative impasses arose that would eventually need to be dealt with. Given that bureaucratic proliferation did not conform to an institutional project, the state spared itself heavy investments in bureaucratic reforms but ended up faced with a multitude of administrative structures that through duplication, neutralization, and a general lack of coordination pushed up administrative costs and were detrimental to the transparency of power.

Concluding this overview of the second period under consideration, it can be said that the politics of administration then adopted was in some ways highly pragmatic and flexible, and as such they contributed to stifling dynamism in the economy and to accommodating competitive social interests. However, what in the short run constituted pragmatism and flexibility was to quickly be transformed into opportunism, into a lack of administrative strategy, and into the erecting of bureaucratic obstacles to development.

While economic growth indexes signalled a reduced dynamism during the early sixties, rising inflation, growing social unrest, and political polarization laid the grounds for a military coup. The quest for state structures better suited to meeting the nation's major challenges played a key role in the dictatorial discourse. In two decades of military rule in Brazil (1964-84), public bureaucracies took on a multitude of administrative, technical, political, and economic functions. The ruling army adopted a new model of modernization from above, one in which policy activities were presented as substitutes for the political disputes that had been despotically brought to a halt. This new political model -- which was adopted in several Latin American countries as well as in other dictatorial experiments elsewhere in the developing world -- came to be conceptualized as bureaucratic authoritarianism, a title earned due to the centrality of state bureaucracies in commanding political, economic, and social life in conjunction with a national development project (O'Donnell 1978: 3-38).

Coherent with the above, the authoritarian regime installed in Brazil in 1964 opted to once again move toward administrative reform. To this end, legislation was approved in 1967 (Decree-Law No. 200) in order to adjust governmental structures to the newly adopted economic model. Since the government was willing to become more responsive to business interests (particularly international ones) in terms of regulation, infrastructure, and services, changes in administrative regulations became strategic. The reforms also aimed to expand state control over society.

The duality of purposes behind the reform measures to some extent explains not only their contradictory, centralizing, and decentralizing implications but also the open dissatisfaction expressed by a number of their earlier supporters who eventually became critical of the changes undertaken.[8] Centralization did occur to the extent that the margin of exclusive executive competence in administrative matters was significantly expanded. Many of the state agencies were in fact subordinated directly to the national presidency and became de facto autonomous bodies protected by the alleged superiority of purely technical concerns over the give-and-take of politics.

Some observers refer to the above phenomenon as a form of Balkanization and call attention to the subsequent increase in the discretionary powers of certain state agencies. Agency employees also earned much higher salaries than their counterparts in the traditional public sector and enjoyed much better pension and retirement plans in addition to many other fringe benefits. In short, this so-called technocratic sector of the state administration, which constituted the back-bone of the military dictatorship, came to constitute a kind of aristocracy within the public service.[9]

A clear illustration of the visible expansion of the 'indirect' administration under the military is the fact that of the 251 federal state enterprises active in 1980, nearly half had been created during the preceding ten years (Trebat 1983: 37). Also revealing is the fact that between 1960 and 1980 technical and scientific occupations (where the government is the leading employer) more than doubled their participation in the economically active population, jumping from 2.5 million (3.1%) to 8.2 million (6.8%). During the same period, the participation of the conventional public sector rose from 3.17n of the EAP to 4.1% (Hasenbalg and Valle e Silva 1988: 16, 22).

Included among the de-centralization measures of the 1967 reform was a move to facilitate contracts with private firms for the supplying of goods and services to the public sector. The justification was the claim that private capital was much more efficient than the bulky state machinery in performing economic tasks. In practice, private firms transformed themselves into clients of the state and made use of non-market resources to secure new contracts, either by invoking their social functions as large-scale employers or by resorting to less honourable instruments of persuasion.

As this brief historical overview suggests, two major attempts at bureaucratic reform in Brazil were implemented by authoritarian regimes eager to increase their powers of control: one under Vargas and the other under military rule. Both experiences have to be understood as part and parcel of statebuilding projects sponsored by dictatorial governments, the first civil and the second military. In between the two, attempts to modernize administrative practices reflected pragmatic economic considerations rather than concerted efforts to expand public power.

There were of course significant differences between the politics of state administration implemented in the period of 1930-45 and those implemented by the ruling army starting in the mid-sixties. In terms of the above discussion, it is possible to conclude that under Vargas, administrative reform and innovation were the key to national development. At that time, the purposes of administrative reform ranged from the intent to alter the bureaucratic ethos and bureaucratic performance, so as to increase efficiency, to the intent to administrate the political market through the distribution of welfare benefits.

Under the military, no all-encompassing administrative reforms were implemented. The modifications of administrative legislation adopted in 1967, although of profound consequences, were basically aimed at making room for the entrepreneurial state as well as for private capital. In coherence with the option for an economic strategy that delayed distribution in favour of concentrated growth, the dictatorial state initially dealt with its own bureaucratic agencies essentially either as production units or as instruments of coercion.

State- and nation-building were of course central concerns for the military but here their project was modeled on the premise that the economic dynamism of state enterprises was to be the major instrument in creating public power and that economic performance would in turn fortify popular support. Only in sparsely populated rural areas was there an explicit effort to expand the administrative machinery. In a way, this led to the conclusion of a process of bureaucratization of power that had long been completed in urban areas. These efforts significantly altered power networks in rural areas, substituting new state officers for old local bosses and strengthening national loyalty among the ruralities through the final granting of minimal citizenship rights to rural workers (Reis 1988: 203-18).

In assessing the overall results of the changes introduced by 1967 administrative legislation (Decree-Law 200), one can see that despite the many failures of the new legal provisions, gains were indeed made in efficiency, reverting mainly in favour of central state authorities. Market interests also benefited (even if in a less obvious way), since an explicit commitment to the acceleration of capitalist development permeated all these moves toward change. It is undeniable, however, that public bureaucracies did not become more responsive to social needs, that unaccountability continued to be justified in the name of national development, and that while state economic initiatives benefited from modernizing changes, the government was never seriously concerned with offering better administrative services to the citizenry.

Bureaucratic structures were so closely identified with the arbitrariness and unaccountability of power that among the most visible of the defunct military regime's moves to liberalize from within was the National De-Bureaucratization Program, established in 1979. Cutting red-tape and making bureaucracies accountable came to constitute (at least at the rhetorical level) official signs of government willingness to embark upon a democratizing experiment (Batista Araûjo e Oliveira 1984). Given that the modernizing dictatorship of this period had been aptly described as bureaucratic authoritarianism, it was obvious that any move toward liberalization would necessarily entail a deliberate effort to improve both the responsiveness and the accountability of the public sector. It is quite clear that the National De-bureaucratization Program mainly fulfilled the symbolic-expressive role of substantiating government concern over the vicissitudes citizens encounter in their dealings with the state

(Reis 1984). The effective impact on administrative routines and bureaucratic behaviour was far from impressive. In any case, the popularity gained by the Program in its heyday attests to the dramatic salience of bureaucratic shortcomings and wrongdoings in the daily life of individual citizens and of collective actors. In this sense, the symbolic attempt to correct bureaucracies, which the military regime used to signal its willingness to liberalize from within, highlighted the tight relationship between bureaucratic practices and the scope and meaning of citizenship.

The Emergence of the Civilian Government

The civilian government inaugurated in 1985, with the explicit task of implementing the democratic transition that had been negotiated with the military, seemed willing to honour the commitment to remedy public bureaucracies. Initially, the survival of the De-Bureaucratization Program seemed to suggest that it could gain momentum and help to improve accountability thus strengthening democratic forces. But the very revalorisation of politics deflated the concerted effort to improve bureaucratic transparency and responsiveness.

In practice, the Office for De-bureaucratization competed with other cabinets and with politicians for brokerage functions; naturally, open competition was not in its favour. While under authoritarianism the National De-bureaucratization Program benefited from a monopoly, under the rules of the political market it could not match its competitors ability to effectively bypass bureaucratic obstacles and to mediate access to public services.

The Program was soon cancelled and its ombudsman-like features were dispersed among a series of more traditional channels of political brokerage. With the revalorisation of the vote-currency in the political arena, politicians disputed opportunities to mediate between citizens and street-level bureaucrats, between interest groups and state firms, and between local governments and top cabinet officers.

This is not to say that public accountability was greater under the dictatorship than under the current civilian regime, nor that bureaucratic oppression has worsened. The mere reestablishment of basic civil and political rights has acted as a powerful deterrent to many abuses of administrative power. However, it cannot be ignored that throughout the seven years that have passed since the military stepped down, the rectification of public bureaucracies has not ranked high on the political agenda. While the drafting of the new Constitution set the stage for a thorough revision of the relationship between politics and administration, little has been done to institutionalize changes in that direction. After twenty years of deliberate intertwining of politics and bureaucracy, the nation is faced with an established bureaucracy that, not surprisingly, over the years came to internally reproduce the fragmentation of interests typical of politics.[10]

This is particularly notable in the ease of state firms, which take advantage of their ambiguous public/private identity and combine market and authority criteria, circumventing the conventional mechanisms through which accountability is enforced. With their own constituencies in civil society, these powerful bureaucracies are sometimes described as states within the state (Reis and Orenstein 1989: 121-33). They have, for example, defied government attempts to enforce new public sector regulations and have successfully resisted anti-inflationary wage policies.

With regard to bureaucratic agencies in the direct administration, and as indicated in the previous section, the long-established tradition of creating bureaucratic agencies parallel to the older state structures confined the latter to a marginal position where poor working conditions, insufficient pay, and low morale have produced an environment prone to extreme inefficiency and irresponsiveness.

The dramatic economic crisis afflicting Brazil hampers the always tense relationship between politics and bureaucracy and increases the complexity of the democratizing challenge. In confronting a multitude of political, social, and economic problems, public authorities must also search for new patterns of interaction between politicians and bureaucrats as a sine qua non to the consolidation of democracy (Reis 1990: 19-30).

In this kind of context, the currently observed temptation to put full blame for the gigantic economic crisis on the public sector constitutes a severe threat to the consolidation of a democratic order. If it is true that the functioning of the public sector is the driving force behind the huge state deficit, it might prove disastrous to opt for the radical privatization scheme that appears to be gaining ever more prestige in the political market.

The persistence of bureaucratic inefficiency, a lack of transparency in government, and despotism have certainly played important roles in recent Brazilian history. However, the emulation of radical liberalism would surely require the state to abdicate part of its legitimate functions in favour of the market. Considering that in most of the third world, capitalism has evolved under 'savage' social conditions that have sanctioned extreme inequalities, re-entrusting the market with functions it has actually never had would jeopardize social solidarity and hinder economic growth.

What has been stated here is not meant as a defence of irresponsible state capitalism or of the patrimonial-like features inherent to the authoritarian welfarism traditionally adopted by Brazil. My argument is that as long as a significant parcel of the population has to struggle fiercely to assure its mere survival, handing social regulatory power over to the market would have explosive consequences.

Given that past experiences reveal the dramatic consequences of state efforts to curb market functions and that these same experiences suggest that the indiscriminate privatization of functions performed by public bureaucracies jeopardizes solidarity, we are left with the same old challenge of reconciling politics and bureaucracy. This might appear to some as an endless regression to nowhere. Yet, I hope the arguments presented here help to clarify conditions that are peculiar to Brazil as well as to other late-developing capitalist societies. These conditions seem to suggest that the knots entangling political and economic crises are perhaps tighter now than ever in such societies. They also suggest that the politics of public bureaucracies will play a key role in forging both the conditions for economic growth and the prospects for democratic consolidation.

Notes

3. The recent upsurge of market forces and the strengthening of social movements in Eastern Europe, while in many respects interdependent, clearly justify analytical differentiation.

4. On the Portuguese patrimonial legacy see Raimundo Faoro, *Os Donos do Poder*, Porto Alegre: Globo, 1958. The persistence of patrimonial features in Brazilian politics is discusse in Simon Schwartzman, *As Bases do Autoritarsmo Brasilero*, Rio de Janeiro, Paz e Terra, 1982.

5. The son and representative of the Portuguese king declared Brazilian independence in 1822.

6. This is perhaps the best-documented aspect of bureaucracy under Vargas. See, for example, Luciano Martins 1976; Robert Levine 1970. *The Vargas Regime: The Critical Years*, 1934-38, New York, Columbia University Press; John Wirth 1970. *The Politics of Brazilian Development*, 1930-54, Stanford, Stanford University Press.

7. Naturally, upon Vargas' return to the national presidency (1950-54), this time through the pools, we witness an attempt to re-establish his past bureaucratic politics. However, the altered political-institutional conditions for enforcing power, on the one hand, and the very dynamics of economic growth, on the other, prevented a complete re-enactment of past administrative projects.

8. Hélio Beltrão, 1967 author of Decree-Law 200 and later to become the first Minister of De-bureaucratization, complained bitterly about the distortion of the original objectives of this law and, chief among them, of the incentives offered to private entrepreneurship.

9. Since the military stepped down, politicians have earned immediate profits from their position to these privileged sectors of public administration. The victorious 1989 presidential campaign was based largely upon an aggressive attach of the privileged echelons of the state bureaucracy.

10. On the inevitable fragmentation of the interests of bureaucratic government, see Guy Peters, "The Problem of Bureaucratic Politics", Vol. 43, No.1, 1981: 55-82.

References

Araujo e Oliveira, Joano Batista (1984), *Desburocratizacao e Democracia,* Campinas, Papirus.

Baer Werner, I. Kertzenetzky and A. Villela (1973), "The Changing Role of the State in the Brazilian Economy, in *World Development*, Vol. 11, No.1.

Belträo Helio (1967), Decree-Law 200.

Carcia, Fernando C. (1983), "Uma Interpretaçao dos Impasses e um Projeto Alternativo", in IPEA/INPES, *Modernizaçao Administrativa,* Rio de Janeiro.

Faoro Raimundo (1958), *Donos do Poder,* Porto Alegre, Globo.

Graham, Lawrence (1968), *Civil Service Reform in Brazil: Principles vs. Practice*, Austin, University of Texas Press.

Haesenbalg, Carlos and N. Valle e Silva (1988), *Estrutura Social, Mobilidade e Raça,* Sao Paulo, Vertice.

Keane, John (1984), *Public Lifein Late Capitalism*, Cambridge, Cambridge University Press.

LaPalombara, Joseph (1963), *Bureaucracy and Political Development,* Princeton, New Jersey, Princeton University Press.

Levine, Robert (1970), *The Vargas Regime: The Critical Years, 1934-38*, New York, Colombia University Press.

Martins, Luciano (1976), *Pouvoir Politique et Development Economique: Formation et Evolution des Structures Politiques au Bresil*, Paris, Anthropos.

Nunes, Edson O. and B. Ceddes (1987), "Clientelism and Political Insulation: Towards a Political Sociology of Contemporary Brazil", in John Wirth, Odson O. Nunes and Thomas Bogenschild eds., *The State and Society in Brazil: Continuity and Change*, bolder, Westview Press.

O'Donnell, Guillermo (1978), "Reflections on the Patterns of Change in the Bureaucratic-Authoritarian State", in *Latin America Research Review,* Vol.13, No.2, 3-38.

Peters, Guy (1981), "The Problem of Bureaucratic Politics", Vol.43, No. 1, 55-82.

Reis, Elisa P. (1979), *The Agrarian Roots of Authoritarian Modernization in Brazil: 1880-1930*, Unpublished Ph.D. dissertation, Cambridge, Mass., MIT.

Reis, Elisa P. (1984), "Bureaucratic Oppression: The Citizen"s View, paper presented at the Third International Conference on Bureaucracy, Gottlieb Duttweiler Institute, Zurich, October.

Reis, Elisa P. (1988), "Mudança e Contnuidade na Politica Rural Brasileira", *DADOS,*Vol. 31, No.2, 203-18.

Reis, Elisa P. and Luiz Orenstein (1989), " The Transparency Issue: Public and Private Access to Information in the Brazilian Transition to Democracy", in *The Journal of Behavioral and Social Sciences,* Vol. 29, 121-33.

Reis, Elisa P. (1990), " Bureaucrats and Politicians in Current Brazilian Politics, in *International Social Science Journal,* 123, 19-30.

Revel, Jean-François (1983), *Comment les Democraties Finissent*, Paris, Grasset.

Santos dos, Wanderley G. (1979), *Cidadania e justica*, Rio de Janeiro, Campus.

Schmitter, Philippe (1971), *Interest Conflict and Political Change in Brazil,* Stanford, Stanford University Press.

Schwartzman, Simon (1982), *As Bases do Autoritarismo Brasileiro*, Rio de Janeiro, Paz e Terra.

Siegel, Gilbert (1978), *The Vicissitudes of Governmental Reform in Brazil: a Study of the DASP*, Washington D.C. University Press of America.

Trebat, Thomas J. (1983), *Brazil's State-Owned Enterprises, A Case Study of the State as Entrepreneur,* Cambridge, Cambridge University Press.

Vieira da Cunha, Mario W. (1963), *O Sistema Administrativo Brasileiro*, Rio de Janeiro, CBPE.

Werneck Vianna, Luiz J. (1976), *Liberalismo e Sindicato no Brasil*, Rio de Janeiro, Paz e Terra.

Wirth, John (1970), *The Politics of Brazilian Development: 1930-54*, Stanford, Stanford University Press.

4 SURINAM'S DEVELOPMENT PLANNING : ADVERSITY OR FAILURE

R. Hoppe

Introduction

Political context

Surinam became independent on November 25, 1975. Latin America had gained a new democratic civilian government - or so it seemed. Less than five years later, the curtain came down on what was in effect a decaying elite-cartel democracy (Hoppe 1976a). A handful of non-commissioned officers staged a coup on February 25, 1980, and a new government consisting of soldiers and non-compromised 'technocrats' was quickly installed. The new regime made known its intentions in a Manifesto of the Revolution, which promised the Surinamese a new social and economic order. Exploitation and other ills of neo-colonial rule would be a thing of the past.

But the dream turned into a nightmare. The logic of power for power's sake gradually drove Surinam to the edge of military dictatorship. In the night of December 7, 1982, that borderline was crossed for all to see, when the new regime's leading opponents were liquidated by the military clique headed by 'Commander' Bouterse. During the seven years that Surinam's political system was slipping from a corrupted variant of democracy into a military dictatorship, the treaty signed by the Netherlands and Surinam at the time of Surinamese independence was being implemented. The Netherlands had promised that development aid amounting to three and a half milliard Dutch guilders would be forthcoming over a period of ten to fifteen years. However, as soon as the events of December 1982 became known, the Netherlands unilaterally suspended the execution of this treaty. Foreign pressures, domestic unrest, and a lack of administrative capability and political vision soon brought the 'revolution' to a halt. In 1984, after short-lived flirtations with radical left-wing groups, Bouterse secretly renewed the cooperation with the political parties representing the 'ancien régime' (Chin & Buddingh' 1987: 65). The elections held in November 1987 restored democracy, but the balance between civilian and military power remained disjointed and unstable. Although no new development plans were drawn up, the Dutch government restored economic aid to Surinam under the terms of the independence treaty.

Present relations between Surinam and the Netherlands call for a thorough reassessment of all aspects of those relations, including an evaluation of the objectives, execution and results of Surinam's development planning up to the present day. Throughout independence, military coup and the gradual restoration of democracy, the complex of socioeconomic problems facing the country have displayed a singular continuity. One thing which was sorely lacking after independence was a new conception of Surinam's economic development strategy. The general attitude was that up to 1975 its development planning had been a failure, and that this failure could be laid at the door of Dutch neo-colonialism. However, if any new strategy is to succeed, the failure of earlier policies must first be squarely faced and dealt with in a creative manner. The following evaluation of Surinamese development in the period 1946 to 1975 is an attempt to meet this need.

Evaluation strategy

There still is little attention for the link between (in-)effectiveness of government policy and administrative and/or political factors. This prompted the formulation of the problem guiding the present study: Have the objectives of Surinam's development policy between 1946 and 1975 been attained, or brought closer to realization? And if not, what is the nature of the political and administrative factors which contributed to that failure?

There are countless problems involved in the formulation of tenable claims as to the relationship between 'policy as plan', 'policy in action' and 'the results of policy'. One need only consider the additional perils of policy evaluation in the Third World, due to the uncertainty which dogs both planners and evaluators (Stolper, 1966; Caiden & Wildavsky 1974: 45-65). Surinam is an example of just such a Third World or peripheral country, and this means that any attempt to arrive at an accurate assessment of all aspects of Surinam's development policy is doomed to failure. A complete assessment must of necessity be preceded by a more approximate analysis, such as we envision here.

The problem may be divided into four main sections:

1. What were the contents of the various development plans drawn up between 1946 and 1975?
2. Did the structural characteristics of Surinam's peripheral economy, i.e. the lack of cohesion, the unproductive interaction between the various economic sectors, and the heavy external dependence, improve or worsen during this period?
3. What does the answer to the second question tell us about the extent to which the official objectives have been met?

4. What are the causes of failure of a political and administrative nature which may help
   to explain the answers to question three?

The first two questions are intermediate steps designed to provide an answer to the third
question, which in effect contains the *explanandum* to which the answer to the fourth question
must provide the *explanans*. Each separate question requires some clarification, and it is
the sum of these clarifications which provides the basis for the evaluation strategy chosen
here.

The core of that strategy is to replace the orthodox 'look for the results' type of policy
assessment by a 'find the culprit' procedure. Thus we are not evaluating a single, isolated
policy program. The problem is not: here is the culprit and his plan, now establish the
consequences of his actions. Sometimes it is preferable to opt for a well-defined situation
as the object of evaluation, and then to examine the effects of policy, seen as changes in
that situation. Thus we can reformulate our problem to read: here is a series of changes
in the given situation, now find the culprit or culprits (Hoogerwerf 1977; Patton 1980:
54-57).

Although we are looking for the 'culprits' responsible for changes in a well-defined situation,
we are still interested primarily in the policies of the Surinamese government. In our figure
of speech, there is always a 'prime suspect'. Hence, our first question. The second question
has two methodological implications for our 'find the culprit' approach. First, it entails
a *series of changes* in a well-defined situation, and this requires a longitudinal approach.
In the present case, the obvious choice was the period 1946 to 1975, which covers the
transition from colonial status to sovereignty. In the area of internal affairs, Surinam had
de facto self-government from 1948 on, and formal self-government after 1954. This is
also the period during which the economic development strategy took shape. The present
leaders must now decide whether to accept or reject the basic tenets of that development
strategy, on the assumption that after four decades the effects of even long-term policies
will have made themselves felt.

Second, this approach also entails a description of the changes within a *well-defined* situation,
and this requires a theory that is both scientifically objective and policy-oriented. These
requirements are met by many of the main propositions of the centre-periphery theory.
This theory is the product of a debate among Latin American economists and policy-makers,
which evaluated the causes behind the failure of the much heralded policy of industrialization
through import substitution. In the sixties this debate culminated in a macrotheory of the
relationships between central and peripheral economies that prevent the latter from breaking
out of the vicious circles of poverty and dependence (Girvan 1973).

According to the centre-periphery theory, a peripheral national economy may be viewed in terms of two structural characteristics:

a. *lack of internal cohesion*: excessive differences between the various economic sectors of a single national economy, and an unprofitable interaction between them.

b. *excessive external dependence*: the dynamics of the economic structure is dependent on the fortunes of a number of centre regions with which the peripheral economy has close ties.

The formulation of the problem and the evaluation strategy to be employed then require that a causal link be laid between the changes in the situation and the actions of the 'culprits'. Because the Surinamese authorities are 'prime suspects', the third question examines the degree to which they realized their own planning aims, against the background of the long-term development of structural characteristics.

This *Gestalt*-type foreground/background sketch reflects what we see as the most important implications of the 'find the culprit' approach. Because the changes in the situation which have been objectively and scientifically described must be traced back to the concrete actions of concrete 'culprits, the evaluator is compelled to employ 'mixed scanning'.

Once the contours of the historical constraints and structural obstacles have been sketched by means of the 'high coverage, low detail' lens of the centre-periphery theory, the third question sends the researcher off in search of the facts that will establish the extent to which the Surinamese authorities have met their self-proclaimed goals. In order to locate the actors who can help to account for the measure of success which has been achieved by the Surinamese government, the fourth question requires the use of the 'low coverage, high detail' lens provided by theories on policy-making and political and administrative systems. Thus the activities of all relevant personae are systematically examined in a double perspective: that of the policy to be evaluated, and that of the wider context within which that policy had to be made.

Not only does this agree with Etzioni's theory on policy-making (1968: 282ff), but this form of 'mixed scanning' also enhances the relevance of the findings for future policies, often the weak point in evaluation studies. This double perspective also helps the researcher to identify the causes of policy failures for which none of the culprits are responsible. He will automatically include in his research other actors alongside the authorities. He will no longer be tempted to clarify policy failures exclusively on the basis of policy carried out in this one field, as a failure to implement some other policy may be equally responsible. In short, through this type of evaluation strategy, the question of adequacy, i.e. policy as a sufficient condition for effectiveness, which is so vital to the development of new policy, is given the attention it merits.

When a policy has failed, moreover, 'mixed scanning' helps the researcher to distinguish between *adversity* (failure outside the sphere of responsibility of the focal actor) and *actual failure* (for which he is indeed responsible). Every policy-maker knows that his freedom to determine policy is in fact freedom in constraint. Prudent policy-making is the art of making optimal use of the scope offered, within the multi-conditional network of constraints, strategies and counter-strategies. Policy-makers may reasonably expect researchers to take into account this conflict between freedom and constraint in drawing up their of necessity somewhat 'academic' assessments. This will in any case add to the relevance of their evaluations 'after the fact'.

Peripheral structure, planning aims and planning effects

Official planning aims

There is no such thing as the development plan for Surinam. The series of plans launched between 1946 and 1975 display significant shifts in objectives, and corresponding adjustments to the means of attaining those objectives. These shifts and adjustments reflect corrections - some of them quite substantial - to the theories on which the original plans were based. Not to mention the unquantified formulations of ends and means, devoid of time scale; the incompatible or, at best, competing aims, and the inevitable seesawing priorities. All these problems are discussed in the section which deals with the contents of the various development plans. But in order to evaluate the extent to which the aims have been achieved, the researcher must distil from all these plans a practical measuring rod. We have opted for the goals contained in the *Tweede Vijfjarenplan* (Second Five-Year Plan) drawn up in 1972, the most representative version of Surinam's development planning. Figure 1, which represents the main objectives contained in the *Second Five-Year Plan*, is in short the answer to the first question.

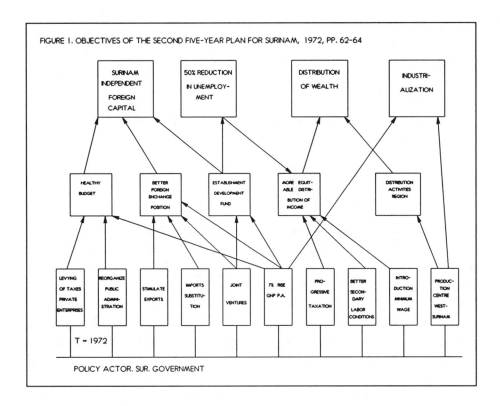

FIGURE I. OBJECTIVES OF THE SECOND FIVE-YEAR PLAN FOR SURINAM, 1972, PP. 62-64

Quantitative time-series analysis of structural characteristics

The answer to the second question requires a longitudinal description of the changes in Surinam's economy. In the early seventies, Nohlen and Nuscheler devoted a critical study to the many well-known indices for 'underdevelopment'. They then developed a series of indicators for a quantitative time-series analysis of the structural characteristics of peripheral economies (Nohlen & Nuscheler 1974: 356-359). Their index reflects the mix of objectivity and policy orientation in the centre-periphery theory, in that certain indicators may also be interpreted as an indication of the extent to which Surinam's official planning goals have been achieved. Thus with the aid of Nohlen and Nuscheler's indicators, we are also able to answer the third question.

In our contribution to Nohlen and Nuscheler's Third World Handbook, we provided a detailed description of the changes which took place within Surinam's economic situation up to 1972-73 (Hoppe 1976b). For purposes of the present chapter, that statistical material has been supplemented with more recent information (De Rooy & Van Schaaijk, 1978; Chin & Buddingh', 1987) and, where necessary, revised. Due to the shortage of space, and the fact that readers are assumed to be familiar with the centre-periphery theory, the text of the next section is not a mere interpretation of the statistical material. We have attempted to provide a concise answer to questions two and three in a manner which does not presuppose detailed knowledge of the centre-periphery theory, nor familiarity with particulars of the national economy of Surinam.

'Plus ça change, plus c'est la meme chose'

During the seventeenth and eighteenth centuries Surinam was a lucrative colony with vast sugar plantations. Its prosperity was based on a combination of three factors: Dutch capital, know-how and management; slave labour imported from Africa; and Surinam's own fertile farmland. From 1800 on, however, developments on the international scene undermined Dutch commercial capitalism, and Surinam became a financial burden. The available capital went instead to the Dutch East Indies, and between 1850 and 1950 Surinam succumbed to a well-nigh prototypical 'development of underdevelopment'. The plantations went into decline, and in the wake of the abolition of slavery and the hasty import of contract workers from India, pre-industrial, 'small-scale' agriculture began to develop. Around the turn of the century, foreign influences led to the development of a raw materials sector, and during the Second World War bauxite was of such strategic value to the Americans that Surinam became in effect a mining enclave. This same period saw the rise of an extensive import-export trade, a modicum of industrial production for the local market, a service sector and a government sector.

By 1950 Surinam was a textbook example of a peripheral economy. The sectors which had developed as a result of outside influences did not form a cohesive 'system', and there was no fruitful interaction between them. Through the influence of the bauxite sector, the national economy was dependent on centre countries, mainly the United States and, to a lesser extent, the Netherlands. Since then, the mining sector has become even more important. Up to 1965, only raw bauxite was mined, but since the Brokopondo investments, a portion has also been processed into alumina and aluminium. The domestic processing of raw materials is relatively small in scale, employing only 6% of the working population, but it has an enormous influence on the economy of the country. If it were to decline, the entire national economy would be in danger of collapse.

The Brokopondo investments had positive if temporary spin-offs in industry and the service sector, where mining led to the creation of jobs for an estimated 20% of the working population (Essed 1973: 76ff). But it is no doubt the government which has profited most, in the form of additional national income. The apparatus of the civil service increased substantially, as a result of patronage, the growth of the working population, and a failure to create the necessary new jobs. In effect, the Surinamese government had become the major allocator of jobs and income. The rhythm of growth points up the significance of the raw materials sector: during the Brokopondo investments, the economy grew at lightning speed, while before and after it stagnated. Between 1946 and 1975, the average rise in gross domestic product was 6-7%. Against the background of an average annual population increase of 3 1/2%, this represents an increase in real per capita GNP of 3%. On the basis of these figures, we can conclude that, on the whole, the growth objectives of the development plan were met.

Although there was a certain cohesion between mining, industry, the service sector and government, there was no fruitful interaction between them. The effect of the burgeoning mining industry on the other sectors was one of quantity rather than quality. That mutual interaction was lacking which is indispensable if a national economy is to generate its own capacity for growth. Moreover, this cluster of sectors within Surinam's economic structure was still highly dependent on centre countries. To the extent that this can be laid at the door of a single policy, then it is the investment policy of the Aluminium Company of America (ALCOA) and its Surinamese subsidiary Suralco. According to reliable sources, the Brokopondo investments were autonomous, that is, they were not elicited by Surinam's pre-1958 policy on infrastructure, taxation and industrialization (Chin 1971: 1452). Thus the government was clearly not the only - or even the most important - 'culprit' responsible for the economic changes.

Surinam's 'industrialization by invitation' policy was no more successful in the years after 1958. Almost no further private investments were forthcoming from centre countries, in spite of the Investment Act and the efforts of the Foundation for the Promotion of Investment in Surinam and, later, the Economic Information Service. This also explains the failure of efforts to boost employment in the productive sectors, to keep pace with the growth of the working population. Thus the Surinamese government was obliged to continue to create jobs, while the employment goals it had set itself were proving less and less realistic. Unemployment, which was approximately 14% in 1960, had by 1974 reached a figure of 20% (De Rooy & Van Schaaijk 1978: 123).

The lack of sectoral interaction is illustrated most vividly by the agricultural situation. (For purposes of the present discussion, we will leave aside such pre-industrial means of production as gathering, hunting, fishing and crop rotation, which were employed by the Indians and maroons in the interior.) The income generated by the mining sector did not lead to any appreciable increase in the demand for basic foodstuffs. It profited the small farmers little or nothing, as a shrewd group of middlemen had positioned themselves between the farmers and the market in Paramaribo. Their low standard of living made it impossible for them to put money aside; they were unable to buy better tools and equipment, which would have increased productivity, let alone to set up a local industry for simple agriculture equipment. The agrarian sector - both large and small - deteriorated sharply during the period of autonomy. By 1970 its share of the GNP had declined by almost half, and it was not until 1973 that an upward trend was again evident, as a result of higher foreign prices for rice (De Rooy & Van Schaaijk 1978: 57). During the Second World War, only half of the working population was still employed in agriculture. After 1960 this figure again declined by half, before levelling off. Although the relative importance of small and medium-sized agricultural holdings has declined significantly, nine out of ten farm labourers are still employed in small-scale agriculture. Many businesses are too small to mechanize and too large to be run by manual labour on a strictly family basis. Moreover, such farms do not provide sufficient income for the often large families who are dependent on them. Many small farmers are forced to take part-time jobs elsewhere, in order to supplement the family income. The younger generation escape these gloomy perspectives by moving to Paramaribo and surrounding regions.

Given the situation as it was in 1950, and the natural decline in large-scale agriculture predicted by the planners who drafted the 1952 *Grondslagen van een Tienjarenplan voor Suriname* (Foundations for a Ten-Year Plan for Surinam), these disastrous developments must be attributed to the agricultural policy of the Surinamese government. This policy ran counter to the logic of economic development, in that agrarian development was not held to be a pre-condition for industrialization, but was seen as subordinate to, and derived from, the development in mining and industry (Stichting Planbureau Suriname 1965: 488). From 1960 on, the emphasis was on attracting foreign capital from private and development-aid sources, in order to stimulate large-scale agriculture. It was such large enterprises as rice, bananas and oil palms which profited most from these investments, often in the form of state companies and joint ventures.

This policy had disastrous effects on jobs and rural living standards. By giving priority to large-scale agriculture at the expense of small-scale and medium-sized holdings, the authorities made it clear that they considered export and economic growth more important than the domestic food supply. Whereas up to the Second World War Surinam was self-suffi-cient, during the period of political autonomy it had to import between 8% and 12% of its foodstuffs (Lagerberg & Vingerhoets 1974: 534).

The lack of cohesion and fruitful interaction between the major sectors of the Surinamese economy is abundantly clear from the above. We will turn now to the country's external dependence. That dependence is reflected in the fact that only one-third of the economy is in Surinamese hands. It is only in forestry and large-scale agriculture that control over the means of production is concentrated in the hands of the state. The Netherlands, which controls only about one-sixth of Surinam's economy, hardly merits the title of 'neo-colonial power'. Since 1950 there has been almost no new investment of Dutch capital in Surinam. The expectation, voiced in trade and industry quarters, that Surinam would provide minor but tangible compensation for the loss of the Dutch East Indies, has never been realized. The United States, which controls approximately half of the economy, has taken over the role once reserved for the Netherlands (Algemeen Bureau voor de Statistiek 1975: 81-82). The geographical distribution of imports and exports is another sign of the country's dependence. There are close ties with centre areas such as the United States and the EC, while those with neighbouring peripheral economies are limited. The export figures show that in the wake of the Brokopondo investments, Surinam is more than ever a bauxite monoculture. For all its development plans, the economic base of the country has not been broadened, and Suriname has remained largely dependent on foreign capital. As regards private capital transactions in the period 1954-1975, the amount leaving the country was 250 million Surinamese guilders higher than the total foreign investments. This was offset by a total of 495.4 million Surinamese guilders in development aid. Despite the not inconsiderable profits accruing to the government treasury from the activities of foreign companies, Surinam would have been unable to balance its budget without that development aid. The price which the country paid was a steadily rising debt, concentrated in the Netherlands.

Leaving aside the practical significance of the official planning aims for the Surinamese leaders themselves, on the basis of the centre-periphery theory it is reasonable to expect that, if successful, the accumulated effect of thirty years of policy implementation would have been reflected in increased cohesion, a fruitful interaction between the various sectors, and a decrease in foreign dependency. The above evaluation of the structure and dynamics of the Surinamese economy leads inevitably to the conclusion that the development planning has been a failure. Even if we were to disregard the two structural characteristics of peripheral economies commonly used as measuring rods, and confine ourselves to the official planning aims, the policy was clearly a fiasco. It is some small consolation that responsibility cannot be attributed exclusively to the Surinamese authorities.

In 1973 former Minister of Reconstruction Essed wrote: 'From an economic viewpoint, not that much has changed in comparison with the period before 1945' (1976: 86). This is a trenchant observation, especially when one considers that it was made by a man who is rightfully seen as the spiritual father of Surinam's own development concept. He admits that the most essential planning aims were not achieved. The question is: why not?

Adversity or failure?

Possible causes of the failure of government policy

In order to unravel the causal and goals-means relationships between government action and policy results, the researcher must have an insight into the immediate causes of the failure of government policy. Failed government policy may be seen as a gulf between the desired effects and those which have actually been achieved. It is only when the gap between the two is attributable, entirely or in part, to factors within the power of the authorities that it is possible to say that *government* policy has been a failure. This is the case when it is possible to identify political and administrative factors in the cycle of policy-making which contributed substantially to the formation of that gap.

Analogous to the stages in policy-making which can be distinguished analytically, there are three types of causes which can be linked to the failure of government policy. Those of the *first type*, which are to be found in the early stages, during agenda-setting, may create a gap between social needs and politically desirable objectives. Causes of the *second type* go back to the stage at which policy is being formulated, where conflicts may arise between issues on the political agenda and the 'policy as plan'. The *third type* of cause, which is found at the stage where policy is executed, leads to a discrepancy between the policy effects envisaged by the planmakers and the actual effects.

Of course, that is not the whole story. For who would maintain that a government is always in complete control of every aspect of its policy from beginning to end? Government power is anchored in more or less durable power bases. But non-governmental agencies establish, maintain and strengthen their own power bases, often in competition with the authorities. Transnational corporations in peripheral countries often use their power to steer government policy in a certain direction, and their actions can further or thwart that policy. In the latter case, is it correct to speak of failed or unsuccessful government policy?

It is my conviction that policy may only be considered unsuccessful if the researcher is able to put forward a plausible and relevant alternative course of policy which would have resulted in a less pronounced gap between the desired and the actual effects, and which was within the range of feasible options open to the authorities *at that particular moment*. Although the construction of a 'relevant counterfactual' is not always easy (Lukes 1974:46-56), in this case the alternative is presented to us on a silver platter, as it were, in the form of the *Foundations for a Ten-Year Plan for Surinam (1952).*

Risks of failure inherent in a neo-colonial elite-cartel democracy

Is it not somewhat far-fetched to point to risks of failure rooted in the process of agenda-setting? Yes and no. Yes, because - unlike the Frankfurt School - we do not lay claim to a 'critical theory, which in the political articulation of social needs, distinguishes between "false consciousness" and "true interests" (Geuss 1981). Yes, because unlike the welfare theorists, we do not claim to have a standard by which the aggregation of political preferences can be measured against a theoretical optimum. But, in the end, no, because we are able to show that certain characteristics of the Surinamese elite-cartel democracy, and of the ties with the Netherlands, exhibit strong 'Wahlverwandtschaft' with risks of failure related to the content, formulation and implementation of the development plans.

In references to Surinam's political system, we have used the term 'a decaying elite-cartel democracy' (Hoppe 1976a). In effect, the system is based on the willingness of the political elites to 'accommodate at the top', and their skill in 'segmenting at the bottom'. Segmentation consists primarily in cultivating and nurturing patron-client relationships between politicians and the rank and file. By means of patronage, the politician is able to transform public wealth into personal power bases, in the form of affection, prestige and sheer numbers. The power of numbers gives the politicians of a particular party their leverage with the ruling cartel. The patronage system is so deeply entrenched in Surinam that the military regime which for seven years replaced the elite-cartel system became just one more cartel, vying with the older cartels for public funds and favour.

Accommodation at the top is based on observance by the elites of certain rules. 'Secrecy' and 'depoliticization' promote compromise, while under the ethnicity-related rule of 'propor-tion' the profits of a successful policy are divided on a pro rata basis, according to the contribution of each ethnic group to the cartel. Publicly earned wealth is thus transformed into patronage and power.

This means that each ruling cartel sets certain pre-conditions with respect to the content and form of economic planning. Concerning content:

1. In the short term, tangible and 'distributable' results must be obtained. (Infrastructural projects, e.g., generally create more jobs than agricultural projects.)
2. In the long term, the potential for generating more public income by means of ordinary taxation must be enlarged. (It is a well-known fact that patronage costs money.)

Concerning form:

1. Plans and planners notwithstanding, the politicians must have sufficient freedom to manoeuvre. (How else can they take into account the changeable wishes of the rank and file?)
2. Plans must be developed within a depoliticized negotiating setting.

The explanation for this latter paradox lies in the link with the Netherlands. From 1948 until independence, the Surinamese government was autonomous in 'domestic affairs', but otherwise bound by the laws of the Kingdom of the Netherlands. Thus, given the composition of the decision-making bodies of the Kingdom, Surinam was tied to the Netherlands (Ooft 1972). The Charter obliged the Netherlands and Surinam to cooperate in economic affairs, but the cooperation between Surinam and countries outside the Kingdom was subject to the unilateral approval of the Netherlands. As regards rights and riches, the power bases of the Surinamese authorities were to some extent derived from those of the Dutch. As far as the economic development of the country was concerned, the position of Surinam was comparable to that of a Dutch ministry: it was a question of fighting for one's share of the Dutch national budget.

These ties with the Kingdom also meant that Surinam's planning was a kind of prelude to bilateral negotiations. Domestic considerations - such as depoliticization and taking a united stand against the Netherlands - dictated that economic planning should be kept out of the day-to-day political conflict. This situation, too, had a number of consequences for the contents of these plans. For Surinamese politicians, this meant:

1. safeguarding long-term development aid from Holland
2. maximizing that aid in the short term
3. minimizing Surinam's repayment obligations.

On the Dutch side, the aims included:

1. limiting the total amount of aid, i.e. it had to be in keeping with cyclical economic policy and with the budget and balance-of-trade policies
2. monitoring the accountability of expenditures in Surinam
3. preventing damage to Dutch economic interests as a result of the implementation of Surinamese plans.

The conclusion to be drawn from this section is that there were indeed *causes for failure of the first type* (during the agenda-setting process). In an elite-cartel democracy, patronage is the politician's major source of power. This puts certain limitations on planning content and form, which may be seen as potential sources of failure. The ties between Surinam and the Netherlands under the terms of the Charter necessarily put planning preparation squarely in the arena of political negotiations. This added another potential source of failure:

the demands of political bargaining are likely to take precedence over those of prudent development planning.

The 'lessons' of Brokopondo

In the present section we will be looking at the *causes of failure of the second type*, those which are traceable to the policy-formulation stage. We will confine ourselves to those factors which led to incorrect policy choices.

It is often maintained that Surinam's development planning is doomed to perpetuate the country's external dependence. This argument is based on the role played by a number of factors which are all but unsusceptible to the influence of government policy:

a. the small scale of the country (both geographic and demographic), which forms an obstacle to the development of a domestic market;

b. the unfavourable geographic location, outside the usual trade routes;

c. the fact that its raw materials are not easily accessible and difficult to exploit;

d. the concentration of the population in and around Paramaribo;

e. the heterogeneity of the population; ethnic segmentation invariably leads to a 'weak nation';

f. the resulting 'weak state';

g. the lack of adequate schooling and the low level of productivity at all levels of the working population.

Admittedly, no government policy is capable of achieving rapid and spectacular changes in the above factors. But it would be incorrect to say that they were so restrictive that no other policy was open to the Surinamese authorities. The evidence offered by the Surinamese policies themselves shows that a different approach was indeed possible. *Foundations* was based on a policy-belief system which differs significantly from that of *Development (1958-63)*. *Foundations for a Ten-Year Plan* envisages permanent structural improvements to the economy. Economic development is not the result of spin-offs from the stimulation of the foreign-capital sectors (mining and large-scale agriculture). In the long run, development 'under one's own steam' can only be attained by focusing Dutch development aid on small-scale and medium-sized agriculture in the form of cooperative ventures. In this way Dutch financial aid can contribute to the development of skilled labour and know-how within Surinam itself. In the end it is these two factors which must counterbalance the bauxite monoculture dominated by foreign capital.

The concrete objectives are: to broaden the economic base, increase spendable income, balance the budget, and strengthen the labour market. Where short-term objectives conflict with each other or with the main aims, these conflicts must be carefully identified and where possible reconciled, through the distribution of planning funds and the scheduling of the various projects. *Foundations* is today in no way outdated, which makes it a remarkable achievement indeed. Industrialization was not given preference over agrarian development, and large-scale agriculture was not automatically considered more important than small-scale or medium-sized enterprises. It stressed the importance of concentrating on developing Surinam's own resources and production potential. These are policy accents which are still advocated by present-day proponents of the centre-periphery paradigm. A viable alternative course of policy had indeed been presented to us on a silver platter.

Which brings us to the sixty-four-dollar question: why did Surinamese politicians not welcome this proposal with open arms? The answer is: because their political self-interest ran counter to the economic priorities set forth in *Foundations*. It was this self-interest which kept them from putting long-term goals before short-term objectives, and made it unacceptable to sacrifice industrialization potential to agrarian development. In the *Tienjarenplan* (Ten-Year Plan) of 1955, short-term objectives were given more emphasis. Officially, the aim was still to lay the foundation for economic development 'under one's own steam'. But the wording is less ambitious than in the original, and there are two preconditions: improving the level of social welfare facilities, and raising the living standards of the most disadvantaged. Moreover, there is a distinct shift of emphasis in the direction of industrialization.

At this time, Surinamese politicians were already entertaining dreams of *the Brokopondo project*. What was needed was a Surinamese state-owned company, which would process the bauxite mined by Suralco and Billiton into alumina and aluminium, partly within the country. The necessary energy would be generated by the state company itself, through the construction of a barrage and a hydroelectric power plant. The electricity thus produced would benefit other economic activities as well.

Without going into details, it has been established beyond doubt that the Brokopondo project was a fiasco. Surinamese politicians overestimated their powers of persuasion, and in 1954 and 1957 the Dutch government refused to come to their rescue with financial support, presumably because they preferred to award the processing of Surinam's bauxite to a number of languishing areas in the Netherlands itself. In their dealings with ALCOA, the Surinamese politicians overestimated the available information and know-how. In any case, no Surinamese state company was ever set up. The barrage, hydroelectric plant, and processing plant were built, exploited and financed by Suralco. The Caribbean expert Girvan analyzed the contract and termed it a textbook example of the manner in which governments of peripheral countries can be duped by transnational concerns (Girvan 1971).

After this fiasco, opposition to the government's planning priorities increased, for the authorities were not to be deterred. The lesson learned from the Brokopondo affair was not: 'this is a dead-end street, and we must shift our priorities back to agriculture', but rather: 'we'll try again, and if we plan our strategy more carefully, we'll get the best of the deal yet.' The government declaration of 1958 states that 'at this stage in Surinam's development, it is of essential importance to raise the people's level of material prosperity.' And in his *Opbouw 1958-1963: de nationale visie* (Development 1958-1963: the National View), the Minister for Development F. Essed, concludes that the time is ripe for a new, authentically Surinamese development strategy.

The as yet undeveloped 'hinterland' of the country must be opened up. The Natural Resources (the capitals are Essed's) which this will unearth will form the basis for the coming economic expansion. The factor 'nature' will then take precedence over 'capital' and 'labour'. These Natural Resources must be processed at home, because this 'will make a far greater contribution to the general prosperity than the production of raw materials alone' (Opbouw 1958-1963: 136).

Then follows the pre-eminent 'lesson' of Brokopondo. The authorities must encourage private enterprise to invest in those ventures which will make the greatest contribution to the fulfilment of the government's objectives. To this end government and industry must collaborate: the authorities will be responsible for external production conditions (infrastructure, tax climate, physical and geographical planning, and land policy), while the entrepreneur will exploit the production unit (Ibid: 195). The industrial processing of raw materials must be stimulated by opening the way to increased profits for companies which locate those processes within Suriname (Ibid: 33).

Clearly, the Brokopondo fiasco did not prompt the Surinamese authorities to mend their ways. On the contrary, they set about designing a new variation on the course they had already embarked upon. The 1959 *Herzien Tienjaren Plan* (Revised Ten-Year Plan) and the 1962 *Aanvullend Opbouwplan* (Supplementary Development Plan) made adjustments to the *Ten-Year Plan* which showed leanings in the direction of the views expressed by Essed. The 1963 *Raamwerk Integraal Opbouwplan* (Framework for an Integral Development Plan), as well as the 1965 *Nationaal Ontwikkelingsplan Suriname* (National Development Plan for Surinam) were preparatory exercises for the 1967 *First Five-Year Plan*, while *Opbouw '70* (Development '70) was an attempt to evaluate the results of government planning since 1958. This led to minor adjustments in what had been the orthodox view on development since 1958, as reflected in the *Second Five-Year Plan (1972)*. (See Fig. 1.)

In actual fact, nothing was learned from the Brokopondo fiasco. Surinam's own concept of development is still based on excessive optimism and a willingness to take risks:

1. 'Large quantities of natural resources are being discovered'. With the exception of bauxite finds, such optimism has proved unfounded.
2. 'The present supplies are - or soon will be - capable of economic exploitation.' This is a miscalculation even in the case of bauxite, as Surinam's share of the world bauxite market has declined from over 25% in 1950 to approximately 7% today.
3. 'Our negotiating position with respect to foreign companies is sufficiently strong, thanks to a thorough stock-taking and a clever policy of concession.' This is another prediction which has not been borne out by the Brokopondo affair, and in the light of the squabbling which has surrounded the search for a partner for the joint venture in West Surinam, there is little likelihood that it ever will be.

It is abundantly clear that the authorities have not learned from their mistakes, when one considers that the authentic Surinamese development plan proposed by Essed is in fact far more 'Western' and traditional than *Foundations*. As we have seen, the latter was based on the assumption that economic autonomy was indeed feasible, provided the conflict between short-term and long-term objectives was recognised. Paradoxically, the new Surinamese development plan actually rejects the idea that Surinam is capable of developing through its own efforts, and confuses short-term with long-term goals. This is a traditionally Western view, for since the beginning of this century the general aim has been to boost Surinam's prosperity by encouraging the investment of foreign capital. The new concept is actually akin to current growth-phase theories on economic 'backwardness'. The greatest good is an industrial society modeled on the West, which can be achieved through massive injections of capital. Against this background, a plan like *Foundations*, which gives priority to agrarian development, is quickly stamped 'neo-colonial'. Moreover, the supposed relationship between capital investment and increased production was an excellent excuse for politicians in peripheral countries to ask for more development aid.

In any case, the inescapable conclusion is that up to now Surinam's development failures have been due largely to the inadequacy of the growth-phase theory on which the country's own development concept was founded. It was this which led Surinamese politicians to hand over their country to transnational concerns. And it was these concerns which distorted the economic structure and, through their high wages and the subsequent effect on demand, impeded the expansion of labour-intensive sectors whose production was intended for domestic markets. Their foreign currency profits brought Western imports and Western patterns of consumption within reach, while their contributions to the national treasury helped to maintain the democracy of elitist cartels.

Looking back on this section, we can conclude that the Surinamese politicians' strategic interests in the content and form of development planning enticed them into opting for the wrong development strategy. It is tragic that at this crucial stage in its history, the country did not have political leaders with sufficient moral courage to resist the systematic temptation to subordinate long-term objective to short-term possibilities. Thus they sacrificed the agrarian sector on the altar of industrial aspirations. The Surinamese government is not the only, nor even the major, contributor to the continuing peripheral structure of the national economy. But through its single-track policy, it is at the very least an 'accessory'.

Planning as a negotiating tool

In this section we will continue our search for *causes of failure of the second type* (formulation of policy). But whereas the previous section brought to light the factors underlying imprudent policy choices, the present section will deal with the causes of failure at the planning stage. Within the sphere of Surinamese development planning, it is almost impossible to divorce formulation from implementation. For this reason, we will also consider here the *causes of failure of the third type* (at the stage where policy is implemented).

Foundations was drawn up in 1951-52 by the Surinamese Planning Bureau (SPS), an independent foundation. Planning preparation was kept separate from the political entanglements of the emerging elitist cartel democracy. Depoliticization was in the interests of both Surinam and the Netherlands. But the planners were out to depoliticize the implementation as well. *Foundations* provided detailed criteria for planning adjustments during implementation, and an elaborate time and expenditure schema. All of which was intended to guarantee the necessary cohesion between the projects, and to avert undesirable macro-economic effects.

But Surinam's politicians viewed this plan as 'ten years of bondage'. They turned the *Ten-Year Plan* into a 'plan of intent', whereby they were bound by the plan objectives, but not by the individual projects. In effect, this dictated the nature of future planning: instead of 'comprehensive planning', Surinam got a fairly loose-knit global plan, with two major guidelines:

1. Each plan will be based on a tentative list of projects, consisting of suggestions for the future expenditure of development aid (Kool 1964:81).
2. Each plan will be based on a tentative distribution code, whereby projects are subdivided into 'directly productive', 'infrastructural' and 'social' projects. Each category will receive a set proportion of the total sum.

In a later stage, such global plans were drawn up by a team of Surinamese and Dutch experts, thus providing the basis for negotiations between the two governments over the total amount of aid. This was, in fact, the sole purpose of the preparatory stage. Admittedly, the modality of the aid (the donation or 'soft loan' and in the Five-Year Plan the 'hard loan' as well) was not a particularly powerful lever to obtain the desired distribution of the total sum over the various project categories. But the global plans were above all a basis for negotiation, and thus a 'weapon' in those negotiations.

The procedural rules for planning implementation were more important to the content and administration of the Surinamese development plans. The nature of the two global guidelines sketched above necessitated a procedure for the further elaboration of existing projects, and the addition of new ones to the project list, which is generally up-dated once a year. We will look first at the domestic aspects of the procedural rules, before turning to their role in the relationship between The Hague and Paramaribo.

Planning procedure was organized on three levels. At the highest level both governments were responsible; initially it was thought that this level would deal solely with disputes. The second level consisted of the Planning Bureau, which was set up by the Surinamese government to act as coordinator. In consultation with the Surinamese government, the Planning Bureau would draw up a budget proposal for a particular year, together with a proposal for the distribution of funds over the various project categories. At the third level, each Surinamese ministry would draw up a project list of its own, based on that proposal. Each year the Planning Bureau would then issue a working plan based on the lists from the ministries, again in consultation with the highest level.

The Dutch government transferred the power to approve the working plans, and to make available development aid funds, to a Dutch delegation. In addition to the responsibility for assessment which it shared with the Planning Bureau, this delegation would, where necessary, lend assistance in the preparatory stages (Van Dusseldorp 1967:62). Once the annual budget was approved by the Planning Bureau and the delegation, and by the Surinamese Ministry of General Affairs, the projects were worked out at ministry level, and then either executed or put out to contract.

The introduction of this procedure ran distinctly counter to normal procedures. No longer was there a single flow of funds from Surinam's Ministry of Finance to the 'spending departments'. There was now a second flow which travelled from planners to spending departments. Understandably, the planners were anxious to create separate agencies for the execution of planning projects. And equally understandably, both the ministries and the Surinamese politicians were opposed to this idea. They, of course, wanted their share of the second flow of funds. In an elite-cartel democracy, where patronage is the major means of exercising power, ministries are doubly out to maximize the budget. But there was a danger that the new flow of money and the new agencies charged with the execution of projects might be detrimental to existing interests. The politicians had to keep their control of the flow of government funds, even though it now came out of two different taps! Moreover, for civil servants and politicians, the execution of plans at the ministerial level served to counterbalance the influence of the planners. The bureaucratic solution to the dilemma was obvious: the creation of separate development agencies, which would operate under the auspices of the existing ministries. The result was the Building Bureau (for infrastructural projects), which was part of the Ministry of Public Works and Transport, and the Bureau for Rural Development (for agricultural projects), which was part of Agriculture, Cattle Breeding and Fisheries (Vroon 1963:44,56).

But there were other, more important factors which motivated Surinamese politicians. The execution of plans by and through the ministries not only maintained existing patron-client relationships, but actually gave them more leeway. There were now two flows of funds, which merged at this third level. From a patronage standpoint, this offered new potential for shifts and combinations. And this was precisely what the Netherlands, in the interests of accountability, had been trying to prevent, by ensuring that the Dutch delegation (and indirectly the Planning Bureau) had control of a separate flow of funds.

This brings us to relations between the Netherlands and Surinam. Up until the period 1957-1958, these were more or less as had been envisaged. But, as we have seen, two Dutch non-decisions involving the financing of the Brokopondo project had embittered Surinamese politicians, who drew two conclusions from the conduct of the Netherlands:

1. Wherever possible, Dutch influence must be minimized.
2. As a sanction for the lack of cooperation, Surinam must do everything in its power to pull in as much development aid as possible.

In 1958 a Creole-Hindustan cartel led by Pengel came to power. The Pengel period lasted until 1968, during which time his successive governments came to view themselves as negotiators with but a single aim: maximum realization of the interests of Surinam at the expense of those of the Netherlands. This was, in effect, the formulation of Surinam's own development concept. On the procedural level, it meant a complete reorganization of the planning apparatus, while from a political-tactical point of view, it represented a switch from 'underspending' to a structural overspending. At present we are interested primarily in the reorganization.

This consisted, in effect, of a general weakening of the intermediate level, whereby the Planning Bureau was given a purely administrative status, and preliminary planning was transferred to a new Ministry of Development. From 1963 on, it was abundantly clear that both these measures were intended to strengthen the grip of Surinam's politicians on the preparatory planning stage. Prime Minister Pengel centralized economic, financial and development policies. Moreover, the Dutch permanent delegation was dissolved; its work would in future be carried out by a single Dutch civil servant, the Representative of the Netherlands for the *Ten-Year Plan* for Surinam.

Surinam's policy of overspending, made possible by the dismantling of the Planning Bureau and the Dutch delegation, and justified by the government's concept of development, met with success during the sixties. Surinam managed to increase the total amount of development aid, while decreasing its repayment obligations. Despite ever more frequent consultations between the representative of the Netherlands and the authorities in The Hague, the Surinamese politicians made effective use of that paradox of power: the tendency for the strong to be 'exploited' by the weak (Olson 1974:29).

Not until 1968 did the Netherlands attempt to turn this unfavourable tide. It announced that temporary projects would be dropped, employed 'hard' loans in order to force Surinam to opt for projects which would show direct effect, and laid down stricter procedures. Nevertheless, the Surinamese politicians were still able to implement their own policy preferences.

They were able to circumvent the stricter procedure, thanks to a number of factors which worked in their favour:

a. Surinam controlled project preparation, and was able to dictate the contents of the alternatives submitted.
b. Surinam determined the number of projects submitted.
c. Surinam determined de facto (if not de jure) the moment at which projects were submitted.
d. Surinam ultimately controlled the execution of the projects.

Thanks to these discretionary powers, the following tactics could be employed:

a. Delay submission of a project until everyone is starting to lose patience.
b. Submit a deluge of projects all at once.
c. Accuse the Netherlands of paternalism when all the projects are not automatically approved.

Since Surinam determined the alternatives, all the projects were in any case acceptable. While the delaying tactics put the Netherlands under the pressure of time, more important still was the moral pressure. This forced the Netherlands to be less critical in its assessment. Even if it had the courage to reject a number of projects, there would still be enough acceptable projects to satisfy Surinam. Projects that were rejected reappeared the next time around, with a few minor adjustments, or were replaced by 'better' alternatives.

In all bureaucracies, weaker or subordinate bodies make use of padding tactics such as these (Caiden & Wildavsky 1974:140), which in the present case enabled the Surinamese government to get round the evaluation criteria of the Netherlands, despite the stricter procedural regulations. Moreover, any attempt on the part of the Dutch authorities to tighten procedures or evaluation criteria was seized upon by Surinam as the occasion for fresh accusations of neo-colonialism. Within the limits of the total amount in aid, Surinamese politicians were able to realize their policy preferences. In effect this situation continued until 1975.

As we come to the end of this section, it will be clear that the causes of failure may also be traced to the policy formulation and policy implementation stages. The organization and procedures of Surinam's development planning had been adapted to the necessity of maintaining political control through patronage. It is not surprising that, for both Surinam and the Netherlands, central planning preparation was no longer a steering wheel, but a negotiating tool. Furthermore, a division was created between central planning preparation and the poorly coordinated implementation within the ministries. In addition to the causes of failure related to know-how, skills and finance, it was due to organizational and procedural factors that the planning apparatus as a whole was incapable of learning from the past.

Guidelines for a better policy

These, then, are the political and administrative factors which, added to the poor economic situation and certain other impediments, may be seen as the causes of the failure of Surinam's efforts to extricate its national economy from the vicious circles of poverty and dependence. Surinamese planning was clearly an attempt to develop the national economy, but it was caught up in and ultimately strangled by, the political and administrative logic of underdevelopment (Hoppe, 1981). To an extent, this also explains why the military were given the benefit of the doubt after their coup of February 1980.

What 'lessons' are to be drawn from our evaluation which may serve to guide government policy in the present situation? The *first* is that Surinam cannot continue to maintain that the failure of its development policy up to 1975 - and even later, for the same road has been followed right up to the present - was due to the evils of international imperialism in general, and Dutch neo-colonialism in particular. The Netherlands need no longer permit Surinam to harangue it into the dock, nor should it allow its political judgement to be clouded by guilt complexes.

The *second* lesson is that the Netherlands should have no illusions concerning its potential influence on the policy measures of any Surinamese government. The simple fact that it provides development aid is a necessary condition, but by no means a guarantee that it can actually influence policy. If this was true during the period of good relations between the two countries, then it must be doubly so in the chilly relations which prevail now.

The *third* lesson could be that, regardless of the nature of the regime in Paramaribo, Suriname itself will have to interpret the causes of the failure of its former policy in a positive manner, transforming them into guidelines for a better policy now and in the future. The present analysis of the causes of failure may provide a number of points of departure: namely, a gradual turn-round of the present policy, in which the key words are mobilization of the country's own resources, small-scale projects, and genuine decentralization.

A gradual turn-round, because Surinam has thrust its head too far into the noose of external dependence to suddenly pull back now. The present leaders are, after all, responsible for jobs and income for approximately half of the working population and their dependents. *Mobilization of the country's own resources*, because up to now self-confidence has been the scarcest 'production factor' of all. It is time to lay aside the idea that development is the result of the application of know-how 'from outside'. What is needed are authentic and original Surinamese answers to specific Surinamese questions. *Small-scale projects*, because they alone will be able to mobilize the country's own resources. We have seen that the planning apparatus of planners and civil servants lacked a built-in potential for learning from the past. Through small-scale industrial and agrarian projects, it will be possible to exploit the learning potential of more and more people. *Decentralization*, because this forms the indispensable institutional foundation for small-scale development, and because, once it has put down roots, it can prevent a return to the old relationships of patronage. Thus causes of past failure can become guidelines for better policies in the future. Our task is nevertheless limited to promoting a critical, and above all objective approach to Surinam's past. Only then will it be possible to learn from the mistakes which have been made.

References

Algemeen Bureau voor de Statistiek, Suriname (1975), *Balansen van de nationale economie en aanvullende staten*. Suriname in Cijfers, nr. 75.

Caiden, N. and Wildavsky, A. (1974), *Planning and Budgeting in Poor Countries*, New York: John Wiley & Sons.

Chin, H.E. (1971), 'Suriname, ontwikkelingshulp en economische samenwerking', *Interntionale Spectator*, 25.

Chin, H.E. and Buddingh', H. (1987), *Surinam. Politics, Economics and Society*, London and New York, Frances Pinter.

Dusseldorp van, D. (1967), *Meerdimensionale overheidsplanning: De overheidsplanning van Suriname in de periode 1952-1967*, Ph.D. dissertation, Wageningen.

Essed, F. (1973), *Een volk op weg naar ontwikkeling*, Paramaribo.

Etzioni, A. (1968), *The Active Society*, New York: The Free Press.

Geuss, R. (1981), The Idea of a Critical Theory: Habermas & the Frankfurt School, Cambridge: Cambridge University Press.

Girvan, N. (1971), 'Making the rules of the game: company-country agreements in the bauxite industry', Social and Economic Studies, 20, 4.

Girvan, N. (1973), 'The development of dependency economics in the Caribbean and Latin America: review and comparison, *Social and Economic Studies,* 22, 1.

Hoogerwerf, A. (1977), 'Effecten van overheidsbeleid', *Beleid & Maatschappij,* 4.

Hoppe, R. (1976a), 'Het politieke systeem van Suriname: elite-kartel democratie', *Acta Politica,* 9: 145-177.

Hoppe, R. (1976b), 'Surinam', in *Nohlen & Nuscheler,* 1976: 415-427.

Hoppe, R. (1981), 'Naar een politieke logica van de onderontwikkeling', *Acta Politica,* 16: 355-381.

Kool, R. (1964), *Agricultural planning in Surinam 1950-1960: An evaluation,* Ph.D. dissertation, Wageningen.

Lagerberg, C. and Vingerhoets, J. (1974), 'Ontwikkelingssamenwerking met onafhankelijk Suriname', *Interntionale Spectator,* 28.

Lukes, S. (1974), *Power: A Radical View,* London: The Macmillan Press.

Nohlen, D. and Nuscheler, F. (Hrsg.) (1974), *Handbuch der Dritten Welt. Band I. Theorien und Indikatoren von Unterentwicklung und Entwicklung,* Hamburg: Hoffmann und Campe.

Nohlen, D. and Nuscheler, F. (Hrsg.) (1976), *Handbuch der Dritten Welt. Band III. Unterentwicklung und Entwicklung in Lateinamerika,* Hamburg: Hoffmann und Campe.

Olson, M. (1974), *The Logic of Collective Action. Public Goods and the Theory of Groups,* Cambridge: Cambridge University Press.

Ooft, C.D. (1972), *Ontwikkeling van het constitutionele recht in Suriname,* Assen: Van Gorcum.

Patton, M.Q. (1980), *Qualitative Evaluation Methods,* Beverly Hills: Sage Publications.

Rooy de, W. and Van Schaaijk, M. (1978), *Inleiding in de Surinaamse economie,* mimeo, Paramaribo.

Stichting Planbureau Suriname (1965), *Nationaal Ontwikkelings Plan Suriname,* Deel 2, Paramaribo.

Stolper, W. (1973), *Planning without Facts,* Cambridge: Harvard University Press.

Vroon, L.J. (1963/64), 'Voorgeschiedenis, opzet en resultaten van het Surinaams Tienjaren-plan', *Nieuwe West-Indische Gids*, 43.

5 POLITICS, ADMINISTRATION, AND THE POLICY PROCESS IN ETHIOPIA : A COMPARATIVE ASSESSMENT OF REGIME PERFORMANCES

H.K. Asmerom

Introduction: Some Theoretical Departures

Formulating and implementing public policy[1] is a routine task of responsible government anywhere in the world. This simple assertion does not necessarily imply, however, that all public policies are successfully implemented without obstacles. Extreme situations aside, worldwide experiences clearly illustrate that some public policies tend to be more successfully implemented than others. Indeed, some public policies are non-controversial and straightforward and do not encounter any opposition or obstacle once they are released into the implementation process, while other policies are complex by nature and entail considerable difficulty in implementation.

Discrepancies between policy objectives as contained in policy documents and plans (i.e. short and long-term development plans) on the one hand, and the tangible concrete outcomes (i.e. schools, health centres, agricultural schemes, feeder roads, supply of electricity to rural areas etc..) on the other, do in fact vary from one developing nation to the next. The explanation of such discrepancies can be found in the unique characteristics of each country or in the influence of natural or man-made problems or in pressure directed from outside the country. Explanations may also be found in the combination of all these factors. In any case, it is generally assumed that "success" and "failure" are complementary attributes of the implementation process in both developed and developing countries. At the same time, there seems to be a general consensus that the success side of the story occurs more frequently in the developed countries than in the developing ones. These are assertions from the implementation literature, which means they have to be verified empirically.

In the context of the developing countries, the data and information acquired to formulate public policies may or may not take into account the demands and wishes of the target groups and other side-line interest groups. All the same, once the available data and information are compiled into a meaningful "document for action" in the form of a draft public policy, they are endorsed by the highest authority structure in the land and publicized as the policy of the government ready to be implemented by the bureaucracy. This means that, although the target groups and the arena for concrete action leading to certain outcomes is located far away from the national capital, the implementation process begins right at the centre, where the policy has been given its final shape as part of the comprehensive national development policy. This situation, in fact, blurs the distinction between the policy-making and the policy-implementation phases. Take, for instance, policies on rural development programmes and policies related to the decentralization. Both are types of public policy which are given their final shape in the form of urgent development policies at the central government level, while the implementation process of both can stretch from the centre down to the grassroots level where the target groups are located. In other words, both policies have to be approved by the central government as part and parcel of the comprehensive national development policy. Once this initial stage has been accomplished, a number of government and non-government organizations, civil servants located at national and sub-national levels, national and local-level politicians, internal and external environmental factors and the target groups, themselves, all come into dynamic interaction. This occurs during the implementation process, before the expected results are realized or failures become apparent. In the face of all these possibilities, the question of how, why and when things go wrong, once a certain policy has been set and presented for implementation, has become a recurrent and often wearisome issue of the administration and politics of developing countries (Grindle 1980, Rondinelli/Cheema 1983, Smith 1985, Forss 1985, McHenry 1979; Quick 1980; Bowden 1986; Love/Sederberg 1987).

In a developing country like Ethiopia, implementation problems are easily detectable because many of the preconditions (political support, administrative and management know-how, adequate financial and physical infrastructure, clarity and consistency of programme objectives, target group co-operation etc.) that are crucial for the successful implementation of a given public policy are not optimally available at the right moment. Furthermore, as has been seen in the design and strategy of many development programmes in the third world, successful implementation of a given public policy could depend on external financial and technical assistance and management know-how of various types. Other factors, such as civil wars, liberation movements, armed regional conflicts, shortage of rain, flooding, and the like, threaten the whole process of formulating and implementing public policy. Whatever the precise combination of factors might be that adversely affect the implementation of public policy, the end results were invariably characterized by failure. What is more, the failures were often realized and detected at a much later stage of the implementation process because the early warning tools (the feedback and monitoring mechanisms) were suppressed or not properly institutionalized. In the worst cases, failures were not openly admitted by the governments in question, or they were simply attributed to forces beyond the control of the state.

In part, therefore, the aim of this chapter is to provide some insight and appreciation of these increasingly widespread problems in the context of the Haile Selassie and the Mengistu Regimes in Ethiopia.

Formulating and Implementing Public Policy during Haile Selassie's Rule

(a) The context : The Political and Bureaucratic Traditions

Ethiopia has had a long experience of traditional patrimonial rulership, the last and the most advanced phase of which took place under the reign of Haile Selassie I (Asmerom 1978; Gebru Tareke 1991: 45-54). Once in power, Haile Selassie made significant departures from the past. He introduced constitutional reforms that were essentially geared to formalize the traditional powers of the Emperor in writing and thus became in 1931, the first Ethiopian monarch to have his powers and prerogatives duly documented and elaborated in a constitution. Having effected this innovation, he began his reign as an absolute monarch, with all the decision-making powers emanating from and culminating at the imperial palace. The ministries and the government departments responsible for each of them continued to operate as mere extensions of the imperial palace. In other words, the system of government and administration were still expressions of traditional patrimonialism. All state activities, from minor to major policy areas, depended upon the whims and wishes of the all-powerful monarch.

After 1942, when the five-year Italian occupation of the country came to an end, Haile Selassie started to rebuild his administration, creating many more ministries and government agencies. The administration of the various regions of the country was also brought under more effective central control with the creation of a uniform system of provincial administration. Starting with the Emperor at the top of the hierarchy, the remaining state institutions consisted of a) the Crown Council, b) the Prime Minister, c) the Council of Ministers, d) the Individual Ministries, e) other Central Government Agencies, and f) the Provincial and Sub-Provincial Administration, which operated under the control of the minister if the Interior. At the same time, it should be noted that the provincial and sub-provincial governors were appointed by the Emperor and were seen as his representatives in their respective provinces. The Emperor was the head of state and the head of government, while the Crown Council was the highest advisory body to the Emperor.

The post of the Prime Minister had a rather vague existence beginning with the last years of Menelik's rule, but it became more institutionalized when Haile Selassie returned from exile in 1942. Gradually, the Prime Minister's Office grew in importance as the coordinator of all government activities. By 1966, the Prime Minister was given the power to choose members of his cabinet, who were then appointed by the Emperor himself. At the same time, the Prime Minister functioned as the trusted and subservient highest official under the Emperor, until the eve of the 1974 revolution. In a similar style of subservience, the Council of Ministers acted as an advisory body to the Emperor. The ministries and other government agencies, including the provincial administration hierarchy, formed the core of the public bureaucracy. All in all, the decision-making process was still highly centralized. No major decision could be made without the knowledge or formal approval of the Emperor. At the same time, however, as we shall see below, the Emperor made use of the technical services and expertise of organizations, like the planning agency, in articulating public policy, especially that which dealt with developmental matters. Long and short term planning activities were recognized as vital preconditions to attract foreign capital investment in the country and to secure bilateral and multilateral development assistance.

(b) The nature of public policies and how they were formulated and implemented

Like most third world countries, the policies and developmental programmes of Ethiopia during the ancient regime were elaborated sector by sector. Ultimately these were integrated into comprehensive national development blueprints, usually in the form of five-year development plans. From 1957 to 1973 three such five-year development plans were launched. The First Five-Year Development Plan (1957-1962) could be seen as a very preliminary attempt at rational planning of public policy in Ethiopia. In fact, the plan was kept confidential for half of the plan period. Even when it was gradually made public, its contents were not accepted by the ministries and other government agencies that were supposed to implement them. In other words, the plan was not taken seriously, the reason being that the Emperor continued to introduce new elements to the plan and to initiate tasks which had to be carried out as a matter of priority. At any rate, at least on paper, the First Five-Year Development Plan devoted its attention to socio-economic infrastructure, such as agriculture, mining, industry, transport, health, and education.

The targets and achievements varied considerably from one sector to the other. Some targets were over-achieved while others were not touched at all. In terms of management and administration, there was a great lack of co-ordination among the various ministries and government agencies.[2] As a policy document, the First Five-Year Development Plan was, to all intents and purposes, a mere attempt and its achievements were very limited indeed.

The Second Five Year Development Plan (1963-1968) was, by and large, a continuation of the First in its emphasis on the development of the country's socio-economic infrastructure. Further, in a manner similar to the First Plan, the preparation of the Second Five-Year Plan was based on unreliable and incomplete data. In other words, the plan was based largely on estimates, even though, from a technical point of view, it was more sophisticated than the First Plan, in that it incorporated an achievement plan in the form of a twenty-year projections of what was to be achieved in the various sectoral policies. Recommendations for administrative improvements of existing organizations and the creation of new departments were also included in the plan. The plan envisaged an investment programme that which would change the pattern of technology and infrastructure of the country for the better by introducing modern equipment to improve the production and distribution of goods and services. For the most part, the industrial sector was expected to adopt capital-intensive patterns of technology instead of labour intensive methods. Similarly, agriculture was to be modernized by the introduction of scientific farming techniques. Capital intensive technology was also seen as the preferred method in exploiting the country's mineral resources.

As with the First Five-Year Development Plan, the actual implementation of the Second Development Plan did not conform with the official investment allocation. The economy appeared to have grown only 4% between 1961 and 1965, while the population increased at 2% per annum. The low level of economic growth was attributed mostly to the low level of agricultural production. The growth rate in manufactured products during the same period was 16.2%. The fast growth rates recorded in some sectors of the economy could not conceal the fact that overall economic growth was still very low. Following sporadic evaluations conducted by the planning agency, the reasons for failure in the agricultural sector were attributed to the antiquated agrarian structure of the country, especially the exploitative and complex land tenure systems, and to primitive farming methods. By the end of the Second Five-Year Development Plan, the Ethiopian economy was still dominated by subsistence agriculture, with only about 5% of the national product entering the market. By the end of the Second Five-Year Development Plan, agriculture was still very stagnant, with a per capita rate of growth only 2% per year, one of the lowest in Africa (Bekele and Chole 1969: 19-25).

The low level of investment also adversely affected economic development. The highly centralized and patrimonial nature of the decision-making process appears to have been one of the major stumbling blocks to the formulation and implementation of development planning, along with the absence of sufficient trained manpower at all levels of the government machinery.

The Third Five-Year Development Plan (1968-1973) was certainly much more sophisticated than the previous two policy documents. Its principal objectives were:a) to raise the general level of the country's socio-economic development by 6% per year; b) to modernize and strengthen the administrative machinery and financial institutions in order to make them fitting instruments for the formulation and implementation of the interrelated goals and objectives of the plan; and c) to extend economic and social development from urban centres to the rural areas. In other words, the plan put greater emphasis to rural development. In terms of economic growth, the Third Five-Year Development Plan envisaged a target increase in overall production of Eth.$ 4.8 billion. This means that, in the course of the plan period, the country's gross domestic product (GDP) was expected to grow at an average of 6% per year, while real income per head was intended to rise from Eth.$ 151 in 1960 to Eth.$ 181 in 1965 (Third Five Year Plan: 42). Further, it was assumed that subsistence farmers would move in the direction of commercial production for the market at the rate of 9% per year. As the result of this move in the direction of commercial agriculture, subsistence production would be reduced from 45% to 37% of the nation's total GDP between 1968 and 1973 (Third Five Year Development Plan: 43-4).

The components of the three consecutive five-year development plans were collected from the various ministries and other government departments in the form of suggested short- and long-term activities. They were then aggregated by the central planning agency as five-year development plans. The integrated comprehensive plan was then discussed in the Council of Ministers under the chairmanship of the Emperor.[3] Finally, after the necessary changes and adjustments,the plan was approved by the Emperor as the comprehensive development strategy of the country for the next five years.

The institution which was closely involved in the planning process was the planning office, which was attached to the Ministry of Commerce, Industry and Planning until 1961, i.e. until the end of the First Five-Year period. The actual preparation of the First Five-Year plan was done by a team of Yugoslav economists who were believed to have produced the plan more or less on their own, using some crude data, but also their own home experience in Yugoslavia. The result was a planning document to be implemented by the Ethiopian government, which was only marginally involved in its preparation. Ethiopian experts were very few at the time. What is more, a major problem encountered by the Yugoslav experts when they arrived in Ethiopia was the absence of organized and reliable information. Apart from incomplete figures on foreign trade, they did not find any reliable data. The experts' primary task was therefore to estimate where the Ethiopian economy stood and thus establish the basis of the plan. There were no institutional or organizational facilities that were concerned with planning at all. Later, when the plan was published, it could be seen that the policy and structural elements necessary for the implementation of any development programme were lacking. Because of the absence of an effective coordinating body, some structural rearrangements were introduced during the First Five-Year Development plan. This rearrangement scheme resulted in the transfer of the Planning Office from the ministry of Commerce, Industry and Planning to the Prime Minister's Office, giving the latter a significant status as coordinating body for the entire planning process of the country.

Further changes were made in 1966 with regard to the organization of the state bureaucracy as a whole with the result that the planning activities were transferred to a newly created Ministry of Planning and Development. The technical agency, the Central Statistical Office and the Economic and Technical Assistance Board were all brought under the supervision of the Ministry of Planning and Development.

In 1970, the Planning Commission replaced the Ministry of Planning and Development. The new Commission itself came under the direct control of the Prime Minister's Office. Accordingly, its position and status as a coordinating body of the planning process was much strengthened, since it remained outside the stream of interministerial competition and rivalry for available budgetary allocations. After 1970, the structure of the planning process was as follows: Firstly, at the top of the pyramid was the Planning Commission. It consisted of the Prime Minister who acted as the chairman of the Commission's meetings. The members of the Commission included all the members of the Council of Ministers, the Governor of the National Bank and the Head of the Planning Commission. The main task of the Planning Commission was to prepare an overall socio-economic development plans for the country, which was to be submitted to the Emperor for his approval before it became a binding document for all government organizations and the private sector. Secondly, there was the Planning Commission's Office (PCO). This was, in effect, the secretariat of the Planning Commission. It was headed by an executive officer appointed by the Emperor upon the recommendation of the Prime Minister. Other state organizations which were closely associated with activities of the Planning Commission through providing technical services to the planning process included: a) the Central Statistical Office. This was a semi-autonomous agency within the Planning Commssion's Office. It was responsible for assembling and processing data needed for the formulation of various sectoral policies that were to be integrated into the overall planning document; b) the Technical Agency. This was also a semi-autonomous state organization. It acted as the consultancy staff organization in the preparation of specific projects to be adopted and implemented by both government departments and private contractors; c) Planning and Programming units, each of which was intended to carry out, more or less, the following uniform tasks: 1. preparation of short- and long-term programmes; 2. project planning; and 3. research and study of economic, statistical and marketing conditions useful to the overall activities of the ministry or government organization to which they belonged. These staff units were intended to function as planning units of their parent organizations, but they were not yet functional by the eve of the 1974 revolution.

At the sub-national level, two regional planning offices, one for the northern regions, and the other for the southern regions, were to be established. Again all this was still a blueprint on the eve of the 1974 revolution.

Formulating and Implementing of Public Policy during the Mengistu Socialist Regime.

(a) The context : The Emergent Political and Bureaucratic Ethos

As it were, the seeds of the revolution had been germinating ever since the attempted coup d'etat of 1960 (Clapham 1988:32-38), but they did not bear fruit until the overthrow of the monarchy in September 1974 by a group of young military officers. This marked the beginning of the much- abhorred 16 years of socialist experiment in Ethiopia.

The military officers did not establish a full-fledged Marxist-Leninist regime from the start, but rather they presented themselves as the Provisional Military Administrative Council (PMAC). Initially, the PMAC acted as a collective head of state and head of government at the same time. In its internal day-to-day functioning the PMAC was divided into specialized committees and sub-committees for the purpose of supervising and controlling the activities of the bureaucracy (Yohannes Abate 1979:20). As a collective body politic, it also started to conduct its deliberations according to normal democratic principles, with decisions being arrived after long debates and by majority vote. It became increasingly clear, however, that the new collective leadership, with its 120 members, was too large and cumbersome to function efficiently. By design or by accident, Mengistu Haile Mariam took over the chairmanship of the PMAC meetings and began to direct its activities along less democratic and more authoritarian lines of decision-making (Blair Thomson 1975:116-7). Within a year after the military takeover, all semblance of democratic decision-making was abandoned and a dictatorial style of rule began to take shape with Mengistu at the top.

Under the supervision of the various committees and sub-committees of the PAMC, the inherited bureaucracy continued to function in the same way as it did during the long reign of Emperor Haile Selassie I. At the same time, however, because of the far reaching changes that were introduced in the socio-economic and political spheres, together with the uncertain and confusion that accompanied these changes, the bureaucracy could not function optimally as demanded by the new leaders (Legum 1975:52; Brietzke 1982:192-215). The Council of Ministers, for example, merely received directives and orders from above, which were expected to be implemented by the rank and file of the bureaucrats. If they delayed or raised questions, they would be accused of counter-revolutionary activity. If things went wrong, however, the ministers and their subordinates would be accused of sabotage and neglect of duty, even if the undesired acts or outcomes were beyond their control and they were powerless to avert them (Ottaway & Ottaway 1978:142-43). Many dysfunctional practices of the previous system of administration including favouritism, rewards and penalties, promotions and demotions and the conduct of government business on the basis of patron-client relationships re-emerged on a greater scale (Brietzke 1982:192-215).

Once it had consolidated the reins of power and was in full control of all state institutions, the PMAC launched a campaign of attack and vilification against the inherited bureaucracy, using phrases like "bureaucratic capitalism" and "petty bourgeoisie" (Ethiopian Herald 1975, 1976, 1977). For purely practical reasons, however, it did not subject the more than 100,000 civil servants and government officials to systematic purges or mass dismissals (Ottaway & Ottaway 1978:74).

As the result of the sweeping nationalization measures, the activities of the public bureaucracy expanded considerably. New ministries and other state agencies were created to administer these new activities, all under the centralized control and supervision of the PMAC. The central government's control over the provincial administration also became tighter. Indeed, as an extension of the central bureaucracy, the sub-national administration was kept as weak as it was during the time of Emperor Haile Selassie I. Still, for some time during the post-revolutionary period, the sub-national administration acted as an arbitrator for conflicting political forces, rather than as the representative of the PMAC in the countryside (Ottaway & Ottaway 1978: 177), due to the upheavals created by the nationalization of all rural lands and the disappearance of the entrenched land lords from the political and administrative landscape of rural Ethiopia.

The newly established grassroots institutions - the peasant associations in the rural areas and the kebels (committees) in the urban centres - although they contained seeds of centrifugal elements, especially during the early years of the post-revolutionary period, were to be effectively controlled by centralized structures such as the Commission to Organize the Party of the Working People of Ethiopia (COPWE), which was converted in 1984 to the

Workers' Party of Ethiopia (WPE), and was, in turn, renamed the Ethiopian Democratic Unity Party in 1990 (Halliday and Molyneux 1981:160-61).

The political turmoil, the widespread assassinations among competing political groupings (in which the PMAC also took part) and the periodic executions and liquidations that were unleashed by the military regime soon after the September revolution resulted in a number of changes in the organization of the PMAC itself. Ultimately, the structural changes that were engineered and sponsored by Mengistu led to his emergence as the most powerful chairman the PMAC had yet known. Indeed, Mengistu accumulated far greater powers than either of his two predecessors (Ottawy and Ottawy 1978:144, Schwab 1985:36-7; Proc.108 of 1976; Proc.110 of 1977). To all intents and purposes, both in theory and in practice, Mengistu became a prototype of a modern third world dictator. The emergence of Mengistu as a dictator has been described in various ways. To some, like Markakis and Ayele, Mengistu represented ruthless authoritarianism and naked dictatorship (Markakis and Ayele 1977). To those like Schwab, who sympathised with his dreams and ideals, he was a true revolutionary directing a true revolution (Schwab 1985:117). To others, he was a ruler who projected himself in the tradition of a strong and popular figure like Twedros (Halliday & Molyneaux 1981:153-54). To the Cultural Survival Group of Scholars, Mengistu was a violator of basic human rights and the champion of misguided plans for human resettlement with all their adverse effects on man and the environment (Jason W. Clay et al 1988). For still other commentators, Mengistu is like Stalin, who clings to absolute power through force, intrigue, and manipulation, aided by a group of loyal henchmen, secret police and terror squads (Dawit Wolde Giorgis 1989:57). Synthesizing all these interpretations, it seems safe to state that Mengistu was indeed a prototype of the third world dictator who thought of himself as someone who legitimately rose to the commanding heights of power and as someone whom Ethiopia could not do without, even if his cherished aims were rejected by the people before his very eyes.

During all these changes, the public bureaucracy continued to carry out its duties in the same subservient manner as in the early years of the revolution. The traditional hierarchical and centralized linkages between the central and provincial components of the public bureaucracy were, however, revised in 1980 (Proc. No. 179 of 1980), presumably to protect the gains of the revolution at both the centre and the periphery. Accordingly, the Minister of the Interior was given a stronger mandate to supervise the administration of the regions, awrajas and wordeda and thereby protect the revolution against its enemies within the country. At the same time, of course, Mengistu had created a parallel line of control and supervision of the periphery. To start with, this was the Commission for Organizing the Party of the Working People of Ethiopia (COPWE) which was later converted to the Workers' Party of Ethiopia. Later, the name of the Party was changed to the Ethiopian Peoples Democratic Unity Party (EPDUP).

By far, the most far-reaching changes with regard to the nature of the state in general and state-society relationships in particular were introduced in 1987 (Proc. No.1 of 1987 establishing the People's Democratic Republic of Ethiopia).Thus, with the announcement of the new socialist constitution, the PMAC transformed itself into the National Shengo (Parliament or National Assembly), apparently a rubber stamp body comparable to Haile Selassie's Parliament (Proc. No.2 of 1987). There were no substantial changes of actors at the highest level; Mengistu and his close associates were still at the top of the political ladder. The National Shengo held only one regular session per year. During the long recess of the National Shengo, it was the Council of State, chaired by the President of the Republic, Mengistu Haile Mariam, that acted as the highest decision-making body (Articles 81 to 83 of the 1987 Constitution and Article 10 of Proc. No.7 of 1987).

Proc. No.8 of 1987 provided a detailed description of the powers and duties of the newly-restructured bureaucracy. According to this law, the Council of Ministers, chaired by the Prime Minister and assisted by five Deputy Prime Ministers, and with some 25 ministers and commissioners as members, was the highest executive and administrative body of the People's Democratic Republic of Ethiopia. Like Haile Selassie before him, Mengistu had the power to appoint and dismiss all members of the Council of Ministers, including the Prime Minister. One can, of course, lament that these constitutional powers in themselves may not look different from of many other third world countries, and, in a society which had lived with authoritarian rule for much of its history such provisions may not look strange at all. On the other hand, the fact that they could easily be misused to simply preserve one's power position cannot be left unnoticed.

In theory, the Council of Ministers was accountable not only to the President but also to the Council of State and, ultimately to the National Shengo in the discharge of its duties. In practice, however, this accountability was ultimately to the President only, since he was the chairman of both the Council of State and the National Shengo. Commenting on the extensive power position of President Mengistu, Dawit Wolde Giorgis has this to say:

The new constitution is of little importance and mostly of propaganda value. Power is completely centralized in a single leader. The   Politburo, the Central Committee and the new state structures under the constitution are window dressings to hide the totalitarian reality. Like the Reichstag of Hitler's Germany, they rubberstamp pre-made decisions (Dawit Wolde Giorgis 1989:66).

To be sure, these statements were made by someone who was once part of the regime, but later, for reasons of his own, became extremely critical of Mengistu's rule, but any one else who has studied the 1987 constitution and the related proclamations would no doubt arrive at similar conclusions.

As a further manifestation of the emergent socialist system of administration and management, an entirely new and highly elaborate control mechanism known as the Workers' Control Committee has been established by Proc. No.12 of 1987. This committee is to operate at national, regional and primary (i.e. at the site of the work place) levels. Its task consists of four broad categories: (a) combatting the abuse of power by government officials, waste and plunder of resources, bribery, administrative injustice, unlawful enrichment and illegal trade practices; (b) ensuring that dignity of labour is appreciated and respected; (c) encouraging workers to safeguard, protect and administer the resources brought under their control and at the same time ensuring their class dominance; and (d) ensuring that the properties of mass and state organizations are protected (Proc. No. 12 of 1987). Although there are no available reports as yet how this committee system has been operating, it nevertheless represents a highly sophisticated instrument in itself and adds a new dimension to the complexity and proliferation of state institutions.

The administrative and autonomous regions proclaimed by the regime in 1987 were intended to offer decentralization of power to sub-national levels so that the people could be intimately involved in socio-economic development according to their own demands and felt-needs. The intensified struggle for self-determination in Eritrea and demands by other political groupings in the rest of the country for the creation of a truly democratic system of government in Ethiopia, had plunged the people in a protracted war with the armed forces of the regime for several years. As a consequence, not all of the new proclamation on autonomy and regional administration could be implemented. This means, for all practical purposes, that the old patterns of provincial administration continued to be applied in the provinces that were still under the regime's effective control. As the many-pronged wars continued unabated to tear up the country, the regime had no other choice but to impose an emergency military rule. The main task of the regime became the mobilization of the available resources for its war efforts. This blind policy was the prime preoccupation of the regime until its downfall in the Spring 1991.

After a long delay, which was mainly due to social and political turmoil fuelled by the regime itself, the Workers' Party of Ethiopia was announced in 1984. With an elaborated hierarchy of committees and subcommittees at national and sub-national levels, it soon established itself as the most powerful institution ever introduced in the country. Indeed, as Article 6 of the 1987 constitution later framed it, the Party was to be the leading and guiding force of state and society and was to be responsible for the overall policy matters of the nation. This provision was a replica of the then-prevailing standard Marxist-Leninist conception of the status and role assigned to the communist party. Thus, since the authority of the party was supreme, the task of the bureaucracy was simply to implement policies that were formulated and approved by the party. In practice, however, the party and bureaucratic hierarchies were not completely separate from each other. There were mergers and overlapping of functions following the Marxist-Leninist system of rule. For instance, the President of the Republic, who had the ultimate responsibility for the activities of the Council of Ministers, both directly and via the Council of State, was at the same time the Secretary General of the Party, a position which made him both key policy maker and chief administrator at the same time. Below that level, members of the Politburo and the Central Committee could be members of the Council of Ministers or hold other administrative and managerial positions in the much inflated bureaucratic apparatus. This duplication of positions and tasks was repeated at every level down to the peasant associations in the villages.

(b) Formulating and Implementing Public Policy during the Post-revolutionary period

The development campaigns of the initial years

In line with its policy of gradual modernization, it took the regime of Emperor Haile Selassie I something like a quarter of a century to institutionalize a form of economic planning in the country that relied on the active participation of both the public and private sectors. As elaborated earlier in this chapter, by the eve of the 1974 revolution, the idea of planned development, despite all its shortcomings, had become part of the Ethiopian body-politic. This enabled Mengistu socialist regime to start with its own version of planned development at a much faster rate soon after it came to power, since the bureaucracy responsible for the planning process was inherited intact, although some work had to be done to reorient it to the new ideological facade. At any rate, during the initial years of the post-revolutionary period, the regime was essentially pre-occupied with its own survival. From September 1974 until September 1978 it had to fight against all forms of internally and externally-generated opposition (Clapham 1988; Harbeson 1988; Dawit Wolde Giorgis 1989). Nevertheless, even during the first few years of the post-revolutionary period, the regime succeeded in introducing far-reaching socio-economic, political and administrative changes. As a basis for the changes, new policy guidelines under the motto of Ethiopia Tikdem (Ethiopia First) were announced in September 1974. The guidelines stressed that the principles of equality, self-reliance, the dignity of labour, cooperativeness, cultural pride and the unity of Ethiopia would be defended and promoted in the new Ethiopia. These guidelines marked the beginning of a socialist-oriented development strategy in the country. Further, the concept of *hibretesebawinet* (freely translated as communalism) was given prominence in order to support the idea that the emerging socialist ideology had its roots in the Ethiopian culture, just as many other socialist ideologies in Africa tried to identify themselves with traditional African values and norms. At the same time, however, it should be noted that these initial ideological commitments were more an outline of the nature of the policy goals rather than coherent policy statements ready to be translated into concrete action programmes. As Clapham aptly formulated it, at best the policy guide-lines gave an indication on how national unity and socialism could be pursued at the same time (Clapham 1988:45-6). In spite of their apparent vagueness, these initial guidelines were kept as central policy statements of the regime's aims for about two years, until they were replaced by the more elaborate document known as *the Programme of the National Democratic Revolution* in April 1976.

As indicated above, the military regime did not rely on the inherited planning machinery to formulate and implement its radical reform programmes. Instead, it introduced an ad hoc strategy known as the National Development Through Co-operation Campaign (zemetcha in Amharic). It was launched in December 1974 especially for the purpose of implementing the land reform programmes. This campaign involved the mobilization of some 50,000 high school and university students and teachers who were sent by phases to the countryside to implement the land reform programme and to indoctrinate the peasants on the need to defend their newly gained rights and freedoms against former land owners. To achieve such aims, the peasants were to be organized into peasant associations. Urban dwellers, on the other hand, were to form urban associations, known as *kebels* in Amharic.They were to serve as units of urban administration and were entrusted with the implementation of the law that nationalized urban lands and extra houses which was announced in July 1975.

The socialist-oriented top-down development strategy

In April 1976, the document known as the Programme of the National Democratic Revolution (PNDR) was announced. This document was more elaborate and had far-reaching consequences in shaping the entire political and economic structures of the country in the direction of a rigid Marxist-Leninist state. In fact, the expressed aims and objectives of the PNDR were to abolish feudalism, imperialism and bureaucratic capitalism, to accelerate the establishment of socialism in the country, to recognize the rights to self-determination of all nationalities and to safeguard the unity of Ethiopia. To this extent, the document was considered as an outline of a socialist pattern of development , although it was assumed that the general theory and practice of socialist transformation would have to be adjusted to fit the specific circumstances of Ethiopia (Keller 1988:197). This means that the socialist pattern of development that was adopted by the military regime appeared to be based on pragmatic grounds, rather than on pure ideological considerations per se (Keler 1988: 198). At any rate, the PNDR envisaged the development of a centralized economy with a strong public sector . At the same time, the programme left some room for Ethiopian nationals to participate in the economic development of the country (Dessalegn Rahmato, in Keller and Rothchild 1987:165). Regardless of its many-sided aims and objectives the PNDR was already being undermined in importance by 1977 and in 1978, it was effectively abandoned as a key document of the regime (Harbeson 1988:160).

A Provisional Office of Mass Organizational Affairs (POMOA) was created in 1976 with the task of coordinating the activities of the various leftist political parties that mushroomed since the military takeover of power. To be sure, some of these new leftist political parties came to existence with the support of the military regime itself. In 1977, the regime announced the creation of the Central Planning Commission, arguing the need to institutionalize a centralized planning machinery as a pre-condition to the transformation of the archaic feudo-bourgeois mode of production and the augmentation and development of the productive forces and to ensure that production satisfied the needs of the broad masses (Proclamation No.128 of 1977, Establishment of the Central Planning Commission). The Commission was to be chaired by an official designated by the Chairman of the Provisional Military Administrative Council (PMAC). The members of the Commission were to include several ministers, especially those who dealt with development related activities. The Commission was entrusted with the task of preparing the country's short, medium and long-term development plans. All major decisions of the Commission were to be submitted to the Council of Ministers for approval. Further, the Commission was required to cooperate with mass organizations at the regional, provincial, awraja (district), woreda (sub-district) and village levels, and with ministries and other government organizations in estimating the general macro-economic parameters and overall investment needs, and in determining the required technical assistance, loans, credits and other financial and economic activities. At this stage, it can be easily seen that the regime was on the road to a highly institutionalized planning process.

Streamlining the Socialist Planning Institutions

In 1978, the Central Planning Commission was replaced by the National Revolutionary Development Campaign and Central Planning Council (NDC and CPSC). This new planning machinery was to be engaged in the formulation and implementation of the annual development campaign(zemetcha)programmes geared to the problems of food shortage and of other consumer items. Further, the campaigns were supposed to tackle declining productivity, correct the shortage of foreign exchanges and stop rising unemployment. Such urgent programmes were to be implemented with year-to-year allocations from current expenditure. The government had assumed that such annual plans would help pave the way for the economic recovery of the country (Mulatu Wubneh 1990:201). However, as Clapham has argued, the National Revolutionary Development Campaigns were merely ad hoc measures rather than well-conceived development plans. This means, despite the fact that ambitious targets were announced, there was no comprehensive ordering of the available resources to implement very specific goals (Clapham 1988:116).

The cardinal aim of the National Revolutionary Development Campaign and Central Planning was to start the process of long-term planning with peasant agriculture serving as the basis of economic development. Industry was relegated to a secondary priority (Keller 1988: 251). During its first year of operation, the CPSC expanded the area of land under peasant cultivation and claimed success in rasing overall economic growth from below 1% at the beginning of 1978 to over 5% by the end of 1979. Despite such impressive claims, however, the economy as a whole appeared to have been facing a deep crisis due to the worldwide inflation spiral, declining coffee prices and Ethiopia's dwindling foreign exchange reserves. These problems appeared to have been exacerbated by huge external debts that had grown to the tune of $ 691 million (Keller 1988:251-2).

In June of 1984, the CPSC was replaced by the Office of the National Committee for Central Planning (ONCCD). Organizationally, this new planning organization had different layers. At the centre, the most influential body was the National Committee for Central Planning. Chaired by the President of the Republic, its main task was to prepare directives and strategies for short, medium and long-term plans. The membership of the National Committee for Central Planning was dominated by people from the politburo,but there were also officials from the bureaucracy. Peasants and workers, however were not represented. Under the National Committee for Central Planning was an Executive Committee, which was to be chaired by the Vice-chairman of the National Committee. At the regional level, there were seven regional planning offices. They represented the National Committee for Central Planning in their respective regions of jurisdiction. Further, below the regional planning office, there were provincial planning offices, awraja (district) development councils and woreda (sub-district) development councils. By and large, the planning bodies, which were located at various sub-national levels, were expected to be engaged in the initiation of various development proposals, including conducting comprehensive studies on economic and social issues. They were also given the authority to supervise the implementation of approved projects (Miulatu Wubneh 1990:201).

When Ethiopia was transformed into a people's democratic republic in 1987, the National Committee for Central Planning was reestablished by Proc. No.8 of 1987, but with a changed structure and composition of its membership. For one thing, the National Committee was to be chaired by the Deputy Prime Minister for National Planning and Research, and not by the President of the Republic as before. Further, the members of the National Committee included, ministers, managers of state agencies, regional planning heads and other officials to be appointed by the President of the Republic. The National Committee for Central Planning was to be responsible to the Council of Ministers and its main duties would be to prepare short, medium and long-term plans and to follow up the implementation and evaluation of approved programmes. The day-to-day activities of the National Committee were to be supervised by an executive head appointed by the President of the Republic.

Other state organizations that were involved in the realization of the centralized planning process included: a) the Central Statistical Office (CSO) which, as in the times of the ancient regime, was concerned with the collection, compilation, and analysis of multi-purpose statistical data needed for the formulation of comprehensive and sectoral policies; b) the Development Project Study Authority (DPSA), which was assigned with the task of developing guidelines for study, preparation and evaluation of projects that would ensure their compatibility with the political, economic and ideological value premises of the People's Republic of Ethiopia; c) the National Mapping Authority (NMA), which was engaged with the preparation of maps on geography, climate, and the distribution of the country's resources by region and the like; d) the Relief and Rehabilitation Commission (RRC), which was engaged in the distribution of food, medicine and other urgent facilities to famine-stricken areas; e) the Water Resources Commission (WRC), which was concerned with the exploration and utilization of the country's water resources; and f) the Building and Transport Construction Design Authority (BTCDA), which was concerned with the design and implementation of public buildings and the transportation system of the country. In one way or another, these agencies, most of which had been functioning as semi-autonomous state agencies during Haile Selassie's regime, became components of the expanded and highly-centralized state apparatus in the post 1974 period, and especially after the creation of the People's Democratic Republic in 1987. By their very nature, these were essentially involved as support organizations in the formulation and implementation of the centrally planned public policies.

In 1984 the regime published its highly publicized document entitled " The Ten Years Perspective Plan". The plan was designed to cover a period of ten years from 1984 to 1994. For purposes of implementation the plan was to be split into phases of three medium-term plans. The first would be a two-year initial plan (1984/85-1985/86), the second was to be a three-year plan (1986/87-1988/89), and the third phase was to be a five-year plan

(1989/90-1993/94). Further, each phase was to be subdivided into annual plan targets (Clapham 1988:115-117).

The ultimate objective of the Ten Year Perspective Plan was to create a full-fledged socialist pattern of development by 1994 with agriculture as the dominant sector of the economy. All commentators agree, however, that the plan was unrealistic from the start. It relied very heavily on foreign aid; so much so that, at the initial stage, it assumed that 55% of all investment would be acquired from external sources. The chances of securing such a massive amount of foreign aid were slim and, even if it could be secured, it would only promote market-oriented economic activities and not the socialist pattern envisaged by the regime. Secondly, since foreign aid funds and loans are usually tied to projects conforming to the wishes of donors, such projects may not necessarily be in agreement with the interests of a regime that was committed to hard-line socialism. What is more, in the face of increased armed confrontation against liberation movements and other opponents determined to overthrow Mengistu's regime, it was almost taken for granted that most of the externally generated funds would be spent in the acquisition of military hardware. Added to all these factors which were deemed to be ready-made traps for failure, the country was hit by a severe famine crisis in 1984/85 just at the time when the plan was due to take effect. At first the regime cynically put aside the famine tragedy and busied itself with the preparations for the 10th anniversary celebrations of the revolution.

After the celebrations were over, the regime returned its attention to the famine problems. By this time, it had become clear that the ambitious Ten Year Perspective Plan was an unrealistic document that could not be implemented as planned (Clapham 1988: 117; Dejene Aredo 1990: 51). The regime had assumed that the financial requirements anticipated by the Ten Year Perspective Plan would be generated from foreign aid and loans. However, since the plan contained highly inflated objectives, the expected foreign capital could not be attracted. In fact, experts from both the socialist countries of Eastern Europe and the West were believed to have advised the government to adopt a more flexible economic policy. At first the government refused to heed to such advice, but at the beginning of 1988 it indicated its readiness to liberalize the economy. The attempted liberalization policies did not go far enough, however, to meet the terms of foreign investment (Mulatu Wubneh 1990:216-217). Indeed, as Wubneh and Abate put it, "the military regime tried to do too much too quickly with too few resources. Process often substituted for results, policies often overlooked contradictions across programmes and impressive legislations conveyed an illusion for significance without achieving objectives" (Mulatu Wubneh and Yohannis Abate 1988:119-120).

As a prelude to its eventual downfall in May 1991 the Mengistu regime had engaged in fierce and devastating battles with the forces of the Ethiopian People's Revolutionary Democratic Front (EPRDF), the Eritrean People's Liberation Front (EPLF) and the Oromo Liberation Front (OLF) in many parts of the country (Gebru Tareke 1991: 207-228). The string of military defeats it sustained in the hands of these combined forces and the swift march towards Addis Ababa by the forces of EPRDF ultimately resulted in the flight of Mengistu to Zimbabwe. The EPRDF triumphantly marched into Addis Ababa on 21 May 1991 and established itself as the new Ethiopian Provisional Administration. At the same time, it announced that its ultimate aim was to prepare the country for a truly democratic multiparty state under a new constitution. In the mean time, the EPLF has established itself as the provisional administration in Eritrea. The EPLF has declared that it would keep its provisional character until a UN-sponsored referendum is held to decide whether the people of Eritrea would stay with Ethiopia under some sort of loose political arrangement or if they wished to be completely independent from Ethiopia. It is generally expected that Eritrea will choose to be independent, at least for the shorter term. In the rest of Ethiopia, the EPRDF-led provisional government has come out with a new regional division of Ethiopia on the basis of nationalities, abolishing the old provincial structure of the country. In addition to the EPRDF, and the OLF (Oromo Liberation Front) there are now more than twenty other political groupings in the country.

Regional elections were recently held in which many political parties were to take part. It appears that these elections were not very successful. There are accusations against the EPRDF that it did not adhere to fair and honest election procedures. Accordingly, tensions and mutual suspicions among the ethnically-based political parties continue to be unresolved thorny issues in Ethiopia. This means, as things are at the moment, that it is too early to speculate about how the democratization process in Ethiopia will develop to the satisfaction of all the parties concerned. In the light of the still uncertain post-Mengistu political developments in the country, it is difficult to assess the policymaking process of the provisional government and indeed the direction of its socio-economic programmes. All in all, the EPRDF-dominated provisional government is still engaged with the unenviable task of creating a stable democratic political climate in Ethiopia while addressing itself to repairing the damages inflicted upon the country by decades of civil war, famine and the misguided policies of the previous regime.

Achievements and Failures in Comparative Perspective

The analysis has revealed a number of obvious similarities and differences between the strategies and approaches adopted by the Haile Selassie and the Mengistu regimes for planning and economic development in Ethiopia. Haile Selassie's regime was essentially a continuation of the traditional past, with the Emperor playing the key role from the pinnacle of the undifferentiated political and administrative pyramid. As such, it was governed by the tenets of patrimonial ideology of centralized traditional rulership. Its primary aim was the preservation of the traditional socio-economic and political relationships brought under the domination of the theoretically limitless powers and prerogatives of the Emperor as prescribed in the 1955 Revised Constitution.

Dictated by the demands of the time, Haile Selassie's government gradually embraced the standard model of five-year development planning as an instrument for the mobilization of resources within the country and for attracting capital investment from abroad. This meant that both the public and the private sectors were to play mutually beneficial role in the economic development of the country. The government launched three successive five-year development plans from 1957 to 1973. The plans paid a good deal of attention to the socio-economic development of the country, clearly defined sector by sector. However, the concrete achievements scored by these three successive five-year development plans were far from impressive. Few sectors were overachieved while many others were ruled off as complete failures. What is more, the attempts that were made to introduce genuine land reforms were very minimal indeed. The antiquated land holding system and tenancy were still intact by the eve of the 1974 revolution. Indeed, the overall standard of living of the majority of Ethiopians remained one of the lowest in the third world.

In the course of his long reign, Haile Selassie I expanded the public bureaucracy to a considerable size. New ministries and government agencies were established at regular intervals, although very little was done to introduce meaningful decentralization of power and the granting of authority to the sub-national adminstration. To all intents and purposes, the latter remained as an extension of the centre until Haile Selassie's overthrow in September 1974.

The expansion of the bureaucracy at the centre was often brought about without adequate study of the shortcomings of existing ministries and other government organizations. The splintering of ministries and agencies or the introduction of new ones had resulted in a plethora of institutions with overlapping and, at times, contradictory functions, which created unnecessary competition for the available financial, manpower and material resources. Indeed, some of the ministries and state agencies were established in haste and without adequate study. Creating and abolishing government departments without real justification to do so inevitably led to redundancy, duplication of tasks and bitter conflicts among ministers and other government functionaries. To take just one example, the proliferation of organizations geared to agricultural activities had made it impossible for the ministry of agriculture to develop a well-integrated sectoral plan for agricultural development within the framework of the five-year national plans. In some instances, two separate organizations were created for the same objective. A good example of this situation was the creation of the Grain Board and the Grain Corporation both to handle a single commodity, grain. This was a mistaken strategy which aggravated the problems of coordination, overlapping and waste of resources (Institute of Public Administration 1973:4).

Another example of splintered and uncoordinated activity was seen in the management of water resources.In this unique case, the Awash Valley Authority, the Ethiopian Light and Power Authority, the Ministry of National Community Development and Social Affairs, the Department of the Municipalities of the Ministry of the Interior, the Ministry of Agriculture and the Ministry of Mines, were all responsible for different aspects of water resources development (Ibidem 1973:6). Similarly, the ministries of Agriculture, National Community Development and Social Affairs and Land Reform and Administration were all working on settlement and resettlement projects, with little or no coordination among them (UN 1972:120).

Other examples of improper planning could be seen in transport studies that mainly concentrated on highways at the expense of feeder and secondary roads; the plan on electricity and power supply that neglected rural electrification; the studies on agriculture, forestry, fisheries, wildlife, manufacturing and handcraft industries that were inadequate; the land tenure system that was not only obsolete, but also extremely exploitative at the same time; and several basic national surveys crucial to planning, such as a comprehensive population census, that lacked detailed and reliable data on the natural resources of the country.

On the whole, the planning process of the pre-1974 period was adversely affected by the absence of proper and well-balanced sectoral studies and the lack of clearly defined tasks, together with the fact that the Emperor could intervene at any time to modify the planning process in response to some emergency situations or to simply divert resources from one sector to another or to a completely new project. In addition to all these, the decision-making process remained as highly centralized as ever with the Emperor making all major decisions. The prime minister, ministers and other government officials were expected to act according to the Emperor's wishes. The provincial and district administrations, headed by officials appointed by the Emperor, were also merely extensions of the central bureaucracy.

Despite public announcements that the bureaucracy would be an agent of planned socio-economic development with a strong involvement of the private sector, the state institutions (including the public bureaucracy) were still primarily oriented to the preservation of the status quo and to a few showpiece programmes. In other words, the attempts at economic and social development that were made by the bureaucracy and other state organizations, with the help of the successive five-year plans and foreign capital investment, failed to satisfy even the elementary basic needs of the people and to eradicate the root causes of famine and hunger in many parts of the country.

The revolutionary process that unfolded in the country following the 1974 military take-over brought with it many radical changes in the economic, political and administrative spheres. It directly affected the system of land ownership in both the rural and urban areas and the role of the private sector in the economy was drastically reduced. On the other hand, the state bureaucracy expanded to a considerable extent and became more complex than it had been in the past. Departing from the past, a political party under the name of the Workers' Party of Ethiopia (later the Democratic Unity Party of Ethiopia) was established at national and sub-national levels. In similar style to other Marxist-Leninist states, the Party was to be the guiding force in the socio-economic and cultural development of the country. Further, various mass organizations and cooperatives were created to participate in the country's socio-economic and political life.

With all the expanded and centrally controlled party and other mass organizations, the planning machinery that evolved after 1974 was likewise highly centralized in character. All policy matters emanated from above, with little or no initiative coming from below. In short, the decision-making process of the Mengistu era, became much more centralized and rigid than it had been during the reign of Haile Selassie I. Regional and provincial planning structures, as well as the state farms, producers cooperatives and villagization schemes, were effectively controlled by the central planning machinery and the party apparatus.

Decentralization of administration and policy making to the sub-national levels, despite the creation of autonomous and regional administrations, was very much restricted to the implementation of policies already decided by the centre. To all intents and purposes, the actual decision-making process during the Mengistu regime was much more centralized and subject to rigid political supervision and control than it was during Haile Selassie's patrimonial system of rule, where provincial governors and other state officials could make some substantive decisions by themselves in the name of the Emperor.

Some Concluding Observations

The pre- and post-revolutionary political and administrative systems were fundamentally different from each other, especially at the level of ideology. The former was essentially geared to the capitalist pattern of development, in which planning was essentially conceived as an instrument of mobilizing the necessary capital from within and for acquiring external development assistance. Although it began as a classic military coup d'etat, the latter transformed itself into a rigid socialist pattern of socio-economic development effectively controlled from the centre. On the other hand, the ultimate objectives of public policy that were pursued by both the ancient regime and by the Mengistu government were similar in the sense that the paramount concern of both was regime maintenance, whatever might be the costs. In other words, despite all the public announcements that the policies were intended to promote the socio-economic development of the country as a whole, the survival and continuity of those in power was the true goal and objective of both systems of autocratic rulership, though the latter was more brutal and repressive than the former.

The changes that were introduced after the overthrow of Haile Selassie were certainly drastic to the point of damaging the very fabric of Ethiopian society. Entirely new socio-economic, political, administrative and planning systems were introduced. They were all conditioned to function in a highly centralized manner under the control of the Workers' Party of Ethiopia, which acted as a watchdog of Mengistu's dictatorial powers. Mengistu's regime and the hollow foundations on which it was built were overthrown in May of 1991, after decades of war, famine and the destruction of the country's socio-economic infrastructures. With the establishment of a transitional government provisional administration composed of the EPDF and the OLF, a *new order* appears to be in the making. The new group in power have promised to introduce multiparty democracy in the country within two years after May 1991. Despite renewed ethnic tensions, mainly between the parties in the transitional government, in spring of 1992, limited regional elections were held in some parts of the country. For some these elections were the right beginnings towards genuine democracy and political pluralism, while for others, the regional elections were a sham, merely stage-managed by the EPDF and its allies for their own benefit to stay in power under the pretext of democracy. In the face of such renewed tensions, it remains to be seen how the incipient democratic trends will be saved and promoted to maturity and how the desperate socio-economic problems of the country will be addressed in the years to come.

Notes

1. The term "policy" has been defined in many different ways. For instance, McDonnel (1980: 1) defines it as a testable theory. On the other hand Hoppe et al ., conceptualize policy as a never ending series of communicative and technical acts by which all kinds of policy actors, collectively engage themselves in the construction of intersubjective political meaning and at the same time, transform these meaning construct into collective projects (Hoppe et al.,1985: 2). According to Wildavsky, "policy" simply refers to both the input and the output of the same decision-making process(Wildavsky 1977: 384).

2. See *Planning and its implementation in Ethiopia* (Report by Syndicate No.4 of the Executive Development) Seminar, Institute of Public Ad ministration, Addis Ababa, November 1963: 8.

3. During the later years of Haile Selassie"s rule, the chairmanship was nominally delegated to the Prime Minister.

References

Asmerom, H.K. (1978), *Emergence, Expansion, and Decline of Patrimonial Bureaucracy in Ethiopia, 1907-1974: An Attempt at Historical Interpretation,* Ph.D. Thesis, Free University Amsterdam.

Bekele, Assefa and Eshetu Chole (1969), *A Profile of the Ethiopian Economy*, Nairobi, Oxford University Press.

Blair, Thomason, (1975), *Ethiopia: The Country That Cut Off Its Head,* London, Robson Books.

Bowden, Peter (1986), Problems of Implementation, *Public Administration and Development,* Vol.6, No. 1, 61-71.

Brietzke, P.H. (1982), *Law, Development and the Ethiopian Revolution,* Lewisburg, Bucknell University Press.

Cheema, G. S. and D. A. Rondinelli, eds., (1983), *Decentralization and Development: Policy Implementation in Developing Countries*, Sage Publications, Beverly Hills, London, New Delhi.

Clapham, Christopher (1988), Transformation and Continuity in Revolutionary Ethiopia, Cambridge University Press, Cambridge etc.

Constitution of the People's Democratic Republic of Ethiopia, 1987, Dawit Wolde Giorgis (1989), *Red Tears: War, Famine and Revolution in Ethiopia,* The Red Sea Press Inc., Trenton, New Jersey.

Dessalegn Rahmato (1987), The Political Economy of Development in Ethiopia, in Keller, Edmond/Donald Rothchild ed., *Afro-Marxist Regimes: Ideology and Public Policy,* Lynne Rienner Publishers, Boulder and London, 155-179.

Dejene Aredo (1990), The Evolution of Rural Development Policies, in Siegfried Pausewang, Fanta Cheru, Stefan Brüne and Eshetu Chole eds., *Ethiopia: Rural Development Options,* Zed Books Ltd, London and New Jersey, 49-57.

Ethiopian Herald (1975), The Former Maladministration and the Future, 13 September.

Ethiopian Herald (1976), The Ethiopian Revolution and the Bureaucracy, 28 and 29 December.

Ethiopian Herald (1977), The Ethiopian Bureaucracy, Yesterday, Today, 1 and 14 January.

Ethiopian government (before 1974), The 1931 Constitution, Order No.1 Ministers' Definition of Powers as amended, The 1955 Revised Constitution, The 1974 Draft Revised Constitution (unpublished).

Ethiopian government (after 1974), Proc. No.1 of 1974, establishing the Provisional Military Administrative Council; Proc. 128 of 1977; Proc. 174 of 1979 establishing COPWE.Proc. 1 of 1987, Constitution of the People's Democratic Republic of Ethiopia; Proc. 2 of 1987 Declaration of Ethiopia as People's Democratic Republic; Proc. 7 of 1987 Establishing the Council of State; Proc. 14 of 1987 Establishing Autonomous and Administrative Regions.

Forss, Kim, (1986), *Planning and Evaluation in AID Organizations,* Ph.D. dissertation, Stockholm School of Economics.

Gebru Tareke (1991), *Ethiopia: Power and Protest, Peasant Revolts in the Twentieth Century,* African Studies Series 71, Cambridge University Press, Cambridge etc...

Grindle, Merilee S. ed., (1980), *Policy and Policy Implementation in the Third World,* Princeton University Press, Princeton, New Jersey, 1980.

Halliday, F. and M. Molyneux (1981), *The Ethiopian Revolution,* Verso, London.

Harbeson, John W. (1988), *The Ethiopian Transformation: The Quest for the Post-Imperial State,* Westview Press, Boulder and London.

Jason, W. Clay, S. Steigraber and P. Niggli (1988), *The Spoils of Famine: Ethiopian Famine Policy and Peasant Agriculture,* Cultural Survival Inc., Cambridge, Massachusetts.

Keller, Edmond J. (1988), *Revolutionary Ethiopia: From Empire to People's Republic,* Indiana University Press, Bloomington and Indianapolis.

Legum, Colin (1975), *Ethiopia: The Fall of Haile Selassie's Empire,* Rex Collings, London.

Love, Janice and Peter C. Sederberg (1987), Euphony and Cacophony in Policy Implementation: SCF and the Somali Refugee Problem, in *Policy Studies Review,* Vol.7, No.1, 155-173.

Markakis, John and Nega Ayele (1978), *Class and Revolution in Ethiopia,* Spokesman, Nottingham.

Mulatu Wubneh and Yohannis Abate (1988), *Ethiopia: Transition and Development in the Horn of Africa,* Westview Press, Boulder, Colorado, London.

Mulatu Wubneh (1990), Development Strategy and Growth of the Ethiopian Economy: A Comparative Study of the Pre- and Post-Revolutionary Period, in Ottaway, Marina ed., *The Political Economy of Ethiopia,* Praeger, New York etc.., 197-219.

McHenry, Dean E. Jr. (1979), *Tanzania's Ujamaa Villages: The Implementation of Rural Development Strategy,* Berkeley.

Ottaway, M. and D. Ottaway (1978), *Ethiopia: Empire in Revolution,* New York, Africana.

Planning Board (1957), *First Five Year Development Plan 1957-1961,* Addis Ababa.

Planning Board (1962), *Second Five Year Development Plan 1963-1967,* Addis Ababa.

Planning Commission Office (1968), *Third Five Year Development Plan 1968-1973,* Addis Ababa.

Planning Commission Office (1973), *Strategy Outline for the Fourth Five Year Plan, 1974/75 - 1978/79,* Addis Ababa.

Quick, Stephen A. (1980), The Paradox of Popularity: Ideological Programme Implementation in Zambia, in Grindle, Merillee S. ed. *Policy Implementation in the Third World,* 40-63.

Schwab, Peter (1985), *Ethiopia: Politics, Economics and Society,* London.

Smith, Somath B. (1985), Evaluating Development Policies and Programmes in the Third World, in *Public Administration and Development,* Vol.5, No.2, 129-144.

Yohannis Abate (1979), *Military Administration and Intra-Military Conflict in Ethiopia,* Paper presented at the 22nd Annual Meeting of African Studies Association , Los Angeles, California, October 31 -November 3.

6 POLITICS, ADMINISTRATION AND RURAL DEVELOPMENT IN EGYPT

J.M. Otto

Introduction

On Tuesday, October 6th 1981, just before 1.00 p.m., Anwar Sadat, president of the Arab Republic of Egypt, was shot by muslim fundamentalists. The murderers had appeared in military disguise from a parade commemorating the 'heroic crossing' of the Suez Canal in October 1973. After Sadat's death, the chairman of the parliament, Sufi Abu-Taleb, automatically became president. On Wednesday October 7th the parliament convened to elect vice-president Husni Mubarak as his successor, and a week later the people of Egypt by referendum confirmed this choice.

This procedure of succession after a dramatic shock of the nation's political life meticulously followed the provisions of the country's constitution of 1971. Sadat had left behind a country with more political and institutional stability than the one he had inherited from Nasser eleven years before. Even now, more than ten years after Sadat's death, Mubarak has basically maintained both the policies and the political and administrative framework established during his predecessor's rule (Ayubi 1989: 12-14; Hinnebusch 1985:302).

In Hanya[1], one of Egypt's 4.000 villages, about 250 km south of Cairo, on that ominous October day about a decade ago, the news about the assassination first remained unnoticed. Most men were in the fields, sowing winter crops such as beans and wheat. Women were working hard in their homes, washing, cleaning, pumping water. And the children, apart from those who were helping their parents at home or in the fields, attended the village's primary school until 1.30 p.m. Only in the evening at 8.00 p.m. when people as usual had gathered around the few television sets in the village, they listened to the astonishing news as it was told them by Husni Mubarak.

People started arguing about what would happen. Old villagers remembered the July Revolution of 1952 that had ended the 'ancien régime' of King, landlords, Wafd-party and foreign interests, which were mainly British. That Revolution had brought a new generation of leaders to power like Nasser and Sadat, men of middle class origin, dedicated to improving the lot of the common people. And to a large extent it had worked : the feudalist patterns of landownership around Hanya were largely eradicated by a series of agrarian reform laws and new policies implemented by new agencies, and many villagers now owned their own plot, albeit a very tiny one.

Upon hearing of the assassination of the *ra'is'*, as the president was usually called, they wondered whether it would bring about another revolution. Nobody in the village hoped so. Maybe the students in the neighbouring town of Minya, and other opponents of the régime, like muslim fundamentalists or communists, cherished hopes for an immediate coup d'état. But not so the farmers of Hanya who in the next week would cast their votes in the referendum for Husni Mubarak, as they had always supported the régime. What else can a *fellah*, an Egyptian farmer who lives at the foot of the pyramids do than obey or avoid the government of his pharao, king or president ?

Hanya is an average village in Middle Egypt, the majority of its people depending on agriculture. Although large landownership was abolished by Nasser , about 85 % of the land is in possession of members of three large family clans who more or less control the village. Most villagers belong to lesser family clans, they own little or no land and lead a poor life. So, in their dealings with political and administrative institutions, increase of income is their major concern.

In all villages of Egypt we find the same eight rural institutions, that form the administrative backbone of rural development.[2] In the field of agriculture there are the agricultural co-operative societies, the village banks and the veterinary units. In the field of social services we find primary schools, health units and social units. And in the field of modern local government there are village councils, and village units headed by village administrators. The government of Egypt under Nasser and Sadat had set up thousands of such institutions continuing a long tradition of state intervention in the rural areas. During Mubarak's rule these institutions have been maintained (Commander 1987: 50-51).[3]

In this chapter Egyptian politics and administration are dealt with both on the national and the local level. To picture the latter, the eight rural institutions of Hanya have been selected as a case study. They are interestingly situated at the interface between state and citizen. Here local administrators and officials must prove every day their actual ability to realize the goals of the state, i.e. to foster rural development.

A study of such rural institutions illustrates a threefold relationship between politics and administration. First, the political system sets the goals for the administration. Formulation of rural development policies with its objectives and tasks and the design of the administrative institutions that are to implement these policies, are all outputs of the national political system. Secondly, the actual functioning of the administration is also subject to influence by political pressure, including local political forces. Thirdly, political success of the régime depends to a considerable extent on administrative performance.

Paragraphs 2 to 6 are devoted to the political history and present power structure of Egypt including village politics. In paragraphs 7 to 11 the administrative organization of Egypt, its rural institutions and people's access are dealt with. In the final part, paragraphs 12 and 13, we conclude with an analysis of politics, administration and rural development in today's Egypt.

Political History

Developing reasonably effective public institutions took today's industrialized countries more than a century, and many developing countries are attempting to compress that process into a few decades (World Bank 1983:115). This is not completely true in the case of the Egyptian state, that dates back to 3000 B.C. The institutions of its New Kingdom (1570-1075 B.C.) were considered by Max Weber as the historical model for all bureaucracies to come.

Egyptian history, which covers approximately fifty centuries, shows a remarkable continuity as far as the relation between state and society is concerned. The political scene has always been dominated by four main political actors : the ruler and his entourage, the military and civil state apparatus, the local leading class and the mass of mostly poor peasants.

On the other hand, there has also been much discontinuity in the nature of the country's leadership over the last twenty-five centuries. After the Arab conquest in the seventh century, Egypt developed into an Arab-speaking country with an islamic majority, since 1517 under Ottoman rule. It was a shock when the French under Napoléon conquered the country in 1798. The non-Egyptian elite of Mamelukes was chased away and Egyptian muslim leaders were drawn into the administration. A few years later, in 1801, the British with Turkish support forced the French to capitulate. From the power struggle that followed an Albanian officer of the Turkish army by the name of Muhammad Ali emerged as the country's new leader. He and his descendants would rule Egypt as monarchs for 150 years, initially still under the formal sovereignty of the Ottoman sultan.

Muhammad Ali (1805-1849) reformed the administration and education, and fostered agriculture, industry and trade. In doing so he was inspired by European, mainly French, models, and many Egyptians were sent abroad for further studies. During the nineteenth century the country's law and administration were increasingly influenced by the French system. European businessmen were attracted to Egypt by the opportunities in trade, investment and public work contracts.

When in 1876 the state's finance turned out to be in disarray, an international consortium led by Britain and France took over the financial administration. This foreign domination led to the first outburst of Egyptian nationalism in modern times, the Orabi revolt of 1882 which gave rise to a British occupation of Egypt under Lord Cromer (1883-1907). In this period the first local councils and agricultural credit cooperatives were instituted under the control of British inspectors, and major infrastructure works, like the Assuan Dam, were carried out. In 1883 a constitutional document was issued providing for a monarchy with two elected representative bodies. At first Lord Cromer merely aimed at restoring political and financial order and at establishing a sound administration. However, after his succession the British considered a more permanent presence in Egypt.

When the First World War broke out in 1914, Britain found itself at war with Turkey, that still exercised the formal sovereign power over Egypt, and unilaterally declared Egypt to be its protectorate (1914-1922). Fierce nationalist uprisings and lack of consensus between nationalists and the British led the latter to , again unilaterally, declare Egypt independent albeit with certain conditions implying a continuing foreign presence.

The Constitution of 1923 established a constitutional monarchy with a parliamentary system. Politics then were dominated by the king, the *Wafd* party and the British. The interests of large landowners and businessmen were represented in parliament, by the *Wafd* and other parties. The countryside continued to be ruled in a semi-feudal manner and the condition of the *fellah* remained mostly deplorable. In the thirties and forties efforts were made both by the state and private associations to help the poor, but only on a limited scale.

When the *Free Officers* overthrew the government in July 1952 they did not yet have a clear cut ideology or policy. They just wanted to get rid of the British and of feudalism. Soon, under the leadership of Naguib and Nasser a major transformation of state and society began. Political parties were banned and the economic forces of the market were curbed by central planning, nationalizations, price distortions and subsidies. The lower classes were freed of their complete dependence from landlords and businessmen and provided with numerous welfare services. Every day a primary school was erected, and every week a rural health centre came into existence (Otto 1987:232-233). The government now considered its ideology and policies to be socialist. Nasser became the undisputed leader, loved by the people, while his fellow Free Officers performed key functions within the supreme Revolutionary Command Council. So the military controlled politics and supervised the administration. In order to create linkages between the state elite and the masses and to mobilize the people behind the banners of Arab socialism, a mass party was created. This was the Arab Socialist Union (ASU) with branches all over the countryside. Rural participatory institutions like village councils and agricultural cooperative societies, that had existed before in some places, were now introduced in a uniform way and manned with ASU-cadres.

Their mission of political mobilization of peasants and implementation of agrarian reform was quite successful (Harik 1974).

Because of the wars of 1956 and 1967, huge amounts were allocated for military tasks. Yet the civil state apparatus continued to grow (Ayubi 1980: 238-270) though with its cumbersome procedures it became an impediment rather than an instrument of development. Economic stagnation was rampant. Relations with western countries worsened after the Suez crisis of 1956 and subsequent nationalizations. Then Egypt sought economic and military support from Eastern Europe but these resulted in heavy financial debts. Nasser's political control with its many intelligence services and concentration camps became more and more oppressive. He used to say that centuries of submission and lack of education had made Egyptians inapt for democracy and that much time and training would be needed to remedy this shortages. Consequently he ruled 'by monologue', instructed his ministers and regarded parliament as a mirror that ought to reflect approval of his policies. (Hopwood 1983: 90, 102).

When Sadat succeeded to the presidency in 1970, he had no new ideology. In his efforts to establish a sound power base, he soon dismissed the left-wing prime minister, Aly Sabri, who had challenged his authority. Politics and administration were purged of supporters of Nasser's leftist ideology and in the provinces islamic groups came to help his security men to carry out this job. With the so-called Corrective May Revolution of 1971, Sadat started a gradual liberalization of both economic and political life in Egypt and in the same year a new constitution was enacted. In 1972 relations with the Soviet Union were cut off. In 1973 Egypt attacked Israel, and though no decisive victory was gained, at home Sadat was celebrated as 'hero of the crossing' and his popularity increased immensely.

Abroad relations with the United States gradually improved and a peace settlement with Israel was prepared. This would eventually result in the 1978 Camp David agreement that would isolate Egypt for some years from the Arab world. In 1976 he started political reforms by dissolving the Arab Socialist Union and introducing a multi-party system. Yet, the dominant position of his own centre party, the National Democratic Party (1978) was unchallenged, since official parties were given little room and a number of parties and movements were banned; muslim fundamentalists, communists and 'new wafd' were kept out of power, and sometimes a firm line was taken with them. In universities, notably those in Cairo, Alexandria, Assiut and Minya, student protests flared up regularly so that special security forces were stationed there. The biggest danger for Sadat's regime came from fanatic muslim groups who intended to create an islamic state in Egypt. Sadat's efforts for peace with Israel, his hospitable attitude towards the exiled Shah of Iran, and his 1979 Marriage Act that greatly improved the legal position of the Egyptian woman, further antagonized these groups. In the late summer of 1981 many of them were arrested. In spite of threats to his régime and himself, Sadat succeeded in closing down the concentration camps and diminished the direct control of the army in political life, appointing less military people in high civilian posts.

In the economic field private investment was encouraged both domestic and foreign, and the most radical aspects of Nasser's socialism were softened. This policy became known as the *infitah* (opening). But as in January 1977 Sadat following the World Bank's advice announced to cut down on subsidies on bread and other consumer commodities, the masses rallied in the streets of Cairo and forced him to withdraw such a plan.

In the country's administration Sadat propagated modern management methods including decentralization. Many young people were sent overseas mostly to western countries notably the US for further training. He also strived to stop the employment policies of pumping graduates into government offices. Foreign technical advisers, mostly from the United States, entered almost all sectors of administration as policy researchers and advisers.

After the assassination of Sadat Mubarak came to power, and he has been president now for about ten years, a period almost as long as his predecessor, but much less characterized by dramatic events and policy changes (Tripp and Owen 1989). No major changes took place in the international political alignments and in social and economic policies. Despite the immense problems Mubarak's government proved to be capable of leading the country in a very clever, careful and balanced way. His foreign policy has brought Egypt back in the Arab camp that was left after the Camp David agreements. The Gulf War of 1991 showed Egypt as a major regional power and a trustworthy ally of the United States. It earned Mubarak's Egypt an unprecedented debt relief by the creditors' Club of Paris (Keesing's R.1991:38209). The country's external debt had been increasing dramatically over the last decade, due to a.o. military purchases from the US by high interest rates, substantial investments in infrastructure, an agricultural trade deficit and the 1986 fall of oil prices. Mubarak's government had already renegotiated and secured reasonably soft terms for coping with the debt problem (Butter 1989:136) but the 1991 agreement achieved a remission of debts to foreign governments worth 14 billion US dollars out of a total of 25 billion (NRC Handelsblad, March 22 1991).

Mubarak's style is generally considered to be businesslike, pragmatic and low-profile. It is less ideological, revolutionary and flamboyant than that of Nasser and Sadat. As one observer put it: 'while he has failed to emulate the glory of Nasser and Sadat, he has managed to avoid their disasters' (Butter 1989:129).

Constitutional Developments

The constitution of 1971, as amended in 1980, has created a logical and solid framework for political action at the national level (Flanz 1984). The main political actors according to the constitution are: the people, the president, the cabinet, the people's assembly or parliament, the political parties, the judiciary, including administrative courts and a Supreme Constitutional Court, and the army.

'Sovereignty is vested in the *people* and they alone are the source of authority. The people shall exercise and protect this sovereignty, and safeguard national unity in the manner specified in the constitution' (Art.3). According to the constitution the people elect members of the people's assembly and of local councils (Art.87, 162). Moreover they cast their votes in referenda and plebiscites on important questions such as who shall be president (Art.76), how to solve a conflict between president and people's assembly (Art.127,136), the amendment of the constitution (Art.189) and other 'important matters affecting the supreme interests of the country' (Art. 152).

The head of state is the *president*. 'He shall assume executive power' (Art.37) and 'in conjunction with the government he shall lay down the general policy of the state and supervise its implementation' (Art.138). He appoints and discharges the prime minister, his deputies, the ministers and their deputies, the civil and military officials, and the diplomatic representatives (Art.141, 143). His entourage includes the vice-president , whose jurisdiction is determined by him, a secretariat of the presidency, a minister for presidential affairs, a secretariat of the cabinet, staffs of advisers and a number of National Councils with advisory functions.

The president has also important legislative functions. He proposes laws to the people's assembly, and after their approval he promulgates them or objects to them (Art.109, 112). When vetoed by the president, draft-laws need a qualified majority (Art.113). In certain conditions the president may even legislate autonomously without the assembly's interference (Art.108, 147).

The *cabinet* is 'the supreme executive and administrative organ of the state. It consists of the prime minister, his deputies, the ministers and their deputies' (Art.153). Cabinet members are appointed and dismissed by the president (Art.141). It is the prime minister who supervises the work of the cabinet but the president himself may also step in chairing the cabinet and demanding ministers' reports (Art.142). The cabinet's functions include the 'laying down of general state policy and controlling its implementation in collaboration with the president', directing the work of the ministries, the public sector and the whole state apparatus, preparing legislation, the budget, the general plan and contracting loans

(Art.156). Ministers are the administrative supreme chiefs of their ministries and lay down the ministry's policy in the framework of the general policy.

The *People's assembly* exercises the legislative power, approves the general state policy, the budget and the general plan. It exercises control over the executive as prescribed by the constitution (Art.86). It is this parliament that nominates the president (Art.76), It can start an impeachment procedure against him (Art.85). In case of a vacancy of the presidential office its chairman will temporarily assume the presidency (Art.84). In the field of legislation the people's assembly in principle has the last word, since it can overrule the president's veto with a two-third majority. Presidential decree-laws need its special authorization (Art. 108) or retroactive ratification (Art.147).

Political parties as actors in the political system have returned to Egypt in the mid-seventies when the monopoly of the Arab Socialist Union was brought to an end. This was reflected in the constitutional system, first by the Law on Political Parties of 1977 and later by the constitutional amendment of Article 5 in 1980, stating that Egypt's political system is a multiparty one.

The Law on Political Parties states that no political party may be established on the basis of class, sect, region, race, religion or belief, and that party programmes may not contradict the principles of *shari'a* law. According to that law , a Committee for Political Parties decides upon applications for the establishment of a political party. The committee consists a.o. of the ministers of Justice, Interior and Local Government and some officials without party affiliations. Appeal from its decision can be launched with an administrative court so that the judiciary seems to have the last word in this matter (Dessouki 1978:86-89; Makram Ebeid 1989:22).

'The *judiciary* is independent, subject to no other authority than the law' and 'no authority may intervene in cases or in justice affairs'. Besides the regular courts of justice , the constitution provides for state security courts, a military judiciary, the Council of State for administrative disputes and disciplinary cases, and a supreme constitutional court to review the constitutionality of laws and regulations , and their interpretation (Art.165-172, 174-8, 183).

The *Armed Forces*' have the duty 'to protect the country, safeguard its territory and security, and protect the socialist achievements of the popular strife' (Art.180).

Thus the constitution has created a presidential system with important parliamentary powers, a firm judicial control and consultation of the people when major issues are at hand.

State Ideology

Most developing countries continue to share a general consensus about the major elements of their respective ideologies: 'The twin goals of development are nation-building and socio-economic progress' (Heady 1984: 253). Although Egypt has known a long history of statehood, both internal and external pressures are quite heavy and urge the regime to devote its attention continuously to nation-building, or at least 'nation-propping'. And socio-economic progress has clearly been the other main concern of the government.

For a closer inquiry into the present Egyptian state ideology, it is not sufficient to refer to the aims recently set by Mubarak, since his rule is actually based on the ideologies of both his predecessors.

Nasser's ideology has often been described in terms of the six principles of the revolution of 1952. These principles were : eradication of imperialism, abolishment of feudalism, eradication of monopolization, establishment of social justice, the building of a strong national army, establishment of sound democratic rule (Wheelock 1960: 55-57). This ideology has been labelled as Arab socialism. Its main policy document was the National Charter of 1962.

Sadat's ideology was a mixture of Arab socialism and some economic and political liberalization. Its main policy document was the October Paper of 1974. Interestingly enough, ideological developments in Egypt went ahead of similar changes that have taken place in other African and Asian countries over the last decades (Vasil'ev 1988).

An insight view of the present state ideology under Mubarak is provided by the considerations of the decision by the Committee for Political Parties on April 14th 1990 when it legalized three new political parties: the Green Party, the Democratic Unionist Party and the Young Egypt Party. At this occasion it turned down the application of a fourth, the Nasserist Party. The committee declared that the approved party programmes were 'in accordance with the shari'a, and aimed at the preservation of national unity, social peace, the socialist-democratic system and the socialist achievements and that the principles of the revolutions of July 1952 and May 1971 were held in high esteem'. An earlier request by the Nasserist Party had been rejected in 1987 on the grounds that its goals were the same as those of the NDP (Springborg 1989:44). This time the committee's rejection was based on its disapproval of the 'totalitarian system that prevailed under president Nasser' (Keesing's H.1990:460).

The constitution itself contains more than a few articles describing the ideological foundations of the state.

In the first part, 'The state', Egypt is declared to be a democratic, socialist state based on the alliance of the working forces of the people (Art.1). Islamic jurisprudence is considered as the principal source of legislation (Art.2). The economic system is socialist democratic, based on sufficiency and justice in a manner preventing exploitation, conducive to liquidation of income differences (Art.4). The political system is a multi-party one (Art.5).

In the second part, called 'Basic Constituents of the Society' the social, moral and economic foundations of the state are spelled out in 33 articles. We can distinguish here many references to a few sets of concepts. The first set includes socialist concepts such as solidarity, social justice, equality of opportunity, fair distribution, central economic planning, the sanctity of public ownership, the social function of private ownership, maximum landownership and agricultural co-operatives. A second set contains concepts concerning cultural and religious roots, such as genuine tradition, religion, family life, morality. A third set is concerned with national unity and patriotism. A fourth set, that could be distinguished, deals with economic progress and modernization, raising the standard of living, the value of scientific facts. So the present constitution still bears very much the ideological signs of Arab socialism. To what extent this ideology is virtually expressed in decision-making, depends of course on those who held political power.

National Power Structure

Titles of books on Egyptian politics such as 'Egyptian politics under Sadat' (Hinnebusch 1985) or Mubarak's Egypt' (Springborg 1989) already reveal the importance of presidential power. No doubt the president of Egypt is the real strong man in the country.[4] Major institutions are headed by his supporters, and regular reshuffling of offices prevent others to build up a power base for themselves. His close advisors supervise the security services both of the army and the ministry of Interior. Yet, under Mubarak a process has taken place labelled by Springborg as 'fragmentation of power'.

During Sadat's régime the pyramid of power consisted of three layers of elites under the presidential apex (Hinnebusch 1981). Besides the president who forms a supreme one-man elite, there firstly was a top elite with an inner ring of a few men including the president's cronies such as Sayed Marei, the parliamentary speaker, Osman Ahmed Osman, the country's biggest contractor, and Husni Mubarak, air marshall and vice-president. A second element of Sadat's top elite was an outer ring made up of the prime minister, top ministers, top military commanders, top party leaders and close presidential advisers. Second, there was a middle elite that included most ministers, provincial governors, many of whom were technicians 'lacking both ideological commitment and constituencies'. Third, there was a sub-elite composed of civil servants, military commanders, public-sector managers, editors of newspapers, religious leaders, leaders of professional syndicates and chambers of commerce, and local notables who head branches of the state party. They 'link the elite to the population'.

'The basic meeting ground for these elites is parliament, the institutional arena (...)' where the concerns of the people are expressed and can be taken into account by top and middle elites'(Hinnebusch 1981: 447). It was a 'sturdy and massive political structure, rooted in the dominant social forces and enmeshed in a web of interests and constraints which militated against any major intra-system change' (idem 1985: 302).To put it more bluntly, patronage, clientelism and cronyism, based on kinship and friendship, kept the system together and the president on top of it. The NDP and the ministries were closely interwoven with this system.

Under Mubarak the top, middle and sub-elites and their composition have to a large extent remained the same. But some parts of it are different, and the whole system operates somewhat differently than in the past. To start with, presidential clients are weaker now. The inner elite of Mubarak is less prominent, less intimate, less cohesive and less powerful than under Sadat (Springborg 1989: 30-33). Mubarak has instead surrounded himself with functionaries generally described as colourless bureaucrats.

He has permitted more political liberalization and freedom of the press, allowing other social and political forces to show their relative strength. These include: the *infitah* bourgeoisie that has retained considerable influence, the military who has established a real economic empire within the state, the opposition parties who number more and receive more votes than before, the islamic fundamentalist groups who have a potential for mobilization of the masses and are supported by some Arab states in the region, the US and other creditors and donors who, according to the 'new orthodoxy of development' would like to see growth of the private sector at the cost of the state (idem:295).

Sadat's relation to his cabinet was characterized by pictures that appeared in the newspapers with the *ra'is* sitting in an armchair with his ministers taking notes : president Sadat giving instructions to his ministers. Mubarak's ties with his ministers seem different and weaker. It has happened more than once that controversial policy initiatives could be launched by a minister but in the absence of presidential or cabinet support, the unfortunate minister had to resign (idem:62).

There are more signs of fragmentation. The central planning machinery has become weaker. The representation of the military in the cabinet has been further reduced (Ayubi 1989 :5). The high-profile presentation of the former Defence minister, field marshall Abu

Ghazala, contrasting the president's own low-profile , contributed to tensions between the military on one side and the president and his cabinet on the other. Although Mubarak transferred Abu Ghazala to the office of presidential assistant - not exactly a promotion - , the expansion of army based industries, the intrusion of the military in tasks of the civil administration and the privileged positions of army officers have continued to aggravate the tension.

The NDP has also received less support from Mubarak than it was used to under Sadat, which damaged the party's standing (Springborg 1989: 157-8). Opposition parties have taken more parliamentary seats than before, and even the Muslim Brotherhood now has a prominent fraction in the people's assembly, through an electoral alliance with other parties (Makram Ebeid 1989; Fisher 1990: 381). However, extremist groups are still firmly controlled, therefore the state of emergency that was promulgated after the assassination of Sadat has been extended by the People's Assembly until now (Fisher 1990:378-9). In the process of political liberalization the 'relatively autonomous courts seem to be playing a major, if technical and by definition limited, role'(Ayubi 1989:18). This has been expressed by several decisions of the Supreme Constitutional Court, for example when on May 19, 1990 the 1987 parliamentary elections were declared unconstitutional; no legislation could be enacted as from June 1990 and new elections had to be conducted later that year (Keesing's H.1990: 550).

The people are sovereign, according to the constitution. In political analysis however 'the mass' could be distinguished from the 'bourgeoisie'. The latter has obtained much influence since Sadat's rule, many of this social stratum being still influential but they do not constitute a clear group with political ambitions. The masses are definitely an important factor in the real power structure. As Sadat was confronted with riots in 1977 about the price of bread, Mubarak learned his lesson with the 1984 riots of Kafr ad-Dawa and the 1987 Central Security forces mutiny, which set parts of Cairo afire. 'The extreme caution with which Egypt has implemented economic reforms has been largely due to fears that they will provoke social unrest and increase the threat to social stability posed by islamic fundamentalists'(Fisher 1990: 383).

In the day-to-day life in rural Egypt, most of the political actors mentioned above do not appear on the scene. The army does not play any significant role here, while the importance of political parties is limited to the NDP's regional patronage practices and electoral interventions. In Ayubi's words 'the NDP has access to a whole organisational network - especially in the countryside - that ensures that there are proportionally more votes cast in the countryside, and that these votes go in the right direction (Ayubi 1989: 16). The two most powerful forces are the administration and the informal systems of patronage, kinship and *wastah* . Both have deeply penetrated into society , and often seem to compete, if not struggle against each other to get things done.

Rural Politics and Local Democracy

Social life in rural Upper Egypt is to a large extent dominated by the family clan (*'aylah*). A villager sees himself basically as a clan member. Big clans may consist of hundreds of members. Social borderlines in most villages thus are not primarily economic but between clans. Rivalries create much tension in villages. It is the traditional duty of the clan's leaders to defeat the others in order to preserve the clan's honour. They are usually rich farmers who are excellently connected outside the village. Actually they constitute a new privileged class, a rural bourgeoisie. Recently also younger villagers with more formal education, salaried jobs and bureaucratic skills have come to the forefront of rural politics. Sometimes they act as a sort of skilled assistant to a more traditional village leader.

Village leaders are supposed to 'solve problems' for people and between people. They often have access to the 'sub-elite', e.g. members of parliament, regional party chiefs and top civil servants in the provincial capital. Among this sub-elite one finds often a handful of powerholders who are well known by the villagers and who are often believed to yield enormous powers. Their informal power may extend to the realm of appointments, transfers and dismissals in various departments. They may also exert control over the results of rural elections (Otto 1987:133; Springborg 1979). Elections are a well-established phenomena in rural Egypt, not only for the people's assembly and regional and local people's councils but also for agricultural cooperative boards, and village headmanship.

Every village has its headman called *'umdah*.[5] While the *'umdah* in olden times was invariably the most powerful man of a village, today, as the state has penetrated the rural areas deeply and with a variety of institutions, the *'umdah* has become only one of the representatives of the state in the village. His legal duties include the combatting of crime, the settlement of conflicts, the implementation of laws and regulations, and various administrative tasks. This involves regular reporting to the nearby chief of police and the reception of officials and other guests of the village. The *'umdah* supervises a few guardsmen and a telephone employee whose job is to facilitate communication with the nearby police unit, either to receive instructions or to report problems in the village. Being *'umdah* may be an honourable office but it takes also a lot of time, energy and money. So sometimes local powerholders leave this job to a family member in order to devote their own time more effectively. The same may apply to other public offices. Yet, to be *'umdah*, or even to be his relative still conveys a considerable social status in rural Egypt. Therefore the political strife for this office takes often place in an emotional or even violent atmosphere.

Just like in the other elections, three stages mark the procedural way to the office of *'umdah*: first the nomination, then the election, and finally the appointment. The provincial top official of the Ministry of Interior, who is the director of Security, is to supervise this procedure.

The law puts certain conditions for candidacy such as literacy, economic independence and a good reputation. Often clans lodge complaints against the candidacy of their adversaries. The latter may be accused of a certain crime, of arrears in tax payments, of being illiterate or of having no secure income. Village leaders have proved to be extremely creative in influencing the nomination decisions of the directorate of Security. If only one candidate remains, according to the law no election is required anymore. But if there are two or more candidates , an election by secret ballot is to be held.

As the government prefers to avoid tensions in the countryside, candidates are often urged to withdraw so that only one candidate remains. If elections have to take place, a committee including representatives of the judiciary supervises the actual election in the village, often in a primary school building, while the police tries to maintain order. In rural Upper Egypt clans often vote as closed blocs following the instructions of their leaders. Larger clans are often divided by internal quarrels, and their opponents will do all they can to add fuel to the fire. Smaller and poorer family clans whose role is limited to supporting one of the main candidates will count on receiving special favours and attention. So clan leaders are particularly busy in fostering their coalitions and breaking the others'. After the election a decision will be taken by the director of Security whether or not to appoint the elected person, and this decision in its turn is referred to the Minister of Interior for approval.

Democracy was one of the slogans of the 1952 Revolution but it was not given a high priority because of the unfortunate experience of instability during the preceding parliamentary period. Only as from 1971 Sadat started to foster democracy as a synthesis of Egypts previous experiences (Boutros-Ghali 1978:4-5). Political pluralism, freedom and decentralization increased. So the Local Government Act of 1979 states in its explanatory memorandum that the ultimate goals of the village councils is to reach true democracy. But is democracy feasible in the existing political culture ?

Nasser had tolerated local democracy only in as far as it supported his revolutionary regime. All local posts were filled with men of his A.S.U. As far as the national political scene and the urban areas were concerned, Sadat felt the need for a democracy but one 'with teeth and claws' in order to survive in a hostile environment where communists, religious fundamentalists and others were all aiming at the downfall of his regime possibly using violent means (Hopwood 1983:90; Fernandez 1983: 90-91, 98). But in the rural areas popular support for him was still enormous. Sadat considered himself as the father of the Egyptian family, that ought to be a peaceful and harmonious family, presumably with obedient children. Such concepts were readily accepted by many villagers (Hopwood 1983: 93). In their traditional views the leader of a state should not be criticized, his policies not attacked. Although Mubarak had allowed an increase of democratic practice, rural political culture has basically remained the same.

This does not mean that the ordinary villager does not wish to have any influence on the governmental machinery. It just takes another route : not through elections and representative bodies, but directly in face-to-face contact with the officials concerned, often with the help of a middleman or *wastah*. If the villager has supported a local leader in the elections, the latter may feel obliged to help him in his dealings with the administration. This could be seen as an Egyptian blend of informal democracy influencing the administration.

Regional and Local Administration

The introduction of Local Government Act 124 in 1960 is generally pictured as the start of modern regional and local government in Egypt (Alderfer 1964:49; Mayfield 1974:71). It was to contribute to Nasser's aims of liquidating the feudal centres of power and implementing his policies in a coordinated way. These first local councils consisted of three member groups: ex officio officials of local state institutions, villagers who were elected from the ASU cadres and villagers who were appointed, also from ASU membership. The chairman was appointed by the minister of Local Government. Subsequent local government acts of 1971, 1975 and 1979[6] have brought several important changes, including a new composition of the councils. At present regional and local councils consists of elected citizens only. Affiliation to the NDP is no official requirement though it does play a role in a more covert way. Today councils elect their own chairman, which is another sign of political liberalization reaching down to the rural areas.

Egypt is now divided into 25 provinces or governorates. In each province a governor acts as the chief executive and a provincial people's council is vested with legislative and supervisory powers. According to the constitution a gradual transfer of powers to the people's councils - not only the provincial but also lower councils - is to take place (Art. 163). Since the 1970s the office of governor has become increasingly important. He represents the president and supervises to some extent all government agencies in his area, including branches of the central ministries. In order to boost his coordinating role, the law has envisaged an 'executive committee' of provincial directors of central government services under chairmanship of the governor. It is a kind of an embryonic cabinet on provincial level. The twenty-five provinces have been subdivided into 150 districts. Until 1975 the district was administered by police authorities, but since then it became a full-fledged body of local government. Like the province, its organs are a chief executive and a people's council, the former also chairing a similar 'executive committee'.

The rural parts of Egypt's districts have been subdivided into 4108 municipalities, usually called 'village' (*qaria*).[7] Each of these municipalities is generally composed of a main village and some other villages and hamlets. Yet, in the Local Government Act the rural municipality is mentioned as 'the village'. Its chief executive is called 'chief of the village' and he heads the 'village unit'. The local people's council at this level is called 'village council'. There is also an executive committee, which mirrors the models of province and district.[8]

So government at the village level manifests itself in three ways. First, there is the traditional village administration with police functions that comes under the ministry of Interior. Through the *'umdah* who reports to the police unit nearby, and the wardman (*shaykh al-balad*) the traditional village administration has a firm grip on the rural areas. Secondly, the massive presence of a large number of institutions and functionaries of central ministries illustrate that deconcentration is a common pattern in Egypt. And in the third place, the modern local government system mentioned above coordinates various sectors and promotes community participation.

Sectoral Administration by Ministries

The number of ministerial departments has increased from 16 in 1952 to 44 in 1964. It decreased to 30 in 1990. Deputy prime ministers are appointed to assist the prime minister. Each of them coordinates a set of ministries. More than 20 ministries are involved in rural development, either directly or indirectly. Some of them have field offices in the villages: the rural institutions that will be dealt with below.

A few ministries deserve a some remarks here. The ministry of Planning has a network of planning units in all ministries, agencies, provinces and districts. Sectoral and local plans are integrated to become part of the country's rolling Five Year Plans, that are actually public investment programmes. Foreign aid is also taken into account here (Ayubi 1989:5-6).

The ministry of Interior, one of the oldest and most powerful ministries, is charged with internal security and order. Once all regional and local government was carried out by this ministry. There is rivalry between 'Interior' and the army, both claiming a share in the country's political and security control system (Springborg 1989:140-1). Under Sadat 'Interior' rose to a more prominent position but Mubarak has reversed this trend. The dominant role of Interior in controlling the rural areas through its police units has not been affected. The ministry of Manpower is responsible for the so-called graduate policy which aims at achieving full employment by giving government jobs to graduates. Although various ministries and public corporations now recruit by merit examinations, the graduate policy is still being implemented. Graduates from universities and secondary schools just have to wait a few years for their turn. Applicants are assigned by the ministry throughout the country 'by a process that is haphazard at best' and affected by *wastah* (Palmer 1988:38).

Within the ministries undersecretaries each supervise a number of line-directorates. The inflation of the state apparatus has raised the number of undersecretaries to almost 7000 (Springborg 1989:138). Directorates are subdivided in bureaus. Most ministries have internal directorates within headquarters in Cairo, and 'external' directorates in the provincial capitals. Central agencies are organizations for controlling the whole state machinery. They are directly responsible to either the president or the prime minister (Ayubi 1989:5). There are various types of councils that do not depend on a certain ministry (Ayubi 1980:200-202). According to the constitution specialized national councils come under the direct responsibility of the president who also determines their formation and function. The Supreme Council for Population and Family Planning for example, has a number of cabinet ministers as its members and an executive apparatus of its own. Some of these councils 'exist partly if not exclusively to top up the salaries or pensions of their members' (Springborg 1989:139).

Public Authorities have been established after 1952 to implement certain government tasks in a more efficient way (Ayubi: 219, 236,239). Some of them are important for rural development. Examples are the Organization for Reconstruction and Development of Egyptian Villages (ORDEV), the Egyptian Public Authority for Drainage and the Principal Bank for Agricultural Development and Credit. Many technical jobs like transport, communications, supply of drinking water and land reclamation have been entrusted to such public authorities. Public companies often operate in agricultural and industrial production and distribution or in the services sector. There are a few hundreds of them. These companies are called 'the public sector'.

Finally, a special administrative organization in the agricultural production sector and closely related to the ministry of Agriculture is the cooperative system with central, regional and local cooperative societies. The local branches of this system prevalent in most villages are the so-called multi-purpose societies.[9]

Rural Institutions for Development[10]

Most rural institutions are basically field offices of the central ministries, e.g. of Agriculture, Education, Health and Social Affairs. This holds even true for the agricultural cooperative society. The village unit is supervised by district and provincial authorities, and to some extent by the department of Local Government.[11] Only the village council is essentially no field office but a representative body. However, in practice it often operates as an advisory board legitimating the decisions of the executive.

For the Egyptian farmers the most important rural institutions are the multi-purpose agricultural cooperative societies and the local branches of village banks. Those are to be found in almost every village and their combined tasks encroach deeply on farming, the more so since farmers are in fact obliged to associate themselves with these institutions. The state takes with one hand and gives with the other. This means, on one side the farmers are compelled to grow certain crops, especially cotton, and sell them through these institutions to the state at artificially low prices. This is often referred to as 'implicit taxation'. But on the other side, the cooperative societies and village banks make efforts to provide cheap seeds, fertilizer, pesticides, credit and tools, everything far below market prices. Efforts to raise procurement prices and to decrease subsidies have had but limited effects (Springborg 1989: 268-270).

The cooperative societies have been existing in most villages for a few decades now. Their tasks and management structure still reflect socialist ideology. They are administered jointly by villagers and civil servants. It is even stated in the constitution that 80 percent of the seats in the society's board of management must be occupied by small farmers.

The society's daily tasks are carried out by professional staff of the ministry of Agriculture. Every society has one director and some supervisors who each oversee a part of the village's fields. They have frequent, often daily, contact with the farmers. The board members, who are farmers themselves, sometimes act as mediators. However, too close connections between certain farmers and officials have in the past led to the cooperative society's resources being used for personal gain rather than real cooperative purposes.

In order to counter this, and in accordance with the changing ideology, in 1976 the government has reorganized this sector , transferring the resource management to newly established local branches of a public authority, the Egyptian Bank for Agricultural

Development and Credit. This bank operates under the supervision of the ministry of Agriculture, and is hierarchically administered without people's participation. Its village branches, he so-called village banks, are now entrusted with the core tasks of agricultural policy: delivering seeds, fertilizer and credit to the farmers and recovering their produce. At least in its initial years, the village bank of Amadi and its branch in Hanya performed well with a dedicated staff and strict supervision procedures. For the cooperative societies a number of technical agricultural tasks remained such as the preparation of crop rotation schemes and tractors and other machinery for joint use.

A third agricultural institution is the animal health centre. These centres are located in main villages and serve a number of other villages from there. By frequent vaccinations, these centres generally manage to prevent cattle plague epidemics. But apart from that, they do not appear very successful in promoting the health of the Egypt's extensive livestock population. This may be partly due to a lack of financial and material resources.

Primary schools, rural health units and social units are to implement the social policy of the Egyptian authorities at a local level. Of these three government institutions in many villages the primary school is the oldest, the most active and the most appreciated by the people in many villages. Almost every village has its own school, whilst only one out of two or three villages possesses a health unit; social units are only to be found in main villages alongside the village unit.

Compulsory education is, in principle, offered free of charge. Yet, classes are not attended by all children. Especially in Upper and Middle Egypt many boys and most girls drop out from the higher grades of village schools. Adult education programmes have not come off the ground there either. By comparison, attendance in the Delta seems much higher.

Only limited use is being made of the fully staffed, if not overstaffed, health units, like the one near Hanya. The majority of the paramedical staff has often little to do, but the doctor's surgery hours are frequently visited. Help in childbirth by the appointed midwives and health education take place but rarely. The unit's family planning activities are not too successful either.

Out of the many tasks of the social units, the payment of benefits to the poor and unemployed turns out to be the most important whereas a dozen of tasks in the field of welfare are mostly passed over. In practice, social and psychological problems are not dealt with at this institution but within the private circle.

The local government institutions, the village council and the local unit, which are located in the main villages, are basically meant for people's participation and coordination of the other institutions.[12] According to modern standards the chosen set-up is logical. Our field studies however indicate that the concept of a local council, based on free elections and representation of the village community has not really matured yet. To the development of ordinary villages like Hanya the local council appears to be of very limited importance (Otto 1987:153-158; Hopkins 1988:65).

The 'chief of the village' is in charge of an overstaffed village unit, consisting of dozens of officials who, are among other things, responsible for preparing and implementing resolutions of the village council. The village unit conducts some socio-economic projects like cattle-raising, a poultry farm and a carpentry workshop, but these are not notably of much profit to the villagers of Hanya. Nevertheless, modern local government is developing, partly due to ample American financial support to village councils (Mayfield 1985).

If we take a closer look at the specific tasks of the eight institutions, it appears that, in all, 68 tasks are to be carried out. These tasks all aim at a few major goals. Most of these goals are people-oriented: increasing the people's affluence and knowledge, improving their well-being, social justice, democracy. But some goals are more state-oriented: improving the economic position of the country and supporting the regime. According to the field studies I conducted, about 40% of those 68 tasks was carried out satisfactorily. They include most of those aimed at state-centred goals. The remaining 60% is done badly or not at all. The agricultural cooperative society, village bank and primary school are performing their tasks comparatively well, at a large distance followed by the village unit, health unit and animal health centre, with the social centre and village council bringing up the rear. Whether these institutions fulfil a given task well or not, is determined partly by their internal organization and partly by their relationship with the people. These two aspects are covered in the next paragraphs.

Internal Organization of Institutions

The officials who direct the rural development process at the local level are the heads of rural institutions, i.e. the directors of cooperative society and village bank, the doctors of the health unit and the animal health centre, the principal of the school, the head of the social unit , and the chief of the village. Their **leadership** qualities are a critical factor. Most of them are overburdened with routine administrative matters such as filling in registers and reports, and solve problems with individual clients and personnel on an ad hoc basis. They are constantly under pressure to deal with a never ending procession of clients and assistants who flock their rooms with requests, big and small, for themselves or for somebody else. There without any sense of privacy everybody is sitting, waiting and listening how the chief performs. Politeness requires that persons who carry more status should be warmly welcomed by them and helped first, leaving the little man always waiting at the end of the queue.

They are much less involved in identifying problems, preparing specific plans and motivating and mobilizing personnel and clients. The political and social environment would actually discourage such kind of leadership, on the contrary it stimulates passive obedience and opportunism. The paradox is that a 'good leader' should be able to escape from the prevailing politico-administrative culture and even 'isolate' himself in order to implement the official goals of state policy. Replacing the prevailing style of personalist, improvising, arbitrary and authoritarian leadership with more modern methods of management would require people with strong, independent characters. This kind of personality however is deemed to meet a lot of resistance in Egyptian society.

To what extent does the *internal structure* of rural institutions hamper their success? Overstaffing has since long been common in the Egyptian administration and rural institutions are no exception. According to field data proper implementation of tasks would have been possible as well after a reduction of the staff with approximately 46 percent. A side effect of the above-mentioned 'graduate policy' is that a substantial number of middle level staff is placed in positions that do not fit their educational background, thus causing much frustration.

Regarding the personal backgrounds, in rural Middle Egypt almost 90 percent of the personnel are farmer's children from nearby villages. More than half of them are obliged to commute. This transport in Egypt's overloaded traffic system takes much efforts, time and a considerable part of their salaries, sometimes up to a quarter. Local officials are preferably not posted in their home villages so that personalist interference is avoided. More than 90 % of the personnel are men. Certainly in Upper Egypt this can hinder a smooth communication between rural institutions and village women, who are according to the prevailing morale not considered to relate to 'other men'. On the other hand, female civil servants themselves may in these areas also be bound to refrain from going around freely.

In most rural institutions jobs are not interesting since they consist of routine paperwork. Because of the overstaffing for many there is often little work to be done, so those civil servants are often bored, read the newspaper and just talk. Results of the work are not seldom disappointing and give them little self-esteem. For a successful career *wastah* or personal connections seem often more decisive than performance. The salaries are desperately low, and it is virtually impossible to make a living without additional income. So, any opportunity to earn something extra is welcomed. As a consequence, the doctors of health units and veterinary units ask their clients to pay them personally. Their assistants open up their own private practices. School teachers give private lessons. The driver of the cooperative society's tractor requests *baqshish*. In many cases this second income exceeds by far the official income, but usually it is illegal, so the official will not talk about it openly.

As important as the extra money is the keeping up of a network of good personal connections within the state apparatus. For, those who decide upon appointments, transfers, promotions and thereby also determine the scope for sideline activities, should remain friends. In order to remain friends with superiors, in general one should not bother them with problems. Therefore , reports often tend to picture the situation somewhat brighter than it is in reality.

So a lot of things, though generally known, are kept in the dark. The civil servant has to live in two worlds, a public world and a 'hidden world'. To what extent a rural institution becomes entangled and destructed in this hidden world, depends of the moral code of individual officials, especially the chiefs, and the opportunities they are given. Strict work prescriptions and supervision may help, but at the same time create other problems : will the supervision be just ? In other words : who inspects the inspectors, and will the motivation of civil servants not be adversely affected by a tough control ? Yet field data show a positive correlation between frequency of inspector's visit and performance.

In the case study of Hanya, this was demonstrated by the organization of the village bank. Not only were there intensive inspections more than three times a week, also recruitment, salaries and equipment helped to bring about a better motivation and good results. Lack of material and financial *resources*, and in some cases lack of human resources, may also contribute to ineffectiveness. However, statements that a lack of resources is 'the only problem' of rural development in Egypt, should be considered cautiously. Increasing salaries and other monetary incentives is of course urgent but could be disastrous from an economic point of view. Furthermore, recent research on the relation between income and motivation of Egyptian civil servants have shown that monetary incentives alone are insufficient instruments to promote better performance (Palmer 1988: 45-71). Shortages of medical drugs, fertilizer, pesticides, telephone connections, vehicles can surely hinder rural development. But experience over the past years has demonstrated that without fair distribution, without proper use, maintenance and repairs the resources problem will not be solved by just bringing in the goods.

State Penetration and People's Access

A wide political gap between ruler and ruled is generally considered to be a feature of political and administrative systems in developing countries (Heady 1984 :257). More in particular, postcolonial Arab governments 'have been weak because they are essentially unconnected to the societies over which they provide'; and 'perhaps state and society in Egypt, having long been divorced, and in fact never really married, are destined to keep their distance from one another, at least for some time to come' (Springborg 1991: 232, 248).[13]

Villagers regard the services offered by the rural institutions with suspicion, and from a historical point of view, they have ample reason to do so. Since the days of the Pharaos, they have been forced to work on the land following the state's detailed instructions, only to see the profits being taken away by the state, or by powerholders protected by the state. In that sense Nasser's socialist land reforms , though mobilizing the population against the former feudal landlords, was an extension of century-old practices. Farmers know exactly how the state uses the cooperative society and village bank to effectively exploit the rural sector in order to be able to accommodate the urban masses with cheap agricultural produce. But at least in Upper Egypt in the early eighties, they were still too afraid of the state's power to resist. Yet, as Baer (1969: 93-108) has suggested, the submissiveness of *fellahin* might turn into revolt if two conditions will be combined : if the farmers feel that the rulers act against islam ànd if they feel that their economic *interests* are severely harmed by the state.

Therefore, the government is quite cautious in trying not to alienate the rural electorate any further. And of course many of the rural institutions' 68 tasks do indeed aim at rural development and improvement of the villagers' life. And people do appreciate many changes that were brought to their villages by the government: land reform, irrigation, education and electricity, to mention just a few examples. Yet, unfortunately, many of the rural institutions' other tasks seem not to appeal to the population. For, the villager judges a rural institution by the yardstick of the profit he or she can get out of it, and a great number of tasks are not at all considered profitable. In those cases they become indifferent or defensive. Other tasks that may be seen as basically useful, have their parallel in the private sector, often in informal or traditional spheres (Otto 1987: 304-5). This is most evident from medical aid, which is offered by countless private individuals; there we find not only witchdoctors, priests and traditional midwives, but also staff-members of the public health unit who are striving for an additional income. In other cases, certain religious norms form an impediment, for instance regarding family planning and women's emancipation.

But even if villagers have decided to approach a rural institution, **access** is often problematic. In many cases there are financial thresholds. Or people are put off with rebuffs by civil servants. Villagers may also lack time, transport or information. Of course the villagers' social position often determines how he or she is treated. Rural notables who can pull the strings in the provincial capital are well treated, at the bank or by the doctor. Average villagers who are often fobbed off, either turn away from the government in disappointment or they look again for access, but then in another way, either by bringing in a village chief or a *wastah* within the government machinery or by trying to approach the private individual behind the official with money or promises. This pressure from the use of *wastah* is considered a major work problem by civil servants (Palmer 1988: 108, 112-3).

Implementation of certain tasks which the villagers take no interest in, can only be achieved by the threat of physical *force* by the state. This mainly happens when national interests are at stake, such as the compulsory growing and selling of crops, and taxation. Such tasks are often carried out rather effectively. Some tasks require civil servants to turn to the villagers, e.g. for the transfer of goods or information like contraceptives, health education or agricultural counselling. A practical problem then is that villagers regularly remain outside their *reach*. In the morning when most farmers are in the fields, it is difficult to make an appointment with them.

We have dealt now with several factors concerning both an institutions' internal organization and its relation with the people. These factors - internal structure, resources, leadership[14] as well as villagers' interest, access, state force and reach - help to explain why so many tasks of rural institutions are not well implemented, or even not at all. In their turn they are influenced by the social, economic and political environment, leaving only limited possibilities for improving the functioning of these rural institutions in the near future.

Mubarak's Leadership in Politics and Administration

Nasser, Sadat and Mubarak have all left their distinctive marks on Egypt's history. Nasser transformed society for the sake of redistributing power, knowledge and income from a feudal elite to the people. Though popular with the masses, he operated in an authoritarian, centralized way and relied on the army, the state apparatus and a single party system.

Sadat, long before *perestrojka*, acknowledging the negative aspects of massive socialist interventions by the state, embarked upon an 'open door' policy. He introduced a multi-party system, though maintaining one dominant political party, named the National Democratic

Party, as his own power base. Furthermore he fostered decentralization and encouraged the private sector to invest in the weakened economy. The role of the military was much decreased and a rising bourgeoisie reestablished ties with technocrats in the state apparatus. Sadat himself however ruled in a paternalist way, exploiting and thereby reinforcing the typical Egyptian social networks of patronage, kinship and friendship. To get things done, *wastah* was commonly used.

Rather than preaching 'revolution' as both his predecessors did, Mubarak has tried to preserve the gains of their work (Dessouki 1990). The socialist welfare state stands still upright whilst the course of economic and political liberalization is still being pursued as well, albeit very cautiously. At the same time he has tried to rationalize political life by a depersonalization of the power structure. Mubarak's attitude towards administration is not one of grand reforms, he has simply stressed that people and civil servants should work hard, be accountable, be not corrupt and do not use *wastah* (cfr.Palmer 1988:13). Who knows the prevailing manners and customs in modern Egypt will acknowledge that this policy aims at a fundamental social change which would actually be a revolution in itself. Whether it will succeed or not, for his efforts to attack the *wastah* system, Mubarak certainly deserves more credit than has been generally awarded to him by scholarly observers[15]. His modest matter-of-factnesss and unobtrusive style has won him less admiration and adoration but certainly also less antipathy and repugnance than Nasser and Sadat.

Yet there is much criticism. International presence and the feeling of being too strongly tied to the United States and other donor and creditor countries has hurt nationalist feelings in Egypt. Policy advisors have attacked established policies. Human rights organizations have criticized the government for abuse of power. The military alliance in the Gulf War of 1991, where Egyptians helped to fight the Iraqi's, may have aggravated what may develop in another national crisis of identity. This could make the regime particularly vulnerable to opposition by islamic fundamentalists. This threat prevents any policy that could be percei-ved as radical westernization. So, while Mubarak has been balancing and not claiming the public's attention with new initiatives, others have been busy in reinforcing or just retaining their position in the nation's power games. They include groups in the army with strong ties with the United States, the 'parasytic bourgeoisie' of the open-door policy (Springborg 1989: 85-87), the opposition parties and especially the islamic fundamentalists, who operate partly through opposition alliances in parliament and partly underground.

Mubarak's style of leadership implicates that he does not have a close inner circle of cronies, no client group ,like Sadat had. Instead he does not associate himself clearly with persons or policies, rather trying to act as an arbiter between parties. He also relies on institutions and functional advisors, mostly military men and a few civilians, his prime minister and his political partymen of the National Democratic Party, which has developed even closer ties with the ministry of Interior (idem:156-170). Reshuffling of cabinets, a familiar practice under Sadat, is still common under Mubarak.

Springborg has labelled these changes in the structure of power relations under Mubarak as 'political fragmentation' and 'weak government'. This may be true to some extent, yet the above-mentioned developments could at the same time be interpreted in terms of administrative rationalization, depersonalization, political liberalization and decentralization? The display of power by the courts, especially the administrative courts and the Supreme Constitutional Court during Mubarak's rule, does support this view. That would mean that the political and administrative order as envisaged by the constitution is steadily maturing in Mubarak's Egypt.

Rural Institutions between Politics, Policies and the People

To a large extent rural development is still controlled and fostered by the administration. Farming is partly guided and supervised by the local institutions of the ministry of Agriculture that impose an implicit taxation through compulsory procurement of agricultural produce, notably cotton. Security and rural political life, including local and national elections and referenda, are closely watched and more or less controlled by the rural police units that are part of the ministry of Interior, with the assistance of the traditional village headmen. The formation and development of private associations is guarded by the ministry of Social Affairs.

But there is much more than only control : at the same time many subsidized goods and services are offered to the villagers, counterbalancing control and taxation. Providing cheap food including bread, the staple food, is a vital element of social policy. Education has reached almost every corner of rural Egypt, giving a significant contribution to upward social mobility. Health services and schemes of social assistance and security have penetrated the rural areas. Electrical power, drainage schemes and infrastructural projects have followed.

Yet, the rural institutions of the state, created under Nasser and extended under Sadat and Mubarak, are effective only to some extent. As each of these institutions performs different tasks, and the results of these tasks vary, depending on many factors, one should be cautious in generalizing. My field study in Middle Egypt demonstrated that about 40% of the tasks was carried out reasonably well; the remaining 60 % did not bring good results (Otto 1987:285). This has for one part been due to deficiencies inside the institutions, which most of all lack dedicated personnel, and for another part to an often understandable lack of appreciation by the people.

Rural development has also taken place outside the realm of state control. Remittances from workers abroad have greatly contributed to the rise of rural incomes, and private agricultural enterprise has created a rural bourgeoisie who combine cultivation of traditional crops with horticulture, trade, services and local industries. Development through the private sector fits well in the new orthodoxy of development which favours market orientation over state intervention. International pressure from aid donors like World Bank, IMF and USAID and from the consortium of Egypt's creditors, the so-called club of Paris, pushes in that direction. From inside the country Wafdists, liberals, the former aristocracy that still owns real estate and the new bourgeoisie of *infitah* entrepreneurs would all welcome it as well. But Mubarak has continued to treat the private and the public sector as 'equal partners' (Springborg 1989: 284), and as yet, the donors and creditors have not had enough policy leverage as to substantially change the economic structure. Plans from within government circles to roll back on agrarian reforms and weaken the tenant's position vis a vis the landowner, have until now only been debated but implementation is not expected in the foreseeable future (Springborg 1991).

Mubarak's calls for budget austerity have also not slowed down the growth of the civil service, on the contrary, its pace seems to have quickened since the days of Nasser (Ayubi 1989: 6-7). Ministries are still expanding, and around the cities many big state companies continue to operate. Over the last decade the military has established a huge industrial system of its own. As for the rural areas, more institutions, overstaffed with middle level officials, will penetrate into the villages, and join the 'sullen and resentful rump at subsistence wages' (Fernandez 1983: 118). It is unlikely that this will narrow the gap between state and rural population that was so aptly described by Springborg (1989). Presence of more 'parasyte' civil servants in rural areas may even lead to more irritation or even hostility. One may remember that the successful mobilization of the rural masses in the 1950s and 1960s was done by only a handful of Nasser's officials. Whether the *fellahin* will continue to accept the ever increasing meddling with their lives will also depend on the attitudes and behaviour of the civil servants towards their clients.

Any expression of popular discontent, whether spontaneous or through elections, is more likely to take place in urban than in rural areas. The high rate of urbanization therefore indicates growing instability. The rural areas comprising more than four thousand villages, are still well under control. First, since the ministry of Interior directly controls the villages through its rural police units and the subordinate structure of traditional village administration. Secondly, because there is little antagonism between rural bourgeoisie and rural mass:

family ties and rivalries unite the rich and the poor of any particular family clan to stand against other clans.

So the preservation of the 'real Egyptian family', as stated in the constitution (Art. 9) helps in maintaining political stability, at least in the rural areas. Political participation of the rural mass through formal channels, like elections, village councils, cooperative boards, remains somewhat problematic. Nasser's efforts to have a substantial representation of peasants and workers in parliament have become something of the past. In the people's assembly peasants are hardly represented now (Springborg 1989:165). Not only because the regime wants them to keep quiet but also because villagers, rich and poor alike, prefer to serve individual or family interests rather than the development of village communities and regions as a whole. In their approach of rural institutions they tend to use and to strengthen channels of patronage and *wastah*. At least in this respect the people of Egypt are definitely 'sovereign' in politics and administration: even Mubarak, the president who has attacked the *wastah* system has certainly not enough control to withhold them.

In sum, Egypt provides us with a fascinating case study for the comparative study of politics and administration in Third World countries. Over the last decades it has experienced dramatic changes reflecting ideological trends that have affected most other Third World countries as well. The Egyptians have been able to maintain political stability, to carry out and sustain an impressive agrarian reform programme and to set up a dense network of rural institutions. In spite of great political and economic pressures, since 1952 no coup d'état has taken place. As has been shown by Sadat and Mubarak, statemanship in today's Egypt entails the art of balancing and integrating. This applies not only to divergent political forces and to the goods and evils of both state apparatus and *wastah* system. It is also true if we consider opposed systems of thought like 'science and faith', control and liberalization, socialism and privatization, modern urban life and traditional village patterns. The harmonizing skills of Egyptian politicians and administrators can be read from the formula's of the constitution itself, they have become manifest in national politics and are also reflected in rural administration. Their approach seems the only one possible. It is bound to be successful as long as they can keep on bringing the basic goods and services to their people.

Notes

1. Hanya is the fictitious name of a real village in the province of Minya in Middle Egypt. Middle Egypt is the northern part of Upper Egypt, which includes the provinces of Bani Suef, Minya and Assyut. In Hanya I carried out a field research on local government institutions and rural development from 1979 until 1981 . I reported about this research in my PhD thesis (Otto 1987).

2. In this article rural development refers to a process of increase of incomes, welfare, information and social justice in a rural area.

3. We are mainly concerned here with institutions that aim at socio-economic development through direct contact with the rural population itself. Those are the so-called 'people-centred' development institutions as opposed to agencies with physical-technical tasks like roads and water services.

4. According to Springborg Mubarak is the 'weak leader of a weak state' (Springborg 1989:285). Of course Mubarak has not been compared to the prophet like Nasser (Saad 1988:55) nor does he behave as a patrimonial monarch as Sadat did in many ways. However, in spite of the fragmentation of the political order and the lack of clarity in socio-economic policies, the presidency and the state still represent the dominant power in this country (Ayubi 1989:1-4).

5. According to the law this function shall be abolished as soon as a village has its own police unit. In practice police units are situated in certain villages from where they serve a number of villages in the surrounding area. The rural police areas are often overlapping with the areas of local government units, that were established afterwards.

6. The present law concerning local government is Act 43 of 1979 which was amended by Act 9 of 1989.

7. Below the district level the Local Government Act distinguishes between town and village areas. If by prime minister's decree some urban area is declared to be a 'town', this town will have its own chief, local council and executive committee. Town governorates and greater towns can be subdivided in 'quarters'. Again, each quarter has its chief, its local council and its executive committee.

8. The village executive committee consists of the local representatives of six ministries: Agriculture, Education, Health, Social Affairs, Housing (including several public works) and Interior (Local Government Act, Executive decree Art.61).

9. This multipurpose agricultural cooperative society should be distinguished from the agrarian reform cooperative society. Between 1905 and 1952 a few hundred agricultural credit cooperatives were established in the rural areas, mainly on a voluntary basis. Yet they were already supervised and regulated by the state. As the agrarian reform took place in the 1950s, its beneficiaries who received the surplus land of former landlords, were obliged to unite themselves in agrarian reform cooperative societies that were actually ran by the government. In this way ownership could be redistributed without the land being cut into pieces, which would harm its productive capacity. An agronomist from the ministry supervised the production. Credits, seeds, fertilizer and pesticides were distributed to the members on the condition that their harvest would be sold through the cooperative society. This system worked well, at least from the government's perspective. Therefore between 1955 and 1964 this system was extended outside the land reform areas to all villages of the country. Gradually all Egyptian farmers were virtually obliged to associate. Besides the app. 300 agrarian reform cooperative societies, there are now more than 4000 'normal' cooperative societies.

10. The following description is based a.o. on the findings of case studies in two villages, respectively in Upper and Lower Egypt : Hanya in Minya governorate and Bani Amin in Dakhliyah governorate. The available literature about similar institutions elsewhere in Egypt has been studied as well.

11. The department of Local Government and/or the separate ministerial portfolio bearing that name, have been created, renamed or abolished several times over the last decades. Recent cabinet changes that were announced on May 20, 1991, again include the 'new post' of Minister of Local Government (Keesing's R. 1991: 38209).

12. According to the Local Government Law, a village council consists of eighteen elected members, at least two of them representing the main village, and at least one for each adjacent village. At least one member shall be a woman.

13. The same message , albeit in simpler words, was conveyed to me during field research as a farmer in Hanya told me once, while pointing to the sky: 'The government is up there, hundred miles high!'. And another one said :'Do you want to know the truth, there are no farmers in Egypt, there is only a plan from above that says what we are allowed to do and what not. Farmers do not exist here. Only the government exists!'.

14. These three institutional variables have been derived from the so-called Institution Building Universe, a model by Milton J. Esman. The four other variables were developed in an effort to formulate broad concepts covering the reality of state-citizen relations as manifested in the Hanya case study (Otto 1987).

15. Cfr. Springborg(1989) calling Mubarak 'a weak lader of a weak state'. Fisher(1990) condescendingly wrote about Mubarak's 'short lived campaign against corruption.'

References

Ayubi, Nazih N. (1989), Government and the State in Egypt today, in: Charles Tripp and Roger Owen (eds.), *Egypt under Mubarak*, London, 1-20.

Ayubi, Nazih N.M. (1980), *Bureaucracy and Politics in Contemporary Egypt*, London.

Alderfer, H.F. (1964), *Local government in developing countries*, New York.

Baer G. (1969), *Studies in the social history of modern Egypt*, Chicago.

Boutros-Ghali, Boutros (1978), Towards a new democratic life: a prologue, in: Ali E.H. Dessouki (ed.), *Democracy in Egypt: Problems and prospects*, The Cairo papers in social science, Vol. 1 Monograph 2: 3-6.

Butter, David (1989), Debt and Egypt's Financial Policies, in: Charles Tripp and Roger Owen (eds.), *Egypt under Mubarak*, London, 121-136.

Commander, Simon (1989), Some Issues in Agricultural Sector Policy, in: Charles Tripp and Roger Owen eds., *Egypt under Mubarak,* Londen, 137-158.

Dessouki, Ali E.H. ed. (1978), *Democracy in Egypt: Problems and prospects*, The Cairo papers in social science, Vol. 2, Monograph 1.

Dessouki, Ali E. Hillal (1990), L'évolution politique de l'Egypte: pluralisme démocratique où néo-autoritarisme, in: Maghreb-Machrek 127: 7-16.

Fernandes-Armesto, Felipe (1983), *Sadat and his statecraft*, Windsor Forest (U.K.).

Fisher, W.B. (1990), Egypt, in: *The Middle East and North Africa 1991*, London.

Flanz, Gisbert H. and Fouad Shafik (1984), Egypt, in: Albert P. Blaustein and Gisbert H. Flanz eds., *Constitutions of the World*, Dobbs Ferry (N.Y.).

Harik, Ilya (1974), *The Political Mobilization of Peasants, a study of an Egyptian community*, London.

Heady F. (1984), *Public administration: A Comparative Perspective*, New York.

Hinnebusch, Raymond A. (1981), Egypt under Sadat: Elites, Power Structure and Political Change in a Post-Populist State, in: *Social Problems*, Vol.28, No.4, 442-464.

Hinnebusch Jr., Raymond A. (1985), *Egyptian politics under Sadat: the post-populist development of an authoritarian-modernizing state*, Cambridge.

Hopkins, Nicholas S. (1988), *Participation and community in the Egyptian new lands: the case of South Tahrir*, Cairo papers in social science, Vol.11, monograph 1.

Hopwood, Derek (1983), *Egypt, politics and society 1945-1981*, London.

Keesings Historisch Archief (1991).

Keesings Record of World Events (1991).

Makram Ebeid, Mona (1989), The Role of the Official Opposition, in: Charles Tripp and Roger Owen (eds.), *Egypt under Mubarak*, London, 21-52.

Mayfield, James B. (1974), *Local institutions and Egyptian rural development*, Ithaca.

Mayfield, James B. (1985), The Egyptian Basic Village Services Program. A new Strategy for Local Government Capacity Building, in: Jean-Claude Garcia-Zamor ed., *Public Participation in Development, Planning and Management*, Boulder (Col.) 97-125.

Otto, J.M. (1987), *Aan de voet van de piramide; overheidsinstellingen en plattelandsontwikkeling in Egypte: een onderzoek aan de basis [At the foot of the pyramid; government institutions and rural development: a study at the grass roots]*, proefschrift, Rijksuniversiteit te Leiden [Ph.D.thesis University of Leiden], Leiden.

Palmer, Monte, Ali Leila, El Sayed Yassin (1988), *The Egyptian Bureaucracy*, Syracuse.

Saad, Reem, (1988), *Social history of an agrarian reform community in Egypt*, Cairo papers in social science, Vol.11, Monograph 4.

Springborg, Robert (1979), Sayed Bey Marei and political clientelism in Egypt, in: *Comparative Political Studies*, vol. 12, nr 3.

Springborg, Robert (1989), *Mubarak's Egypt : Fragmentation of the Political Order*, Boulder (Col).

Springborg, Robert (1991), State-Society Relations in Egypt, The Debate over Owner-Tenant Relations, in: *The Middle East Journal* 45, 2, 232-249.

Springborg, Robert (1988), The President and the field marshall: civil-military relations in Egypt today, in: *MERIP Middle East Report 147*, July-August 1987, 4-16.

Tripp, Charles, and Roger Owen, eds. (1989), *Egypt under Mubarak*, London.

Vasil'ev, A.M. (1988), Egipet: evoljucia politiceskoj sistemy [Egypt: the evolution of the political system], *Voprosy Istorii*, 11, 22-44.

Wheelock, Keith (1960), *Nasser's new Egypt, a critical analysis*, London.

World Bank (1983), *The, World Development Report 1983*, New York.

7 POLITICAL EXECUTIVE AND THE BUREAUCRACY IN INDIA

R.B. Jain

Introduction

The emergence of the bureaucratic organization in modern governments has laid the formation of a body of civil servants who work for the government as a lifetime career. The very presence of such professional body of trained men is expected to exert a 'rational' influence on the entire decision-making process. Consequently, the element of 'rationality' has come to be recognised and emphasized as the characteristic working approach, and is regarded as an outstanding contribution of the modern governmental organization, no matter whether the state is liberal or totalitarian.

However, despite the superiority that the so called 'rationality' imparts to a bureaucratic organization, and its constant obsession with it, occasionally it has a negative effect, especially when it attempts to stimulate self-sufficiency. Rationality is not only linked to methodological analysis but also to an objective point of view. "Objectivity, in examining issues, an occupational habit" observes Professor Marx, "puts value on a retreat from active partisanship". Indeed, in the realism of public administration the career bureaucracy serves, as a permanent instrument of government under conditions of changing party control, only by acknowledging and adopting an attitude of neutrality. Such a neutrality is the working premise for the loyal support of any legitimate government - whatever be its ideological stance. On the other hand, "it may and does foster a personal disengagement from any kind of political choice, including the difference between constitutional means or ends in the actions of the government of the day"(Marx 1967:25).

With these introductory remarks an attempt will be made to explain the meaning of neutrality within the framework of the Indian bureaucracy, and to show that its interaction with the political executive after Independence has led to its greater politicisation.

The Concept of Neutrality

The tradition of the 'neutrality' of the career service, has often been hailed as the secret of the success of the career-service in Great Britain. Indeed, the concept of 'neutrality' coupled with 'impartiality', 'anonymity', and 'obscurity' has not only become synonymous with the operation of the British Civil Service but is also regarded as "one of the strongest bulwark of democracy" (Attlee 1956:5), essential to the system of parliamentary democracy where the political complexion of the ruling party is subject to periodic, if not frequent changes. However, after World War II, the concept of a neutral bureaucracy has been subjected to vehement criticism in quite a few democracies in the West who had adopted it as a permanent feature of their governmental system. Even the British have become sceptical about the continued utility or validity of the neutral career-service in its ability to implement the objectives and goals of a welfare state.

Ever since the Crichel Down Affair (1954), the British Civil Service came in for a good deal of criticism for its failure to meet the growing needs of a complex welfare state. And this for a variety of reasons, a) its amateurism, rigidity and inefficiency, and b) frequently for its obstructionist posture especially in the way of the implementation of 'progressive' (mainly due to its being supposedly neutral) policies. Similar criticism is also being heard in the context of many Commonwealth and Continental countries which had been influenced by the British tradition of a 'neutral' bureaucracy. This is particularly true in the Indian situation today, where the bureaucracy has been under criticism from the ruling party for not being able to effect the social transformation, which was envisaged in the plans and numerous welfare or progressive legislation. The bureaucracy in India, with its background, education and training has isolated itself totally from the masses and thus is neither able to feel their ambitions or hopes in its veins. Only a "committed" bureaucracy in place of the old indolent, passive, apathetic and apolitical one, could possibly bring about the changes implied in the Plans, is now the widely held view regarding its role.

The idea of 'bureaucracy' as a neutral instrument in the conduct of public affairs thus stands generally refuted - and with it also its 'rational' basis of superiority. The new thinking considers that in any system of government, the bureaucracy must be wholly in sympathy with the basic social philosophy of the party in power. In other words, 'bureaucracy' is now regarded not a value-free but a value-laden instrument of political power. In short, the bureaucracy is being 'politicised'.

Breakdown of the 'neutrality' concept:

This neutrality concept has run into difficulties in the last three decades or so and the demand for a 'politicised' bureaucracy has grown on the grounds that, the British 'concept' has become outmoded and outdated. The so-called 'neutrality' is really a myth and the neutrality of bureaucracy cannot be beyond criticism when the divergence of views between the ruling parties ceases to be narrow, especially when the traditional division of functions between the political masters and civil servants in terms of policy and its implementation is really more imaginary than real. And since, both functionaries are concerned with policy as well as implementation; it is impossible for any enlightened individual capable of judging problems 'pragmatically' to maintain intellectual neutrality. Further, it now appears essential that thinking about the functioning of bureaucracy, particularly in the exercise of its discretionary powers and recommendations, it should normally be guided solely by the national policy objectives.

Causes for the Breakdown of 'neutrality'

The break-down of the classical theory of 'neutrality' has been due to several reasons. First, the processes of policy decision-making are no longer confined to the political executive: they spread over the entire fabric of government, resulting in inescapable delegation and zones of such policy, where the political executive does and need not come into the picture at all and yet the decisions presumably reflect the ethos of the party in power. Secondly, the leadership role of the public bureaucracy is explicit in all political systems, but is more pronounced in the setting of developing countries with a democratic constitution. In the context of a large-scale welfare programme undertaken by them as part of a modernizing process - neutrality is neither possible nor desirable. A certain commitment to the goals and objectives of the state policy is inescapable; neutrality cannot be allowed to degenerate into disinterestedness; nor political sterilization allowed to slip into political desensitization. Thirdly, in the sphere of policy advice and execution, modern bureaucracy cannot afford to remain aloof without involving itself in the prevailing politics. Quite often as has been pointed out "practical and political considerations are indistinguishable"(Chaturvedi 1971: 41-42).

In the legislative sphere particularly, the area of demarcation between what is political and what is non-political becomes extremely tenuous. Fourthly, at the top levels, even the performance appraisal of public bureaucracy is done by political heads and an element of political assessment is bound to creep into such rating. Finally, as human being, no civil servant can be psychologically neutral on issues and problems which confront him; he is a child of his time with a certain degree of subjective bias which simply cannot be eradicated from his judgements.

Thus, the basic assumptions behind the concept of bureaucratic neutrality i.e. (a) that it is the product of 'merit' system and therefore seeks to reflect it in those systems where this concept is recognized in the behaviour of the bureaucrats, and (b) that the advantages of permanency, continuity, reliability, and professionalism, which are supposed to obtain in a neutral bureaucracy far outweigh the disadvantages viz. conservatism, reluctance to a departure from routine, and the performance for incremental change obstructing public policy making in a turbulent environment; - have virtually been refuted in the modern times in practically all political systems - including those western democracies where such ideas were for decades deeply entrenched.

The Indian bureaucracy

The Indian bureaucracy, modelled on the British pattern, where the politico-administrative differentiation should have been as distinct as in Britain, presents a somewhat hazy picture. The consensus of opinion in post-independent India, reflected in the accepted policies of successive governments in the country, was that the Indian society should be built on the socialist pattern of the basis of democracy, secularism and social justice. Such policies need the existence of a higher civil service which is intellectually in sympathy with the policy objectives of the government. Clearly, there seems to be no place in the civil service hierarchy for those who believe in maintaining the status quo. It is possible for an individual to subjugate his personal wishes to carry out the categorical imperative of a superior authority but as observed by a senior civil servant, "where the thought process has to be invoked, where an element of discretion is involved, it is contrary to human nature to expect that he will be able to substitute his own thinking by that of the rulers and exercise discretion fully consistent with all the nuances of the original policy objectives. But, for a civil servant functioning at the higher levels, such an exercise of discretion is essential, for no policy directive can cover all the circumstances which may arise from day to day on the basis of which numerous decisions have to be taken"(Dutt 1973: 13).

A study of the Indian bureaucracy has pointed out that the "Indian bureaucracy has been involved in politics and political activity in a number of ways". They were "not only not neutral in politics, they exercised more powers in reality than the law permits. Many times ministers were found wanting in effectively controlling their departmental bureaucracy"(Bhambri 1971 :267). Another similar study about the relations between the politicians and administrators at the district level in India has stated "that the conventional notion of a clear-cut and precise division of functions between administrators and political leaders does not obtain in practice"(Kothari and Roy 1969: 160). This is also the contention of a senior civil servant, who maintains that the "classical doctrine of the neutrality of the civil service has broken down in the modern times and especially in the Indian situation". The only connotation in which this doctrine can exist further is an idea of non-partisanship and impartiality (impartiality in the sense that where the civil servants are expecting a corpus of statutory laws and regulations, they shall act impartially and will not import into these operations any political considerations which are not contemplated in the statutory law). However, for the large bulk of their activity that is not non-statutory, a new doctrine ought to be propounded to suit the modern times. In the absence of a better phraseology we may say that in place of the doctrine of neutrality, there should be encouraged or adopted a doctrine of political responsiveness which may have the generic name of "commitment"(Chaturvedi 1971: 445).

Following certain basic traditions of the British Civil Service, the Indian bureaucracy is largely neutral in politics. The Central Services Conduct Rules forbid government servants to be members of or be otherwise associated with any political party or any organization and in fact is required to prevent every member of his family from taking part in, subscribing in aid of, or assisting in any other manner in movement or activity which is directly or indirectly deemed to be subversive of the government. The Rules also prohibit the civil servants to participate or canvass on behalf of any political party in its election campaign, but he can vote in the elections without giving any indication of the manner in which he proposes to vote. Although, the aforesaid retirement, however, the fact that many civil servants in India have associated with one political party or the other after their retirement and become its active members, has given rise to the general and somewhat erroneous contention that during the post-independence period the Indian bureaucracy has been involved in politics (Bhambri 1972: 266). Similarly, it is also argued that the Indian bureaucracy during Congress Party rule from 1947 till 1974 was in collusion with Congress Party leaders, even factional leaders and those who actively worked for personal or party interests of the Congress leaders. This was done, it is alleged, in return for the benefits of promotion and better prospects. Further, it is also stated that the Indian bureaucrats - both civil and military - have maintained close liaison with political leaders. Dissatisfied officials, even supplied facts to the opposition party leaders in parliament to criticise various policies (Bhambri 1972 :266).

Political and party interference may also manifest itself in other directions. For example, the political leaders may be able to harass public officials in their functioning through the issue of such directions which may cut across the prescribed rules. On the other hand, many administrators put political pressure to influence decisions in service matters, which are favourable to them. In India many public officials have known to be only too willing to exploit the weakness of the political masters for their own personal advantage (Rao 1970:125). Quite a few have come out of their anonymity and have addressed press conferences. Not only that the political leaders themselves, frequently, have not observed a neutral posture, there are instances when they have openly named civil servants in parliament. Ministers have too often blamed their secretaries for mistakes committed by their ministries.

Civil servants, who are not obliging enough, soon find themselves in trouble. The simplest way is to record an adverse report in the confidential dossier of the civil servant. The power of transfer may be used to harass an officer. Frequent transfers can cause considerable harassment, as they involve uprooting of the whole family. A more dangerous method and yet frequently adopted - is to promote direct indiscipline amongst the different cadres of the civil service. The power of posting may be used to thwart a superior officer's control over his office and extend the minister's influence in the field where his legal power may not stand him in good stead (Rao 1970 :125).

Although, the Indian system prescribes procedure for an aggrieved government servant to seek relief, but the procedure forbids attempts to influence final decisions through outside channels including members of legislatures. This rule, as P.V.R. Rao comments, is more frequently broken than observed, and is a major cause for the deterioration of discipline and efficiency. When a minister himself intervenes in breach of a rule, or connives at it by pressing the request made by a member of the legislature, it is difficult to initiate action against the government servant, who is guilty of breach of discipline. Such interventions erode the authority of the immediate superiors of the government servant concerned. As normally, the government servant in whose favour there has been intervention will be working in the constituency of the member of the legislature, that government servant will have compromised his capacity for impartial action (Rao 1970:128).

A retired IAS officer, R.S. Varma makes the following sharp and pithy comment on political bureaucratization in India:

> In a major breakthrough, politicians are moved by a determination not to allow officials to stand between them and the exploitation of even the details of administration for political cum personal ends. In the war of benefits and concessions for clients, the dividing line between the policy making and field administration

has been eroded. The bureaucratic fort has given way and officials are adjusting themselves to new ways even to the extent of doing and saying what might please the political masters. This indication is leading to blurred roles of the two wings. The one abets the other's corruption (Varma 1973:63).

There is no doubt that in all administrative systems there are frequent political interferences through a very convenient device of being over-critical or simply adopting a fault-finding posture. This may render the task of the public officials more uncomfortable and in disgust he may either become susceptible to the political pressures for sheer survival or may devise attitudes and strategies of self-defence. In both cases he cannot remain neutral and has to act as a "political man".

Minister, Civil Servant Relations in India

An important aspect of the complex relationship and the dichotomy between politics and administration is the issue of relationship between ministers and civil servants. Policy as generally thought in traditional terms involves politics, and therefore, it is argued that it should be the concern of the ministers alone, and the civil servants should only have the responsibility for its execution in a dispassionate and detached manner. But the issue is not so simple and deserves to be examined in greater depth.

Kingsley observes that the traditional view of the relations between Minister and Civil Servant will not, in fact, withstand close examination. In his words "the higher civil servants are not technicians or experts in any strict sense, though expert advice is available to them in the technical branches of the Department. Nor do they so much work under the direction of a Minister or work with him. Their functional position is best described, perhaps, as that of permanent politicians. Because they are permanent, they are competent, for it is this characteristic which enables them to master those details which form the essence of policy. And because they are politicians, they are responsible; for it is this characteristic, above all else, which assures that they will not translate their position of functional dominance into one of domination"(Kingsley 1944:269).

The minister is rarely an expert in the special work on which his department is engaged, or for that matter, in the techniques of public administration. He has general ideas in line with the political ideology of his party, but he often is not sure what is the best solution to a particular problem with which he is faced. He must rely on his permanent officials for facts and advice, for it is the official who has the information which will show whether or not an objective can be realised. If it cannot be achieved, it will probably be quietly abandoned.

The minister is not a superior civil servant and is likely to approach problems in a different way. He is recruited, trained and promoted to office through very different channels. He is likely to have little or no knowledge of his post and if he is ambitious he may hope not to remain in it for very long. On the whole, a Minister is more likely to be interested in positive action in the short-term than in long-term planning. He is unlikely to be well-disposed to decisions that are going to be unpopular. Some appearance of conflict between them is, therefore, unavoidable if advice is to be tendered frankly and Ministers made aware of all the consequences of their proposed actions.

In many fields governments do not have a clear-cut policy. They have a general purpose which becomes more specific, and often is altered, in the process of being achieved. It is only in the day-to-day application of policy that its full implications come to light. Almost inevitably, major adjustments will result from administrative decisions made within a very broad framework of government policy; and quite often, apparently insignificant decisions on minor points, may create new precedents which, with the passage of time, will result in new policies, not previously contemplated. Normally, significant issues are referred to the Minister for decision, but at the periphery much must be left to the permanent official in actual contact with the citizen. And what he does materially influences the practical effects of government policy.

Apart from parliamentary business, the Minister is like the head of any other organization. He sees papers that his senior advisers think he ought to see. A good deal depends on the training and experience of the civil servants and on their ability to anticipate the Minister's wishes. They know the pressures on his time and see their job partly as protecting him from being deluged with official files. No question of any importance however, is likely to be settled in the Minister's name before he has seen the files and he had a fair chance to intervene.

Clearly, a Minister must rely heavily on his permanent staff. When major changes have been introduced and have been accepted, or when a government has no major alterations in mind, initiative in policy formation passes from the politician to the public servant. This is only to be expected. The process of government is not a series of sudden and swift innovations.. Rather, it is a process of gradual and minor adaptations to changing conditions. This fairly smooth progression is broken at rare intervals by a flood of important legislation, brought about because, (with the passage of time) the marginal adjustments that have been made tend to fall short of the people's expectations. The public servant who deals with individual citizens, day after day, is in a good position to see what they want. Normally, he will initiate more policy changes than his Minister, who will be concerned primarily with major and spectacular issues; but because as the public servant is by training and tradition cautious, he is likely to recommend less than the public expects or demands.

In certain aspects of government the logic of events tends to force the Minister into the role of an approving or rejecting authority rather than that of an active controller. More change of scale of government business has shifted even the higher responsibilities from ministry to civil service. As has been well said, owner-drivers have become owners with chauffeurs as the car of the state has grown more complex. The ministerial owners decide destination, pace, the colour of the car or what else they will, but it depends on the their chauffeurs to deal with technical detail and with choice of roadways! The problem of maintaining positive control is aggravated somewhat by the politician's closeness to the people. Because of his pre-occupation with satisfying the personal representation of individual electors and pressure groups, a Minister does not have to supervise his department closely. He is kept busy attending Cabinet and Cabinet Committee meetings, listening to debates in the House, and discussing complaints or proposals with deputations. Most of the major issues facing his department are brought forcibly to his notice by individuals or pressure groups, but in other cases he must rely on his permanent head to advise, initiate and recommend policy agenda. In these instances, the permanent head is in a key position. It is he who decides what the Minister is to see, how material will be presented to him and what the recommendation will be. If he is a strong man with a policy of his own, he may influence materially what is to be done.

Although the public servant works within the framework of politics, service, and legal controls, in some respects so detailed and minute as to sap his initiative, there still remain areas in which he is comparatively free from supervision. In some cases, the existence of political and legal controls creates an excessive fear in the minds of the official that the work on which he is currently engaged might be discussed in Parliament or in the courts. This fear is reinforced by the possibility that the Minister may let him down to lend him support on any public criticism of what is being done. There have been ministers who in order to evade responsibility have taken decisions orally or to use a metaphor "in pencil and used a rubber if things went wrong". Others have chosen the path of evasion (Bhambri 1971: 113-74). However, not all public servants are obsessed with fear of review, for when it does come, it is often difficult to prove that an official has disobeyed instructions wilfully, or acted contrary to that rather nebulous criterion, the public interest.

A Committed Bureaucracy

From time to time, there are criticisms of the political loyalty of the public service as also claims that it frustrates the policies of governments. Usually, these statements are false. Some are based on inadequate knowledge; others are motivated by the desire to find a scapegoat for a political decision that has proved unworkable or unpopular. Nevertheless, such criticisms do raise the question of whether it is desirable that seniorposts in the government services should be filled through recruitment and promotion on merit by a politically independent staffing authority. Independent control of employees in the public service is based partly on the assumption that the public servant is a politically neutral instrument for carrying out government policy. However, analysis of policy formation has shown that even though he may be neutral as far as party politics is concerned, the administrator helps to shape policy and legislation. He assesses public demand and public responses; and in doing so he is the centre of various pressures.

Today, political influences tend to pervade every nook and corner of Indian national life and the administration is inevitably drawn into it. Young people entering the administration have been worried about political developments in the states and the frequent interference by politicians. The relations between civil servants and ministers in India have rapidly deteriorated and few conventions of administrative behaviour have been established in this area.

The formal theory of civil servant-minister relationship is for many ministers an indication of the civil servant's subordinate position: he is the servant while they minister to the public! Civil servants on their side have often a contempt for the politician. This attitude emerges clearly in a study undertaken by Richard Taub in the State of Orissa (Taub 1969) and another study on the attitudes of officials in Meerut district undertaken by S. Kothari and Ramashray Roy (Kothari and Roy 1969: 21). Frequent political interference by politicians with the processes of administration and their over-critical and fault-finding postures, both within Parliament and outside, have led bureaucrats to devise protective attitudes and stratagems of self-defence.

Not long ago civil servants in India were criticised for a lack of commitment to socialist goals. This is a dangerous trend which will inevitably force civil servants into a declaration of their political loyalties. It is easy to see that such a trend will, in the long run, undermine the very foundations of the civil service in a parliamentary system. The controversy had arisen in India over a reported statement made by Prime Minister Indira Gandhi, who at a meeting of the Congress Parliamentary Party on 16 November 1969 referred to the administrative machinery as the stumbling bloc in the way of the country's progress. She wanted officials who would think and see that certain things which are necessary for the progress of the country are implemented properly. She was of the opinion that the country would fall into a rut if it followed the British system in which civil servants were not supposed to be concerned about which political party was in power nor its ideology. In other words, she wanted the public services to be politically committed. In her subsequent statement, however, she modified her earlier stand and said, " We need government servants with 'commitment' - to the development of the country and personal involvement in the tasks"(Indira Gandhi 1969). She emphatically denied that she wanted politically committed or servile government employees, but felt they should be committed to the objectives of the State-which has been approved by Parliament. They should have faith in the programme they are to execute.

These views question the very basis on which the Indian administrative system has been built and cast doubt on its ability to effect social transformation. Basically, there are three assumptions on which the present system is founded: (a) every civil servant implements faithfully all policies and decisions of ministers even when they are contrary to the advice tendered by him; (b) the civil servants enjoy full freedom to express themselves frankly in tendering advice to their superiors including ministers; and (c) the civil servants observe the principle of political neutrality, impartiality and anonymity.

Have these principles vitiated the implementation of government policies? Where they stumbling blocs in the way of the country's progress? Was a committed bureaucracy necessary, feasible or desirable? What were the identifiable factors that affected the implementation of policies and programmes? These were some of the questions which were posed by a team of the correspondents of *Hindustan Times* to some public men and members of the Services. According to the Report of the correspondents, some of the answers revealed that those who criticised the administrative machinery betrayed a lack of their grip over the civil servants. There was also the belief that if a government failed to give shape to its policies and programmes, the neutrality of the civil service tended to be inefficient. Problems in the relationship between the minister and the civil servant arose in India when certain ministers started taking undue advantage of their position through the agency of the civil servant. If a minister took even a small obligation from the secretary, he would not heed the ministers, however high-sounding his declarations may be. In the same Report, a distinguished public man , described the plea for a committed civil service " a partly unintelligent and partly conscious endeavour to assume dictatorial powers". He was categorically opposed to the view that the civil service should have an ideological commitment. The civil service had to be loyal to the Government of the day; carrying out its programme with efficiency. He feared that the entire machinery would come to a halt if the services were to make their decisions, according to their predilections, in carrying out the tasks assigned to them. He was firmly of the opinion that if one seriously tried to implement the commitment plea, there was no doubt that the new result would be "to replace efficiency with patronage". He conceded that the administrative apparatus needed to be improved and methods could be devised to weed out inefficient officers. But the demand for ideological commitment could not be a part of any administrative reform programme(Chaturvedi 1975).

The Administrative Reforms Commission's (ARC) Views

Referring to the relationship between political executive and the civil servants, the ARC felt that "there has been a basic failure on the part of the administrative leadership which has contributed to the present situation in the administration and not all of it can be attributed to the impact of democratic institutions. There has also been a recognizable fall in service standards for which full responsibility must be accepted by the heads of the administration. There is no valid explanation for failure to exercise supervision, for the various instances of administrative slackness and for the tacit acceptance of the present state of the administrative machinery by a fraternity who had been in a better form in the past. It does not seem to have led to any heart-searching amongst them and to any effective move on their part to improve conditions" (Government of India 1969: 198).

At the same time political interference over the administrative head in service matters, incapacity to tolerate unpalatable advice, and a feeling in the districts that the view of the local bosses abut them was a determining factor affecting their future, have altogether continuously resulted in a general fall in the standards of administration. Although the ARC refrained to apportion specific blame for this result, but it did emphasise that correct lessons from the past experience should be drawn and ways and means be devised to secure improvements in the future. It however, suggested certain concrete steps in this direction: first "(a) that near ideal conditions prevail between the Minister and his Secretary and Departmental head; (b) that the services are encouraged to offer advice undeterred by the fear that it may not be liked; (c) that in the field of administration, they are able to maintain impartiality and honesty and are not haunted by the fear of tales being carried about them, which may affect their prospects and (d) that a new confidence is created amongst them, that their prospects depend entirely on their hard work, honesty and merit and need no other prop or support"(Government of India 1969: 182).

The ARC thought that such a relationship could be regulated only if certain general considerations are accepted both by the political leaders as well as the civil servants. Both of them should clearly and sympathetically appreciate the rule of the other, and attempt at a maximum accommodation of each other's view. On the part of the political executive there should be in its words "(a) a proper understanding of the administrative functions and recognition of its professional nature (b) as little interference as possible in service matters e.g., posting, transfers, promotions etc. Discouraging officers of the department to see him personally for redress of service grievances, (c) no requests for departures from declared and approved policies to suit individual cases either as a result of political considerations, or other considerations, which cannot be reduced to general principles of actions" (Government of India 1969: 183).

Similarly on the part of the services it asserts "(a) there must be a sincere and honest attempt to find out what the political head wants and make the necessary adjustment in policies and procedures to suit his wishes; (b) a readiness to fall in with his political chief in all matters, unless strong grounds indicate his dissent and if he is overruled in writing he should willingly carry out his orders; and finally, the minister usually has a department, and it frequently happens that the head of the department, and the secretary are different individuals; frequently they differ in the advice they give. In such a case, the best course is for personal discussion with both, frequently in each other's presence, and no secretary should consider such action as any encroachment on his personal relationship with his minister" (Government of India 1969: 183).

Increasing Politicisation after Independence

From the above discussion it is clear that the civil servant must, in the first instance, be committed to his professional loyalties and encouraged to perform them without fear and understanding. More than this, should not be required from him. To ask for a political or ideological commitment is to import, as the Masterman Committee in England rightly warned, "factionalism within the civil service, undermining team spirit and professional norms" (UK Masterman Committee 1949:6). Such trends are all the more undesirable in view of the complex role which civil servants are called upon to play. Above all, in the context of political fluidity and ministerial instability what permanent political commitment can civil servants be expected to display? - is the fundamental question that is highly debatable.

In India, one of the most important and perceived development of the post-independence period has been the increasing amenability of politics to the administrative process. The introduction of the adult suffrage and the democratic parliamentary institutions brought into fore a new breed of political leaders who ran into the entrenched political administrators in the districts and the secretaries at the state and the central levels. Relationship between these new democratic politicians and the bureaucrat administrators representing an older tradition were bound to be uneasy. The higher echelons of bureaucracy who since the British days were accustomed to functioning within the framework of law and established procedures, found it difficult to bend the universality of rules to the convenience of individual ministers, governors or the local politicians. The new situation was seen by many administrators as political interference. From the very first day of independence, the administration and administrators learnt to be sensitive to politics (Rai 1976: 52). While many district officers and secretaries were able to cope with this new form of pressure, but to survive the rough and tumble required political skills. Thus in the first two decades of India's Independence, there was a continued preoccupation on the part f the bureaucracy with 'political interference' with the result that the political aspect of administrative life became more important. Consequently, the administrators did not find enough time to devote full attention to other matters like improvement of the administration itself including its organization and techniques. The last few years of the decade of 1960s saw the Congress Party leaders making an open call for a 'civil service' committed to their programmes and policies.

In the early 1970s, it seemed that loyalty to the party in power became part of the reward structure of the civil service, which had not been hitherto practised. Those who were loyal were now much more likely to get promotion and desirable postings. The events leading to emergency (1975-77) and thereafter have almost rendered the bureaucracy completely subservient to the political masters of the day. Many district officers obediently carried out the orders and instructions emanating from politicians and extra-constitutional political authorities, as they had no choice. They were helpless for fear of the consequences of not obeying (Potter 1986: 150-167). The advent of the shortlived Janata Government and later the re-entry of Mrs. Gandhi back to power at the Centre in 1980 had firmly established the principle of political loyalty an even more important value than before as one of the norms for advancement to plum jobs at least in the higher bureaucratic echelons. One of the reasons for the declining standards of the administrative performance has been the deterioration in working relations between the ministers and civil servants. In order to fulfil the generously rather than rationally given electoral promises, the political executive wanted the bureaucracy to do certain things, but the bureaucracy in advising the political executive and in fulfilment of their responsibilities has to point out the pitfalls and obstacles in carrying out those orders. Although experienced and confident political executives should have welcomed that advice, but many others and less experienced thought that advice as mere obstructions put up by the entrenched bureaucracy. As the breed of such politicians increased, there also grew a breed of civil service, who would curry favour with ministers, anticipate their views and make recommendations to please them (Potter 1986: 158). They get the promotion and increasingly fill coveted posts, while others who give correct and factual advice are pushed aside or penalized or being transferred from post to post. Those who did not become a part of the system had found it very uneasy to stay in their positions. The examples of the cases of A.K. Chatterjee (1980), A. Appu (1980), D.S. Rawat (1987), A.P. Venkateswaren (1988) and Subhash Kashyap (1990) are too well known to substantiate these trends. All these officials had to resign from their high civil positions because of their clashes or differences with the political executive.

All these cases are indicative of the trend of a difficult and uneasy relationship between elected democratic politicians and the permanent bureaucracy, which is bound to be detrimental to the attainment of administrative and political goals and economy and efficiency in delivering the rewards and services to the public at large. The policy of the government to identify backwardness by a reference to a certain castes and tribes a la Mandal Commission, and to distribute favours to them on that basis has further intensified the traditional social divisions and further widened old gaps among communities and castes.This is bound to have some disastrous repercussions on the performance of the administration. It will not only affect the morale of the bureaucracy due to the merit being discounted, but it is doubtful whether a caste-based democracy can even sustain any modern administration based on the rule of law (Misra 1986: 378). Unless the growing nexus between politicians, criminals and administrators is checked effectively, there is going to be less respite to the aggrieved poor citizen who has still to run from pillar to post to get his legitimate work done.

In one sense, however, the British Imperial traditions of the bureaucracy influenced the political executive. After independence, both the ministers and bureaucrats tried to copy the British Imperial tradition by attempting to have their prestige and status measured in terms of their salary, the quality of their furniture and furnishings, the size of their lawns and office rooms, their allowances, privileges and perquisites. Their approach to life remained elitist and far from Gandhian. Ministers and their officers both flourished independently of the state of the national economy. Though outwardly clad in Khadi, even Congress ministers, with certain exceptions, developed attitudes which differed but little from the general pattern of administrative culture. It is the bureaucracy and its ethos that set the norm for ministerial behaviour (Misra 1986: 375).

The rise of competitive populism and spread of rampant corruption are threatening to destabilise the bureaucratic state. Politicians have been mounting increasing pressures on civil administration to violate norms, disregard procedures, and break rules to their benefit. Those who toe the line reap handsome rewards, and those who try to uphold the rules of law[1] are hounded from pillar to post. A stage has reached in India, where chief secretaries are kicked around for their uprightness, the Home Secretary of a state is arrested on the change of government, an honest IAS officer is slapped by an irate M.P. This has played havoc with institutions and has broken the back of the civil services. India could have survived the impending collapse of bureaucracy if it had fostered some alternate structure in its place. But people-oriented institutions were not allowed to blossom. And now the only mainstay of the polity, the bureaucracy, is crumbling under the hammer blows of populist and corrupt politics (Gill 1992:12).

The divergent opinions of the administrators and the politicians emphasize the strong stresses and strains in their relationships and apparently predict mutual hostility in any programme of activity which compels them to work together. However, in spite of the predispositions of the politicians and administrators certain programmes did succeed and the immediate tasks on hand implemented well. Through a case study of the administration of drought prone areas in Maharashtra between 1970 and 1973, Kuldeep Mathur has demonstrated that individual roles of bureaucrats and politicians are determined by the structural constraints and demands of the situation (Mathur 1974: 844-45). Roles are not played in a vacuum where mutual perceptions are stable for all time to come. Technology of work and demands of environment on the organization shape the pattern of individual roles. The new nature of organizational goals and the demands made by scarcity situations on the state changed its character to adopt itself to the new circumstances. Administrators and politicians were the same individuals but their mutual relationships changed considerably with the change in the demands of the task system (Mathur 1974: 844-45). Mathur's conclusion may well be true in respect of emergent and crisis situations, but in the light of the above discussion it seems unlikely to be the case in normal circumstances.

Conclusion

In conclusion, we will do well to understand clearly that the meaning with which the concept of commitment was sought to be invested, was an emotional and a mental acceptance by the bureaucracy of the ideology of the governmental policies to be executed by it. Although it is neither possible nor seemingly desirable to restore to the old values of strict political neutrality on the part of the bureaucracy, but there is certainly a need on the part of both the political executive and the bureaucracy to recognize that each of the institutions has certain core areas of its operations and transgressing them frequently will only lead to ignoring the basic and more fundamental goals of society. The success of any policy depends on its effective execution, from which flow all benefits to the masses. The execution of the policy being in the hands of the bureaucracy the need exists for commitment at both levels: i.e. at the level of the framers of the policy and those who execute them. Lack of enthusiasm on the part of the executors could lead to half-hearted implementation of them which might defeat the very purpose of planning. Thus as stated by Rao in a recent article "the need for such enthusiasm becomes greater in a country where even after four five-year plans the mistakes committed at the level of implementation are being repeated, not removed. If these mistakes are merely mistakes of commission, resulting from laxity in morals and greater laxity of the government in imposing penalties, there is no need to talk of commitment. All that the government would be required to do then is to enforce all penal mistakes of omission as well as which flow directly from the lack of enthusiasm and lack of foresight"(Rao 1974: 4). The term "commitment" will then have to be understood with reference to three of the well-known limitations of the bureaucracy caused by (a) the need for elaborate procedures, (b) indecisiveness and (c) the absence of self-correction. Removal of these limitations can be only true meaning of commitment (Rao 1974:4).

Notes

1. This is so despite the frequent exhortation and advice by the political leaders to the young recruits to public services to stick to the rule of law and be frank and without fear in tendering their advice to the ministers. In a recent address to the IAS probationers at the Lal Bahadur Shastri National Academy of Administration at Mussoorie on 12 June 1992, the President of India, R. Venkatarama urged them to be "nothing to be afraid of, save and except the law of the land"(The Hindustan Times, 13 June 1992: 12).

References

Attlee, Earl (1956), Civil Servants, Ministers, Parliament and the Public, in Robson, W.A. ed., *The Civil Service in Britain and France,* London, the Hogarth Press.

Bhambri, C.P. (1971), *Bureaucracy and Politics in India,* Delhi, Vikas Publishing House.

Chaturvedi, Mrigendra, K. (1971), Commitment in the Civil Service, in *The Indian Journal of Public Administration,* Vol.17, January-March.

Chaturvedi, T.N., (1975), *Commitment in the Civil Service,* Government of India, Department of Personnel, Training Monograph.

Dutt, R.C. (1973), Committed Civil Service: The Problem, in *Seminar Report,* No.168, New Delhi, August.

Gandhi Indra, Prime Minister of India, (1969), Indra Gandhi's Statement as reported in *The Hindustan Times*, New Delhi, December.

Gill, S.S. (1992), A Withering State? in the Hindustan Times, 15 June, 12-6.

Government of India, Administrative Reform Commission, (1967), Report of the Study Team on Personnel Administration, New Delhi.

August.Kingsley, J. Donald (1944), *Representative Bureaucracy: An Interpretation of the British Civil Service,* Hellosprings, Ohio.

Kothari, Shanti and Ramashray Roy (1969), *Relations Between Politicians and Administrators at the District Level,* New Delhi, Indian Institute of Public Administration and Centre for Applied Politics.

Marx, Fritz Morstein, (1967), *The Administrative State: An Introduction to Bureaucracy,* Chicago, The University of Chicago Press.

Mathur, Kuldeep (1974), Conflict or Cooperation: Administrators and Politicians in a Crisis Situation, in *The Indian Journal of Public Administration*, Vol.20, pp.

Misra, B.B. (1986), *Government and Bureaucracy in India, 1946-76,* Delhi, Oxford University Press.

Potter, David C. (1986), *India's Political Administrators, 1919-1983,* Oxford, Claredon Press.

Rai, E.N. Mangat (1976), *Patterns of Administrative Development in India,* London, Institute of Commonwealth Studies.

Rao, P.V.R. (1970), *Red Tape and White Cap,* New Delhi, Orient Longmans.

Rao, K. Subhas, (1974), Bureaucracy: Inhibitions and Fears, in *The Economic Times,* 14 April.

Taub, Richard B. (1969), *Bureaucrats Under Stress: Administrators and Administration in an Indian State*, Berkeley, Berkeley University Press.

UK, Masterman Committee, (1949), *Report of the Committee on Political Activities of the Civil Servants*, Cmd. 7718.

Varma, R.S. (1973), *Bureaucracy in India,* Bhopal, Progress Publishers.

8 BUREAUCRACY DEVELOPMENT AND THE UPAZILA SYSTEM[1] IN BANGLA-DESH : CONFLICTS AND CONTRADICTIONS

N. Mahtab

Introduction

Bureaucracy is an important and characteristic institution in modern society. The study of bureaucracy has assumed importance in all relevant fields of study in social sciences. The main concern for those interested in the study of public bureaucracy has been the part played by the bureaucracy in the formulation, shaping and implementation of public policy. The importance of the role played by the bureaucracy in development is now a well established phenomenon, especially in the developing countries. The concern about the role of bureaucracy in development is especially important in Bangladesh where the government has taken very important steps to bring about development of the country. The role of bureaucracy in bringing about development has been focused in the efforts of successive regimes in the country. During the British and Pakistani rule, the bureaucracy had been actively involved in the development of the country. The period (1940-1970), saw the *district* as the main seat of development administration and the deputy commissioner (a central bureaucrat) was the highest authority, yielding enormous power with respect to all development programmes. In the latter part of 1970, *thana* was made the main seat of developmenmt administration and the Circle Officer Development (C.O. Dev.)was entrusted with all power at the thana. From 1972-1982, during the first decade of the post-liberation period several attempts were made to change the administrative system to be responsible to people's needs, but all attempts had very little impact on the rural masses which comprises about 87% of the total population of Bangladesh.

Although the role of bureaucracy as an instrument of development is generally acknowledged, there are many misgivings about its position vis-a-vis rural development. Bureaucracy has often been characterised as a soulless, inflexible machine which seems to be unsuited to the needs of the rural people. It is commonly associated with red-tape, rigidity, and never ending rules and regulations Bureaucracy has been also criticized as urban oriented and elitist in nature and unrelated to the needs and responses of the rural areas (Bhattachgarya

1979: 2). These criticisms against bureaucracy reveal some of the structural weaknesses as well as the behavioural consequences that flow from the structure.

After the promulgation of Martial Law in 1982, the government of Ershad took massive steps to reorganize the administrative system of the country, required to cope with the rural problems. The Thana was up-graded to Upazila from 7th November 1982, with the view to bring the administration to the door-steps of the people and to bring about proper development of the rural areas of Bangladesh.

Development has to depend on political management, at the impulse for change comes more often from the political leadership. To accept the supremacy of the politician and to work along with him as co-partners in development work are the built in requirements of development. Again, bureaucracy has to work very closely with the people. Popular participation in development has to be looked at as a resource in its own right. At the same time, the bureaucracy has to elicit the support of the people for various development tasks (Bhattacharya 1979: 14).

It is therefore interesting and essential to examine in how far bureaucrats and political leaders have acquired new orientations and adapted themselves to new methods of work, and also how far the system has been modified and transformed to suit development goals. To what extent do the basic attitudes and orientation displayed by political leaders and bureaucrats change their perception, evaluation, and acceptance of their new role, and in how far they have internalised, legitimised new goals, norms and values? And what is the nature of the relationship between bureaucrats and political leaders during this process of change?

Viewed in this perspective, the present study addresses itself to the empirical study of bureaucracy as an operation mechanism in the process of bringing about development at the *upazila* level. Because bureaucrats and political leaders have to interact within the framework of the newly created upazila structure for the realization of development goals, the study was confined to the following three areas of investigation : (i) the upazila structure, (ii) the political leaders, (iii) the public bureaucrats.

At present, there is a lot of debate on the role and position of the bureaucracy in our country and a good deal of the government's failure to accomplish goals is being attributed to the bureaucracy at various levels, particularly the lower ones. Bureaucracy is being condemned as inefficient and corrupt. Against this background, the study was very important in discovering the impediments and hurdles that bureaucrats experienced in the performance of their tasks. Instead of accusing the bureaucrats for their failure in performing assigned tasks it was fruitful to examine their perceptions, evaluations and judgement of the *upazila system* and of the political leaders in order to find out how far these elements provided their needed support.

The Historical Background

A brief discussion on the historical background of the emergence of different administrative units in Bengal is vital to the study as the units are inter-related and provide the basic for the institutional arrangements (Ali 1982: 29) of the Upazila system to bring about development in Bangladesh. The British inherited the provinces (Subas) and districts (Sarkars) from the Moghuls (Abedein 1973: 1), and created divisions, sub-divisions and thanas. Districts were headed by collectors and thana used to b e the police outpost geared to maintain public order and peace. Between the thana and district, sub-divisions were created for facilitating the administration of criminal cases. Until 1983, these units were headed by sub-divisional magistrates more popularly knows as SDO. The need to supervise the revenue functions of the collector formed the basic unit above the district level and so divisions were created. A division consisting of four or five districts were placed in charge of a functionary called Commissioner. Thus, we find that police, revenue and magisterial functions of the government led to the emergence of different administrative units in Bengal (Ali 1982: 29). According to the recommendations of the Royal Commission upon Decentralization in India (1907-1909) and Bengal District Administration Committee (1913-1914) the *Circle System* came to be introduced in Bengal. One or more thanas were grouped into a circle under the charge of a government officer called the Circle Officer (C.O.).

From the beginning of this century rural development began to become important and in the 1920s and especially in the 1930s it gained considerable importance and the attention of the government, with the result that the concept and philosophy of administration began to change fast and the government began to adopt a new outlook on administration and its functions (Abedin 1973: 116). A resolution of the Government of British Bengal which constituted the Rowlands Committee in December 1944, observed that the main emphasis in the activities of the government henceforth will be in the field of development (Abedin 1973: 166-167).

Pakistan inherited an administrative system created by the former British rulers. Divisions were the immediate units of administration below the national level. Their main role was to guide and supervise the district administration, coordinate certain activities at the district level and hearing appeals on the decision of district revenue officials regarding revenue matters. The district assumed the most dominant role in the governance and administration of the country. With the passage of time, the head of the district administration designated as District Magistrate or Deputy Commissioner assumed increasing responsibilities in the sphere of development activities. It was made clear that development was one of the principal concerns of the District Officer. No development schemes would be implemented unless they were pushed "vigorously, continuously and uninterruptedly", by the District Officer (Abedin 1973: 118).

By Presidential Order Number 18 of 1959 Ayub Khan introduced the system of "Basic Democracy" in the country on October 27, 1959. Under this new system, a four tier system of local government was established - Divisional Council, District Council, Thana Council and Union Council. For the first time a local government unit (Thana Council) was created at the *thana level*. Towards the beginning of 1960 the government began to undertake massive rural development programmes and decided that the administrative machinery of various departments which were connected with development activities would be extended to the thana level. As a result, the various "nation building" departments were gradually posted at the thana level. In 1961, the post of Circle Officer (Dev.) was created at the thana level to undertake and supervise development activities of the thana and union councils.

A thana council consisted of representative members (Chairmen of Union Councils) and officers of the various nation building departments. The council was chaired by the S.D.O. - a central government official. The Circle Officer (Dev) was its ex-officio Vice-Chairman. The thana council was entrusted with the responsibility of drawing up development schemes relating to the thana. Its functions included coordination of activities at Thana level, management of Thana Training and Development Centre, Rural Works Programme and Thana Irrigation Programme. This means the officials played a very important role in the construction of roads, bridges, culverts and irrigation projects.

The Commissioner and Deputy Commissioner - the heads of the general administration of the division and district respectively, were the ex-officio chairman and deputy-chairman of the local bodies at these level. Thus, in addition to the Union Council, the entire local government was under the control of central government officials.. Ayub's initiative of *Basic Democracy*, brought with it a lot of bureaucratic controls over the villages and the 'basic democrats' amassed and misused the government resources on such a scale that they became easy victims in the popular upsurge against Ayub in 1969 and also during the war of liberation (Abedin 1973: 118).

After the emergence of Bangladesh as an independent nation, Majib abolished the system of Union Council in early 1975. He replaced it by an advanced system of co-operative institutions which was part of his one party rule. In the new arrangement, local government was to be placed in the hands of 61 appointed District Governors (Blair 1986). However, after the overthrow of Mujib regime, the Union Council was revived again. The Local Government Ordinance 1976 created a three tier system of local self-government namely *the Zila Parishad, the Thana Parishad and the Union Parishad*. Later in May 1978, Thana Development Committee was constituted of Chairmen of Union Parishads to enable preparation of local planning and implementation of development projects. Although the objectives behind the creation of TDC was to transfer some power from government officials (bureaucracy) to the elected representatives (Chairmen of Union Parishads) of the rural people, it was never implemented. The bureaucrats still retained enormous power while the Circle Officer became the nerve centre. He was usually described as the "leader of the thana and the people", and the "man on the spot". He held a key position in matters of various development activities undertaken by the thana and union Parishad (Abedin 1973: 309-313).

An entirely new scheme called Swanirvar Gram Sarkar was created during Zia's period of rule. Accordingly, in May 1980, the government announced that a new village government or Gram Sarkar would be established for each of the country's 68000 villages by the end of the year. After a period of considerable confusion, the Gram Sarkar were set up early 1981 (Blair 1986). The Gram Sarkar consisted of 11 members with one Gram Pradhan (Village Chief) elected by the village people. But before the new institutions were in a position to implement the expected development programmes, Ziaur Rahman was assassinated by a hail of machinegun bullets (Blair 1986). With the resultant political change and bureaucratic conspiracy, the Gram Sarkar was discredited as unworthy institution. Eventually it was abolished altogether.

The goal and purposes of the colonial structure of administration which Bangladesh inherited were totally unsuitable to the needs of the new nation. The experience gained from the efforts of successive regimes made it clear that if rural development is to be effective, the target groups, i.e. the rural population should actively participate in the decision making process. Apparently, in order to avoid the mistakes and the shortcomings of the past, a high powered Administrative Reorganization/Reform Committee (ARC) was formed in April 28, 1982 with the following terms of reference:

(a)   to review the structure and organization of the existing civilian administration with a view to identifying the inadequacies of the system for serving the people effectively and

(b)   to recommend an appropriate, sound and effective administrative system based on the spirit of devolution and the objective of taking the administration nearer to the people (GPRB 1982: 1).

In its study, the Committee came with the conclusion that bureaucratic dominance at all levels of government cannot fulfil local needs and aspirations under all circumstances. The committee found that (i) popular participation in administration was lacking; (ii) coordination of field services was totally absent especially at the thana level; (iii) there were too many levels of administration creating problems of communication and access to government services (GPRB 1982: ii).

The Committee felt that it was necessary to introduce decentralized system of administration in which the devolved powers of decisionmaking would be exercised, controlled and directed by popular representatives of the local area.

On the basis of CARR Report, the government prepared an ordinance in December 1982, to reorganize the administration. According to the Ordinance a total of 460 thanas were upgraded during the period of November 1982 and February 1984. This gave birth to the Upazila - an integrated system of local self-government with the twin objectives of democratic decentralization and local participation in planned programmes.

The Upazila structure within which officials and political leaders had to work jointly for realizing the developmental goals provided the basic framework for local administration.

The Upazila Structure

The most distinguishing feature of the Upazila system was the provision for an elected chairman for the Upazila Parishad. For the first time in Bangladesh history, the chairman of a thana level representative body would be directly elected by the people. The elected official was somewhat similar to the Collector or Deputy Commissioner at district level, but he had even more authority to supervise thana officialdom for the Upazila Nirbahi Officer (UNO). Technical officers were under the control and supervision of the Upazila Parishad Chairman and not of the line ministries in Dhaka (Blair 1986: 25). Besides the directly elected chairman, the Upazila Parishad consisted of the following:

(a) All chairmen of Union Parishads within the Upazila, who were representative members with voting rights.

(b) Twelve official members representing various government departments at the local level, but without voting right.

(c) Three nominated women members.

(d) One government nominated member most usually belonging to the freedom fighter.

(e) The chairman of Upazila Central Cooperative Association [UCCA] (BPRB 1982).

The bureaucratic kingpin of the Upazila administration was the Upazila Nirbahi Officer (UNO) who combined the role of chairman as well as the principal executive officer of the Parishad. Government officers who worked with the old system in thana, sub -division and district levels were all posted at the Upazila and were required to adjust themselves to the new arrangements.

In the process of upgrading Thanas into Upazilas, the responsibility of all development activities at the local level were transferred to the Upazila Parishad, while the national government had retained the responsibility of regulatory functions and development activities of national and regional coverage (BPRB 1982).

The transferred subjects included Upazila health and family planning, education, agriculture, co-operative, livestock, rural development, fishery, social welfare, mass communication and engineering etc. The regulatory functions on the other hand, were Upazila accounts, magistracy, revenue, law and order and statistical affairs.

The second schedule of the Local Government Ordinance 1982 listed 17 functions of the Upazila Parishad (BPRB 1983). Accordingly, the Upazila Parishad were to coordinate all development activities, initiated, formulated development-related policies, identify projects and schemes, and in general be responsible for the implementation of government policies and programmes within the Upazila.

The above job description reveals that a wide range of development activities were expected to be undertaken by the Upazila Parishad. The whole spectrum of work was designed in such a manner that the dependency of the rural people on national government could be reduced, available and untapped resources could be mobilized and the involvement of national government at the local level planning and development could be greatly reduced.

Thus it is evident that the task given to the Upazila Parishad was massive as well as very important and far reaching in scope. The Upazila Parishad was the final authority to take decisions in the local development activities that were under the control government officials in the previous *thana administration*.

The Upazila at Work

With the theoretical and generally prescriptive presented so far as a background, we now proceed towards an empirical analysis of the actual working of the system. Our main focus will be to assess the extent of development work undertaken at the Upazilas. The sources of success of the Upazila system depended to a great extent on the proper role of officials and non-officials alike. They had to act as partners in the functioning of the system, and wherever this partnership failed, complications would arise.

Non-official leadership (Chairman) and official guidance were essential for the smooth and efficient functioning of these institutions. With this assumption our research examined the specific relationship among the various categories of official and non-officials at the upazila level. The important relationships that were identified included:

1. Relationship between the Chairman and the Upazila Nirbahi Officer (UNO)
2. Relationship between the UNO and the functional officer relationships and
3. Relationship between the Chairman and the functional officer.

(1) *Relationship between the Chairman and the UNO*

To study the complex set of relationships between the non-officials and the officials at the Upazila level it was essential to know the socio-economic political context in which they were operating and functioning. Besides differences in family background between the two groups, we noticed differences in respect of their personal attributes like age, education, income, rural versus urban exposure etc. The non-officials (Political leaders) were by and large younger than the officials. The officials had spent a longer part of their life in urban areas as compared to political leaders who had lived largely in the rural areas. The officials were by and large more educated than the political leaders. On the whole, however, the chairmen were economically better off than the officials. They depended on agriculture as means of their livelihood although a few of them were engaged in business and legal practice. Almost all the chairmen in our study had strong political affiliations in their family which may be the main reason for their coming into power.

To understand the proper role of the Chairman and the consequent relationship with the UNO, it was essential to know their functions. The Chairman was the chief executive officer of the Upazila. In the past, this post was held by Community Development Official. Our analysis revealed that the Chairman had multiple functions (GPRD 1983). Besides development-related functions, he had to perform routine administrative tasks such as supervision and control of the staff of the Upazila Parishad, and coordinating all development activities of the Upazila. He was also responsible for the implementation of governmental policies and programmes within the Upazila. Most importantly, he was to initiate the Annual Confidential Report (ACR) of the UNO.

On the other hand, the UNO was the elected Chairman of the Upazila Council. Further, he was the chief executive officer of the Upazila Parishad. As such, he was responsible to the Chairman of the Parishad whom he assisted in supervising all Upazila level development and administrative work. The UNO was an officer of the Administrative cadre and he had to ensure that the Upazila programme was in agreement with the rules and directives of the Government.

Theoretically the officials should give advice and guidance to the non-officials who were expected to 'value' such advice. They should act as friends, philosophers, guides and promotors of the newly decentralized democratic institutions. But their actual position was far from the expected norms. There existed important areas of conflict between them. The Chairman, with strong political background, and sound economic position and young in age, had the ambition to exercise more and more power. Consequently, he came into conflict with the Upazila Nirbahi Officer (UNO). The chairman felt that he was the elected head of the Parishad and as such his approval was required for everything that happened in the Parishad. On the other hand, the UNO thought that as the highest executive officer of the Parishad, the chairman had accumulated too much power in his own hands. What is more, the fact that the UNO had dual loyalty, there was additional source of conflict. The UNO was responsible to the Chairman who was empowered to write Annual Confidential Reports (ACR) about of the UNO. At the same the UNO was responsible to his departmental superior with regard to his activities at the field. Most often the UNO was inclined to seek guidance from his superiors at higher levels of the bureaucracy rather than follow the instructions of the chairman. All the interviewed chairmen were of the opinion that they were given more responsibility but not sufficient power to carry them out. Further, the chairmen were not happy with the arrangement that all retained subjects belonged to the government. On the other hand the UNOs were not happy with the situation that all development activities were the main concern of the Chairmen, while in the previous thana administration the government official alone was in change of all developmental activities at the thana level. As such he was in full command of all the financial resources. The UNOs were of the opinion that their authority was greatly curtailed in the present decentralized scheme.

The chairmen of the Upazila Parishad were given the status of the government official equal to the Deputy Secretary. On the other hand, the UNO who was one level below the chairman, had the status of Senior Assistant Secretary. This became a source of great frustration among the UNOs. On the other hand, the Chairmen held the view that although the UNOs were subordinate to them in status, nevertheless, they commanded more authority than the Chairmen. Some of the conflict situations created between the Chairman and the UNO had to do with issues related to the selection of development projects, selection of primary school teachers, issues related to law and order, and issues related to service cars.

To understand the conflict situation between the *chairman and the UNO*, we had to interview the UNO and Upazila Chairman of each Upazila under study. These interviews showed that there was lack of mutual understanding with regard to their respective interest. The dual leadership pattern at the Upazila had created conflicts and contradictions in their relationship. During our interviews with the Chairmen and UNOs we identified that the conflict between them arose mainly because of the distribution of power and authority. The Chairmen complained that the UNOs were interfering and dominating. On the other hand, the UNOs complained that the chairmen, who were assigned with enormous powers by law, had the tendency of bossing over. On their part the Chairmen alleged that the UNOs had not adjusted themselves to the new situation. They could not forgo their colonial tradition, urban and elitist outlook.

(2)   *Relationship between the Chairman and the functional Officials (Deputed Central Government Employees)*

The deputation of the central government employees to Upazila Parishad was resented by the Chairman. Section 91 of the Local Government (Upazila Parishad and Upazila Administrative Reorganization) Ordinance 1982 laid down that the Parishad may appoint such officers and employees as it deemed necessary to assist in the discharge of its functions or such items and conditions as may be prescribed (Khan 1986: 16-30).

On the other hand, the field functionary heads were in a difficult position. There was a problem of *duality of control*. The field functionary heads were accountable to the Parishad and at the same time carried out the instructions of the departmental heads. This duality of control exposed them to situations of role confusion and role conflict. Also the officials who were expected to work under the administrative authority of the Chairman, had not developed the necessary predispositions for this, and hence continued to owe allegiance to the superior officials in the administrative hierarchy. In effect, the Chairmen were unable to regulate the behaviour of the officials working in the Upazila since they had few real sanctions to apply. In this case it may be mentioned that it was the UNO who was empowered to write the Annual Confidential Report (ACR) of the deputed officials, and not the Chairman. Again the deputed officials although being nominated members of the Upazila Parishad did not possess any voting rights and this hampered their initiative in the decisions of the Parishad., This situation led to inefficient and corrupt administrative practices. Again, the Chairmen felt that they should have more control over the departments dealing with retained officials, specifically Police and Revenue Department. These subjects were retained by the government and as such the Chairmen had no say over the law and order situation at the Upazila.

(3) *Relationship between UNO and Functional Officials*

Two types of conflicts were inherent in this area of relationship: (i) generalist - specialist conflicts and (ii) intra cadre rivalry.

Thus in the first type, there was a conflict over official leadership between the generalists represented by the Upazila Nirbahi Officer, Assistant Commissioner and Upazila Magistrates and the specialists representing the functional heads. Placing of a senior officer as UNO from the Bangladesh Civil Service (BCS) [Admin.] cadre was not taken heartily by officers of other cadres, especially the "technocrats". The technical departments especially, the engineers and doctors, organized themselves to challenge the leadership of the UNO. There existed conflicts of power and authority among the officers in the Upazilas. Fear and reluctance existed among the officers of the technical services, since they had become prey of dual control and authorities. For their performance they were under the control and guidance of UNO and Chairman, and on the other hand for their promotion and transfer they were under their line ministry and virtually linked offices (Desh 1984).

During our interviews with the technical officials many issues were highlighted in which the resentment and dissatisfaction of the officials were expressed. The professionals resented the power of the UNO to initiate the Annual Confidential Reports (ACRs) of all departmental heads, grant C.L. to them and coordinate the work of departmental heads. Apart from this, there were problems regarding financial and accounting system. The procedure demanded that salaries and allowance of deputed officers and staff be submitted in parishad office which needed to be checked by finance officer first, then signed by both the UNO and the Chairman. Finally, these bills were went to Upazila Accounts Office and local branch of Sonali Bank which functioned as treasury, and back to Upazila office. From there the bills were sent to the respective departments to be cashed. This cumbersome accounting system and authority of the UNO was viewed by the professionals as a method of control awarded to the UNO by the Government thus rendering more authority to the generalists.

Another important area of conflict between the generalist administrator (UNO) and the technical services was brought forward by the Engineer of one of the Upazila under study. This had to do with the resentment that in the absence of the Magistrate, the UNO was empowered to take his place. This arrangement was resented by the technical Specialists who also wanted to act as Magistrates. The technical experts felt that they were passed and indeed degraded.

From our research it became clear that there was a vital area of conflict between the Upazila Magistrate and UNO . There were at least ten major instances where the UNO tried to interfere with the normal function of the field level judiciary. Further evidence showed that at least in two Upazilas the situation was so grave that the normal function of the Upazila Parishad was hampered. In an answer to the question of whether the administrative machinery and the judiciary be separated, every UNO we had interviewed stated that the administrative machinery should have some level of workable control over the judiciary whereas the Upazila Munsifs were of the opinion that they should be separated.

The intra service cadre rivalry was very acute in the Upazila system. In one of the Upazilas there were 24 class I officers; 15 Class II (all Class II officers are non-cadre); 18 cadre and 6 non-cadre belonging to Class I. This intra cadre rivalries would continue to haunt the Upazila Parishads (Khan 1986: 25).

Observations and Analysis

The above description of the actual relationship between the officials and non-officials at the Upazila level made it clear that much of the conflict and contradiction was due to the inexperience of the two sides. Many conflicts arose due to the confusion and the vagueness of the duties and job descriptions of various office holders. In so far as the inter-relationship between officials and political leaders were concerned the former were largely inclined to consult the latter but only a few were willing to be guided by their advice. The problems in this area were openly manifested and there existed a good deal of incongruence in the perceptions of officials and political leaders regarding their respective spheres and boundaries of their activities and authority. Whereas a large number of officials thought that broad policy decisions were taken jointly, the political leaders contended that such decisions were largely taken by the officials alone. On the whole, it was evident that a clearcut division of functions and allocation of responsibilities was not recognized by the participating actors.

It was further observed that so far as officials were concerned a majority of them considered that the political leaders mainly worked in the interest of their supporters and did not pursue wider interests of the community. However, political leaders denied this assertion. The relationships between officials and political leaders were marked by tension. Each actor tried to work for his personal gains rather than for institutional goals. The political leaders and officials instead of becoming pateners in the system, working for common goals, turned out to be rivals for gains and opportunities.

The system of supervisions under the Upazila set-up was the most important controversial point over which there was great resentment among the officials. The dual or rather multiple supervision and control had an averse effect on the working of administration and development.

The Upazila Parishad which was conceived as a mini parliamentary unit for initiating, planning, organizing and executing welfare and development programmes in response to local needs and resources, had not in fact evolved successful. This was largely due to the tussle between the officials and non-officials. To analyse further the relationship between the political leaders and the bureaucrats and to assess the role of bureaucracy in development at the Upazila level, we studied how development projects were undertaken at the Upazila level. This study was divided into *two* broad phases:

i)	Project identification and selection phase
ii)	Project implementation, monitoring and review phase

i) *Project Identification and Selection phase*

The Upazila Parishad was required to identify/select and implement only those projects which fell within the overall framework of Upazila planning. During the field survey selected officials as well as non-official members of the Parishad, including the Chairman, were asked about the procedure of project identification and selection and about the role and involvement of bureaucracy in the process. The study showed a wide gap between the prescribed procedure of project identification and selection and the actual practice.

Each Upazila prepared its Annual Development Plan (ADP) taking into consideration the project proposals received from Union Parishad Chairmen and proposals received from the concerned departmental officials who were taking part in development activities. The Planning and Evaluation Committee chaired by the UNO and including certain officers and Union Parishad Chairmen as members, prepared draft project proposals. These were then placed and discussed in the Upazila Parishad meetings for approval. The Upazila Engineering Bureau prepared final project proforma for the approved projects. Final decision on the project was then taken on the basis of technical feasibility as assessed by the Engineering Bureau, keeping Union and sector-wise allocation in proper perspective.

Theoretically, the decisions about project identification and selection were taken by Upazila Parishad and the decisions and choice of the Upazila Chairmen and Union Parishad members would have existed - they being voting members of the Parishad. But in practice, the situation was quite different. It needs to be mentioned in this connection that in the Upazila Parishad, the departmental representatives had no voting rights. They could express their free will, thought, ideas, views and help the Parishad to identify the projects on priority basis. But it was revealed from the discussion with the Union Parishad Chairmen that in selecting and approving of projects, their opinion was not given total importance. Rather it had been found that it was the officials who made the decision and managed to carry them in the meeting using skilful arguments, their educational and technical superiority. The Engineering Bureau and the Planning and Evaluation Committee played a significant role in favour of bureaucracy in this regard. Thus, the selected projects actually turned out to be those which the bureaucracy and administration wanted to be selected. The people at the grassroots level, had a very limited role in this process and the Union Parishad Chairmen were often sidetracked. Through informal discussions with local people it was learnt that they were not normally informed earlier by the Chairman or members as to when and how the decision on certain projects would be adopted. In the final analysis, with regard to the identification and selection of projects, the officials view remained predominant.

(ii) *Project Implementation, Monitoring and Review phase*

With regard to implementation, supervision and monitoring of projects, the prescription was to have two committees. The bureaucrats were closely interlinked with the project implementation phase since they lended whatever administrative and technical expertise was required at this state. After a project was selected it could be implementated either through employing contractors, i.e. tender committee, or by constituting a project implementation committee.

The tender committee was chained by the UNO, with the Upazila Engineer as member Secretary and the Finance and Planning Officer as its member. The project implementation committee had the Upazila Project Implementation Officer as the Member Secretary. During the implementation stage it was the UNO, the Upazila Engineer and the Project Implementation Officer who played a crucial role in the effective supervision and execution of projects. There was very limited participation by the local population, in identifying, selecting, and implementing development projects. Only few people, usually those belonging, or having access to the power structure, were involved through the project committees. The people at large remained alienated from the administration and development activities undertaken at the Upazila level.

Conclusion

The purpose of introducing the Upazila system was to bring the development administration out of bureaucratic control and into the process of participatory development with the elected Upazila Parishad as the focal point of the decision making process. Bureaucratic grip over the local level planning and development was sought to be broken by vesting the Chairman with adequate degree of administrative control over the deputed functionaries, appointed by the government (Ali 1968: 190-191).

There is no denying the fact that the Upazila system provided a circumscribed space for political competition. But the strategy was rather complex. The whole process was at the behest of authoritarian rather than democratic interests. The politico-administrative as well as the cultural contexts did not provide optimism for a situation where bureaucratic involvement in Upazila administration could be minimized, let alone discarded. The bureaucratic behaviour was rather autocratic behind the facade of a democratic institution of the Upazila. Anti-participatory bureaucratic state did cast a long shadow over a vital local institution.

The necessity and importance of official initiative and control cannot be denied (Abedin 1973: 308-309). Although, with the introduction of the concept of Upazila, it became rather acceptable to denounce or minimize the active bureaucratic participation in the process of rural development, such participation is indispensable, and without it, no development can succeed. But this does not indicate that the role of bureaucracy should be dominant.

The present government, under the leadership of Begum Khaleda Zia, dissolved the Upazila Parishad on grounds of its close affiliation with the previous autocratic regime. What is more, the system was found to be unfair while the Upazila Chairman is believed to have had committed unforgivable economic atrocities. In the light of the experiences so far, the government has now created a powerful committee to review the structure of local government and to recommend a new one which is conducive to the spirit of participation and development. Until the new system is legally established, rural development activities will be carried out by the government officials stationed at the Upazila level. They are expected to carry out these activities under the overall supervision of the UNO - the all purpose generalist civil servant.

The analysis presented in this essay reminds us that sustainable development and accountable administration are inter-related and interdependent agenda points of most third world countries. What is required is the establishment of participatory democratic institutions capable of breaking bureaucratic entanglement. Although a worthwhile effort, a mere introduction of electoral politics is not enough to speed up the participatory process. More substantive questions of jurisdictions, the powers and the constitutional guarantees of the local bodies and their sustainability should enter the discourse.

Notes

1. The Upazila is to be renamed as *Thana* with effect from July 1, 1992.

References

Abedin N. (1973), *Administration and Politics in Modernizing Societies - Bangladesh and Pakistan* -(National Institute of Public Administration (NIPA, Dhaka.

Ali, S.A.M.M. (1982), *Field Administration and Rural Development in Bangladesh* - Centre for Social Studies, University of Dhaka, Dhaka.

Ali, S.A.M.M. (1986), *Politics, Development and Upazila,* National Institute of Local Government (NILG),. Dhaka.

Bhattacharya, M. (1979), *Bureaucracy and Development Administration*, Uppal Publishing House, New Delhi.

Blair, H.W. (1986), "Participation, Public Policy Political Economy and Development in Rural Bangladesh, 1958-1985, *World Development*, Vol. 13, No. 2, Pergamon Press Limited, Great Britain.

Dainik Desh, 3 June, 1984, Government of the People's Republic of Bangladesh (1980b), *The Second Five Year Plan 1980-1981,* Planning Commission, Bangladesh Government Press, Dhaka.

Dainik Desh, 3 June, 1984, Government of the People's Republic of Bangladesh (1982), *Report of the Committee for Administrative Organization and Reform.* Dhaka.

Dainik Desh, 3 June, 1984, Government of the People's Republic of Bangladesh (1983a), *Manual on Thana Administration,* (Bangladesh Government Press, Dhaka).

Khan, A.A. (1986), Conflict and Coordination Problems in Upazila Administration - A Note" - *Journal of the Bangladesh Young Economists' Association*, 3dr Issue, Dhaka.

9 SUMMARY AND CONCLUDING REFLECTIONS

R.B. Jain and H.K. Asmerom

Introduction

This study was launched with the aim of assessing the linkages and relationships between the administrative and the political institutions in a number of nations in Africa, Asia and Latin America. As a point of departure, the politics/administration dichotomy and the relevant theoretical developments have been succinctly reviewed in the *introductory chapter*. It can be reiterated that the usefulness of both concepts in helping to understand human institutions ever since people began to live in organized communities carrying out mutually supportive tasks and obligations as demanded by the laws of survival and continuity is abundantly clear. Indeed, as could be demonstrated in many of the essays, state/society relationships effectuated via the political and administrative systems have undergone various transformations. The ups and downs of state/society relationships, the uniqueness and similarities of the transformations, the attempts that have been made to correct and reform nation-building programmes, and the balance sheet of successes and failures of nation-building as of this date have been dealt with in the essays presented in this volume along with lessons for future developments. Each case presented in this study is unique in its historical and present environmental setting. Countries like India, Egypt, Bangladesh and Surinam have comparable colonial histories, while others like Ethiopia, and to some extent, Brazil have had traditional patrimonial and personal rulership. On the other hand, almost all the cases are multiethnic societies with diverse cultures, languages and religions, which can cause insurmountable problems for institutionalizing democracy or can become instruments for cultivating accommodative and balancing elements in building democratic institutions. In this sense, many of the cases are comparable on several fronts. Almost all the cases have demonstrated engagement with the democratization process, though some of them like India and to a certain extent, Brazil and Egypt, are already functioning democracies, while others, like Ethiopia, are still struggling to come to terms with the democratization process.

Summary

The remaining *six chapters* are arranged by theme and by regions. The essay which is most general in its orienttion is presented in chapter two. Here Elsenhans explores the linkages and relationships between rent and development administration. In doing so, he has made an original attempt at establishing the link between political economy and the comparative study of administration. Elsenhans begins his analysis by asserting that the behaviour of political and administrative processes cannot be understood without reference to the overall political and economic systems of a society. He argues that the transfer of western administrative norms to developing countries is adversely affected by the non-capitalist sector of the economy which is controlled by capitalist forces. In this sense, Elsenhans holds the view that the rationality in administration has been achieved through goal limitation. He contends that it is not the size of administration that brings change to its mode of operation, but rather it is the scope of goals to be pursued that has a decisive role. This phenomenon can be explained in terms of *rent* or *tax* - a type of surplus available for investment. He goes on to explain that rent is dependent on the political and administrative decision-making and on the concurrent influences of various groups. In this connection, he argues that the cultural traits of the decision makers cannot be fully integrated into the decision-making process even though they can prove to be useful in the day-to-day running of the administration. He goes on to assert that when rent is channelled into specific programmes, the cultural values prove to be useful for both the formal aspects of decision-making and for the final outcome of the programme. Further, he contends that, in the developing countries, the administrative systems are not very sensitive to the interests of the masses, but rather simply reflect the values and norms of the dominant elites, with often negative consequences for reform.

On the other hand, the allocation of surplus is influenced by disparate social groups, while revenue, rent and production are controlled by those in the upper echelons of the social hierarchy. In the face of this complex process of interaction, any attempt at comparative study of administrative systems should take into account the origins and types of rent, the linkage between strategy of development and the relative importance of rent versus profit. In the essay the author has examined the various types of rent and how they are controlled by the production forces and how rent is related to the global economy, including monetary policies and fluctuations in the business cycle. From there he went on to elaborate the various actors who control rent. He feels that the interaction among the actors does not necessarily entail policy-oriented cleavages among them. In this connection the author claims that patronage and clientele systems play a key role in strengthening personal relationships.

According to Elsenhans, the only force capable of checking this patronage would be opposition groups who are powerful enough to impose their own will.

Passing to another vital issue in the essay, Elsenhans is of the opinion that decentralization serves as a means of promoting and maintaining democratic control over resources, including rent. The argument here is that, if integration fails at the national level, local governments and related grassroots organizations can be given the necessary power to control local taxes and central government grants.

Elsenhans concludes his essay by stressing the relevance of the political economy approach to the understanding of development administration and decentralization through considerations of rent and the manner of its appropriation. He is also of the opinion that the Weberian type of control is a useful instrument in limiting the discretionary power of bureaucracies. At the same time, however, the authors is of the opinion that, in the context of developing countries, discretionary power cannot be completely avoided for the simple reason that the expectations imposed upon development administration are so enormous in most developing countries. He asserts that development administration may be analysed by recognizing the role of rent and discretionary power in the overall allocation of resources. Finally, the author stresses that development administration which functions according to stated goals and objectives can be geared to a market-oriented and diversified economy capable of meeting the needs and demands of society as a whole.

Coming to the Latin American Case Studies, in chapter three Elisa P. Reis examines the ups and downs of the relationship between politics and administration in Brazil. To begin with, the author examines the role of bureaucracy in socio-economic and political development in the third world and the manner in which the bureaucracy was expanded to meet these challenges. She then goes on to explain how the Brazilian bureaucracy, after three decades of expansion, is now being held responsible for the country's economic malaise, financial mismanagement, arbitrary allocation of public services and for the inhibition of social creativity. Reis continues with her introductory review by stressing that the criticisms levelled against bureaucratic inefficiency all over the world have generated a new trend in the direction of privatization and de-bureaucratization. In this sense, she argues that public bureaucracies in developing countries have been facing problems similar to those of the developed capitalist and socialist states, while projecting their own peculiar characteristics.

In the second part of her essay, Reis presents a detailed analysis and interpretation of the role of the bureaucracy in the Brazilian economic growth. She stresses that the present Brazilian bureaucracy is very much the product of the Portugese patrimonial legacy. She makes it clear that while the expansion of the bureaucracy took place after the 1930 revolution, meaningful administrative reform measures were only carried out after 1938. Further, during the so-called liberal period from 1945 to 1964, various ad hoc measures were undertaken to streamline the working of the state bureaucracy. These measures were, in fact, part of the state-building strategy. The relationship between politics and administration during this second period of Brazilian history was characterized by pragmatism and flexibility, which, in time, were transformed into opportunism, lack of administrative strategy and obstacles to development. Reis argues that in the two decades of military rule, Brazil had adopted a new model of modernization which came to be known as *bureaucratic authoritarianism*.

Reis went on to explain that state and nation-building were the central concerns of the Brazilian military regime. With this goal in mind, the regime promulgated nation-wide Administrative Reforms in 1967. Efforts at National De-bureaucratization Programme were launched in 1979. However the author is of the opinion that this programme had a primarily symbolic value in the sense that the attempts that were made to correct the bureaucracy signalled the military regime's willingness to liberalize from within. These early liberalization efforts were continued by the civilian government which came to power in 1985 and which made explicit attempts to implement the transition to fullfledged democracy. During the current civilian government, the restored basic civil and political rights have begun to act as powerful deterrents to many abuses of administrative power, despite the fact that no serious attempts have been made as yet to reform the bureaucracy. What is more, the current economic crisis has aggravated the tense relationship between politics and the bureaucracy, a situation which in turn has become a challenge to the democratization process. In the final analysis, the author is of the opinion that the programme of radical liberalism implies that the state will eventually have to surrender part of its legitimate functions to market forces. The dilemma here is that privatization of the economy under current circumstances could have explosive consequences and ultimately result in the same old challenge of reconciling politics and bureaucracy. On the positive side, however, the politics of public bureaucracy may act as a catalyst for economic growth and enhance the irreversibility of the democratic process in Brazil.

The second contribution in the *Latin American Case Studies*, presented as chapter four, is Hoppe's critical evaluation of Surinam's development policy from 1946 to 1975. He does this against the background of the country's colonial and post-colonial setting. To deal with the subject-matter in historical perspective, Hoppe has identified four distinct phases: (a) the contents of the various development plans announced between 1946 and 1975; (b) the structural characteristics of what he calls Surinam's peripheral economy; (c) the extent to which the official objectives have been met; and d) the causes of failure which are political and administrative in character. The author views the first two phases as intermediate steps designed to provide answers to the problem areas raised in the third phase.

With the help of theories of centre-periphery relationships, as well as other theories related to policy-making, administrative and political systems, Hoppe explains the historical constraints and structural problems to Surinam's economic development strategy. He argues that the series of plans launched between 1946 and 1975 revealed significant shifts in the declared goals and objectives. Using available historical and contemporary sources on various economic undertakings, the author has concluded that Surinam's development planning during the prescribed period was a failure. To substantiate this assertion, the author identifies three types of causes that were detected (a) at the agenda setting phase; (b) at the policy formulation phase; and (c) at the implementation phase, i.e. the discrepancy between policy effects envisaged by policy makers and the actual effects. The author goes on to clarify that the causes of failure could be traced to what he calls a *neo-colonial elite-cartel democracy*. This means that the organization and the procedures of Surinam's development planning and public resources were utilized to build patron-client relationships. In this connection, the author underlines the sort of love-hate relationship that had emerged between Surinam and the Netherlands - the former colonial power and the present major benefactor of Surinam in providing resources for socio-economic development.

Further, Hoppe identifies a number of factors that adversely affected the planning process in the country. These include harsh geographic terrain, difficulty in locating and exploiting natural resources, excessive concentration of the population in and around the capital, heterogeneity and ethnic segmentation with its consequences for the creation of a *weak state*, lack of adequately trained manpower, and the government's unwillingness to learn from past mistakes. The insistence of the Netherlands' government that the resources delivered to Surinam be utilized for development in the most rational possible manner coupled with Surinam's determination to use the aid in its own way had created such a climate of misunderstanding that the Surinam government felt that it was under Dutch neo-colonial control. The author argues that the weaknesses and hazards associated with political, administrative, socio-economic and environmental factors were instrumental in keeping Surinam in a vicious circle of poverty and dependence. The author is of the opinion that Surinam should not continue to wrongly accuse the Netherlands and "international imperialism" for all its mistakes. He further believes that the Netherlands' government should not in any way try to prescribe how Surinam should develop in the future and the latter should be ready to learn from its own past mistakes. At the same time, the author pleads that Surinam should make relentless efforts to mobilize its resources - it is high time that Surinam begins to *seek original Surinamese answers to specific Surinamese questions by concentrating on small scale industrial and agrarian projects based on decentralized institutional foundations.*

Coming to the *African Case Studies*, Asmerom presents in chapter five an analysis of the linkages and relationships between politics and administration in Ethiopia. Within this framework, the author pays special attention to the comparative evaluation of the decision-making process during the Haile Selassie and the Mengistu regimes. As a prelude to the central theme, the author gives a brief sketch of the meaning of policy and policy implementation in general. He also pays attention to some key internal and external factors that favourably or adversely affect the policy process. The type of general policies and the relative difficulty of implementing them are dealt with in these preliminary discussions. Attention is also given to how various sectoral policies and projects are aggregated at the centre in the form of a comprehensive policy or development plan and how the same comprehensive plan is split into sectoral development policies for implementation by the relevant state organizations.

The author then goes on to highlight the nature of the centralized political and administrative structures that were designed by Emperor Haile Selassie I in accordance with the theory and practice of traditional patrimonialism. The main subjects covered in this discussion include (a) the dominant nature of the traditional patrimonial political system in defining public policy, and (b) why and how the emergent bureaucratic apparatus was an integral part of this political framework, linked as it were by the rules of patronage and superior-subordinate relationships imbedded in the cultural values of highland Ethiopia. It is specifically stressed that the emergent bureaucratic apparatus, including the crown council, the prime minister, the council of ministers, the ministries and the administration at sub-national levels, was designed to carry out their respective functions following rules and guidelines formulated by the centre in the name of the Emperor. In spite of its traditional outlook, Haile Selassie's government was not altogether indifferent to the trends of the time. Accordingly, successive five-year development plans were undertaken from 1957 to 1973. The nature of the planning mechanism as well as the successes and the failures of the various development programmes and projects are critically evaluated in the context of the prevailing bureaucratic and political traditions.

The author next examines the post-1974 period in Ethiopia. The overall changes that were brought about by the military regime in re-structuring the political, economic and administrative systems of the country according to the Marxist-Leninist conception of the state are analysed. Further, the continuity of the centralized pattern of decision making and the emergence of authoritarian and centrally guided command economic planning with its disastrous outcomes, are duly treated in this part of the essay.

In the final part of the essay and in the concluding observations, an attempt is made at a comparative evaluation. This means that the similarities and differences of the nature of politics and administration between the old traditional order and the emergent socialist state, their respective approaches to public policy and planned development, and the subservient character of the public bureaucracy under both systems are systematically reviewed. The continuity of the highly centralized decision-making process, the similarities and differences between Haile Selassie's patrimonial system of rule and Mengistu's Marxist-Leninist state, and the significance of all this to the democratization process in Ethiopia are given the attention they deserve.

The next contribution in part two of the essays, is chapter six, in which Otto presents a detailed analysis of politics, administration and rural development in Egypt. The approach adopted by the author is historical in perspective. Accordingly, in paragraph two, the author provides a well-balanced sketch of Egyptian political history, beginning with the time that Egypt was one of the cradle nation-states in the art and science of administration. Continuing his discussion on the historical past, Otto pays special attention to the development of political and bureaucratic institutions in Egypt that were influenced by periodic external interventions, including the forces of Islam and the eventual subjugation of the country by the Ottoman Empire, the French conquest under Napoleon, the march of the combined forces of Britain and Turkey, and finally by the British alone when the United Nations decided to put Egypt under British protectorate at the end of the Second World War. He goes on to examine how the long period of external domination came to an end, how the country was quickly transformed into a one-party dominated political system known as the Arab Socialist Union, and how a gradual process of liberalization of the economy and the political system took place.

In paragraphs three to five of the essay, the author elaborates the changes that were made to the country's constitution. The issues he examines in this connection include the position and role of the main political actors in the country's political, cultural, economic and administrative life. In part four, Otto elaborates the contents and orientation of the Egyptian state ideology as it underwent change from the original version of *Arab Socialism* to the current more liberal and pluralist political agenda legalizing additional political parties, even though the state is still declared to be a democratic socialist state based on the alliances of the working people. He further underlines the fact that Islamic jurisprudence is the principal source of legislation while the economy is guided by socialist principles based on justice and freedom from exploitation. The author then proceeds to examine the country's pyramid of power which consists of three layers of elites dominated by the presidency from above.

In paragraph six of his essay, the author deals with rural politics and local democracy. In this connection a number of issues are cogently discussed, including the nature of family clans, rivalries and tensions that are manifest in village life and the role of the village headman as an instrument of state penetration into the rural periphery. The author argues that despite attempts at political pluralism, freedom and decentralization, rural political culture has remained basically unchanged - dominated by clan politics and controlled by state agencies.

In paragraph seven, the author examines the Egyptian regional and local administrations, while in paragraph eight he elaborates the structure and functions of central government ministries and other state agencies. The field agencies of the central government ministries and their interaction with the target groups are examined in paragraph nine. The nature of rural institutions and the preconditions for their success are dealt with in the tenth paragraph of the essay. The issues of state penetration into the rural periphery, and the efforts made by the state to motivate or force the people to take part in various local project are examined in paragraph eleven. In paragraph twelve, the pivotal role of the country's three last presidents - Nasser, Sadat and Mubarak in the administrative and political life of the country are handled in comparative perspective. In paragraph thirteen, by way of a conclusion, Otto reassesses the linkages and relationships between politics, policies and the people at large. In doing so, Otto underlines the fact that state institutions are not only concerned with the maintenance of law and order tasks but also with various rural development projects which they carry out in cooperation with other village-level private institutions.

Part III which is devoted to *Case Studies from Asia*, begins with chapter seven, in which Jain examines the relationship between politics and administration in the context of India. Within this broad theme, the author concentrates on the issue of neutrality of the civil service vis-a-vis the political leadership. As a departure point he elaborates the meaning of neutrality as it works in Britain. He argues that, with time, the idea of neutrality has become rather outmoded because there is no such clear division between the formulation and the implementation of policy. He goes on to explain that the causes of the breakdown of the classical theory of neutrality are attributed to the following facts: (a) the processes of decision-making are no longer restricted to the political executive, but rather they are spread over the entire fabric of government; (b) the leadership role of the public bureaucracy is explicit in all political systems although it is more pronounced in the context of the developing countries with democratic constitutions; and (c) in the sphere of policy advice and policy execution, bureaucracy cannot remain aloof without being involved in the prevailing politics. Coming more to the Indian setting, the author argues that, following the inherited British tradition, the Indian bureaucracy is basically a neutral institution in the sense that civil servants are not allowed to participate in the campaigns of political parties, although they are entitled to vote in elections provided they give no indication of the manner in which they cast their votes. Civil servants can, however, become active members of political parties when they retire. In spite of these well-defined limits and possibilities, the author argues that there are many other informal mechanisms by which civil servants and politicians can and do interfere in each other's areas of competence.

In appraising the precise relationship between ministers and civil servants in India, Jain makes it clear that apart from parliamentary business, the minister is the head of his ministry and he is expected to scrutinize documents and papers presented to him by his advisers. No question of any significance can be settled in the name of the minister without his approval. Jain makes it clear that, since the minister is preoccupied with global political matters discussed in parliament, most major policy issues facing his ministry are scrutinized by top permanent civil servants in the ministry. They decide which policy matters are to be presented to the minister for his decision. All in all, Jain's argument is that civil servants in India function within the framework of politics, but there are also areas in which they can act comparatively free from political supervision. He goes on to argue that despite occasional criticism with regard to the loyalty and commitment of civil servants, the Indian bureaucracy on the whole has been more or less *a politically neutral instrument* carrying out government policy regardless of which political party(ies) is in power. Ultimately, Jain is of the opinion that civil servants must remain committed to their professional loyalties and should also remain free from political or ideological commitment. Jain concludes his essay by pleading that there is a need on the part of both the political executive and the bureaucracy to recognize that each has a certain *core area of operations*, the infringement of which would necessarily undermine the fundamental goals of society which both parties are legally and morally committed to achieve.

Jain's views about the political commitment of the administrative elite are in a sense supportive of Etzioni-Halvey's (1979) observation, that, while political commitment of the administrative elite may conceivably contribute to a country's economic development, it is most unlikely to help that country along the road to democracy. This perhaps explains why, in most developing countries, bureaucracies have usually been politically committed rather than politically neutral. On the other hand, it would also help explain why such countries mostly have not adopted the democratic pattern, or if they have, have not been very successful in its implementation (Etzioni-Halvey 1979: 90). The Indian case study proves that in democratic situations, commitment on the part of bureaucracies would mean commitment to their own political executives to maintain their own professional values and political obligations respectively, and to cooperate with each other in realizing the importance of each other's contribution in achieving societal goals.

In chapter eight of Part III, *Case Studies from Asia*, Mahtab explores the politics of development administration and decentralization in Bangladesh. In the introductory section of the essay, the author provides an overall picture of bureaucracy as an instrument of development, both in general terms and in the specific context of Bangladesh. Also outlined in the introductory part are the objectives of the study and its methodology. In the second section of the essay, the political and administrative development of Bangladesh are presented in some detail. The issues raised here include Bangladesh's status during the British rule, its subsequent historical links with Pakistan, and the nature of political and administrative changes introduced in the country since independence in 1975. In this context, she pays special attention to the various political decisions which ultimately led to the establishment of the *upazila* (to be renamed *thana* after July 1, 1992) in 1984. The upazil is a type of an integrated system of local government designed to promote democratic decentralization and grassroots participation in decision making.

In sections three and four of her essay, the author elaborates the structure and the functioning of the upazila system with the help of a number of case studies. She pays particular attention to questions of representation in the upazila council and the tasks it has to coordinate, to issues of the relationship between the chairman and the upazila officials, the relationship between the upazila officers and the field representatives of central government ministries and the relationship between the council chairman and the field representatives of central government ministries.

On the basis of empirical observations and findings, Mahtab presents the conflicts and contradictions in section five of her essay. In doing so, the author brings to light how the interaction between politics and administration can be vividly demonstrated at the grassroots level. She shows how the people at the grassroots level play a very limited role in the decision making process, even with well-conceived mechanisms for participation. She concludes her essay by stressing that, despite its democratic framework, the upazila system seems still to be governed by authoritarianism rather than by democratic interests. She doubts that the politico-administrative and cultural contexts provide much optimism for a situation where bureaucratic involvement in upazila administration could be minimized, let alone discarded.

Concluding Reflections

The above case studies by no means exhaust the discussion on the diverse pattern of relationships between politics and administration obtaining in countries of the Third world. They

are, however, indicative of the general trends in one of the most crucial aspects of public
policy formulation and implementation, particularly in the realism of development. It was
more than a century ago that Woodrow Wilson raised the issue of politics/administration
dichotomy. Since then the controversy appears to have come full circle, inasmuch as after
one hundred years, the same question and its implications, after having gone through a
long period of acceptance of the notion of politics/administration fusion and cooperation
as essential to the process of development, is still at the centre of debate.

The case studies in this volume make amply clear that there is no one single model
of such a relationship which could produce optimum results in the process of development
in Third World countries. Much depends upon the socio-economic and political milieu
in which administrative action in these societies takes place. The recent trends of
democratization in many developing countries may perhaps help in our quest to discover
a more uniformly valid scientific-theoretical construct of politics/administration relations.
Still, perhaps the politico-administrative-cultural ethos would be a significant variable to
reckon with in any meaningful discussion of the complexities of the relationship between
politics, administration and development in any particular context.

The essays have illustrated that the links and relations between politics and administration
can be studied in many different ways and from different perspectives. On the one hand,
each of the essays is an *autonomous academic exercise* on the interaction between politics,
administration and the policy process, stressing the unique characteristics of the case under
consideration. On the other hand, the essays collectively portray the ever-changing political
and administrative institutions of Third World countries as they make desperate attempts
to cope with society's demands for socio-economic development.

Finally, individually as well as collectively, the essays reveal the tremendous challenges
faced by many Third World countries as they try to fulfil the demands of the democratization
process. These renewed challenges for change in the direction of democracy can be detected
in each essay in a variety of ways. For instance, Elsenhans' contribution is intended to
show how the linkage between politics and administration in Third World countries can
be explained from the perspective of political economy, with special attention to *rent* as
a key instrument in the overall allocation of resources for economic development within
the framework of democratic institutions. Other essays in the volume, on the other hand,
examine the *waxing and waning* of political systems in historical perspective and how the
regimes currently in power have come to realize that they ultimately have to yield to forces
of popular change and democratization. In a case like India, on the other hand, where
democracy has already taken root, the focus of attention is on the neutrality of the civil
service vis-a-vis the political leadership. From all the contributions one thing seems very

clear, i.e. that the link between politics and administration cannot be separated from nation-building, democracy and decentralization of the decision-making process. The essays reveal that these are still difficult and yet rewarding research projects that can be undertaken in the context of the rapidly changing social and political climate of Third World countries. Indeed, *fresh analysis* of their political and administrative problems in historical perspective along the lines attempted in this volume, is a step in the right direction of prescribing a theoretically and empirically well-founded partnership between political and administrative institutions to tackle the multitude problems that adversely affect Third World countries.

References

Etzioni-Halvey, Eva (1979), *Political Manipulation and Administrative Power,* London, Routledge & Kegan Paul.

INDEX